Distinguished Conduct

Copyright 2019 Melvin E. Page

All rights reserved. No part of this publication may be reproduced, stored in a retrieval system, or transmitted in any from or by any means, electronic, mechanical, photocopying, recording or otherwise without prior permission from the publishers.

Published by
Mzuni Press,
P/Bag 201, Luwinga, Mzuzu 2, Malawi

ISBN   978-99960-66-37-5
eISBN   978-99960-60-36-5

The Luviri Press is represented outside Malawi by:
African Books Collective Oxford (order@africanbookscollective.com)

www.africanbookscollective.com
www.luviripress.blogspot.com

Cover: Daniel Neuman
Cover art: Based on an image found on the website "Soldiers of the Queen," http://www.soldiersofthequeen.com/MounatinsOfThe Moon-SergeantKings AfricanRifles.html and used with permission.

Distinguished Conduct

An African Life in Colonial Malawi

Melvin E. Page

Luviri Press
Mzuzu
2019

Author's Preface

As a practicing historian for more than four decades, I want to make clear this book is not exactly a work of history. Rather, it is the true story of a real African hero, reimagined in the context of Malawian history. To paraphrase accomplished historian J.H. Hexter's definition of history, it is a story about the past intended to *ring* true. Juma Chimwere was a real person, though there are precious few historical details about his life, most related only to his active military service. Wellington Rangely is a character of my invention, although some details of his interactions are loosely based on actual experiences of others. Some other characters were real persons or have very close historical counterparts, but that is not true of all the people who, in this book, interact with Juma. Most of the battles and other engagements of the Kings African Rifles actually took place, as did some other events, though not every detail may have been precisely as I've described. Many of the other anecdotes are based on real life accounts taken from published works as well as archival documents and interviews with living persons, though I have sometimes changed details for dramatic and narrative effect. What I have attempted is to place a real person squarely in the center of what, as a historian, I believe is the trajectory of Malawi's last seven decades prior to independence from British colonialism.

As this is, above all, an African story, I've throughout introduced words and phrases from three African languages—*Chiyao*, *Kiswahili*, and *Chichewa*—to interject a further sense of authenticity. *Chichewa* is the principal language of Malawi, while *Chiyao*—Juma's native tongue—is widely spoken in some areas.

Kiswahili is not now in wide usage within the country, but was the language of command for the Central African Rifles and then the King's African Rifles, though superseded by *Chichewa* after World War One. Elements of each are used in this book only in those contexts where they would most likely be used. As all three are linguistically related—part of the Bantu language family—similar sounds and spellings conveying the same meaning are not uncommon. I've chosen to use differing forms in their most appropriate contexts rather than homogenizing them throughout.

I am obviously indebted to many other writers and scholars, but as this is not a formal historical account they are not specifically mentioned. My thanks to them are nonetheless immense. However, I do want to mention Brian Maxson, Joey Power, Yusuf Juwayeyi, and my wife Grace who were instrumental in helping and encouraging me in the writing process.

Mel Page
Asheville, North Carolina
July 2019

Book One

Somehow, it really didn't seem strange to Wellington Rangely, learning about the worsening health of former Regimental Sergeant Major Juma at a dinner party. After returning to Nyasaland with his wife Sarah just a few weeks before, this was the first major social event on what was becoming a busy official calendar for the soon-to-be Commandant of the Malawi Rifles. The entire officer corps, and the wives of the most senior among them, had come together to welcome their newly appointed commanding officer with a formal dinner in the officers' mess at Cobbe Barracks in Zomba. Despite the importance of the occasion, Colonel Rangely knew there was no question but that he needed to attend to the old soldier who had been his comrade, and yes, his friend, years before. Making his apologies to the gathering, he kissed Sarah goodnight, seeing to it she would be escorted to their new home further up the mountain should he not return before the dinner concluded. He then made his way, with an aide and a driver for his staff car, toward Majowa village. His officers would understand, though he was uncertain if his wife would be as forgiving about his departure this evening. Certainly after thirty-five years of marriage she had become accustomed to the uncertain demands made on a military wife.

Initially it was an easy drive south on the main Blantyre highway. Having already made that trip many times, Rangely was lost in thought. Just ten months ago, he had been on home leave from India, likely his final posting before retirement. After just over a week in Northamptonshire, he was called to battalion headquarters and asked, not ordered, to report at the Colonial Office in London within two days.

"Why?" was all his wife said when he told her shortly after returning home.

"I have no idea!" His honest response was the only one he could manage.

Sarah Rangely knew her husband was a good soldier, so he would report as requested. Indeed, the next day he took the train to London and then a taxi to the Colonial Office. He first met an assistant under secretary, waited a few moments, and was then escorted into the office of Nigel Fisher, Parliamentary Under Secretary of State for the Colonies. He remembered little of the pleasantries they'd exchanged, but Mr. Fisher's offer remained crystal clear in his mind:

"Lieutenant Colonel Rangely, Her Majesty's Government—in consultation with Nyasaland's leaders, and in anticipation of that Protectorate being granted independence a year from now—hopes that you will accept command of the First Battalion, King's African Rifles and, on the independence of the Protectorate, become commandant of the Malawi Rifles, the new nation's primary defense force. Should you accept you would, of course, be promoted to Colonel prior to assuming those duties. Any further promotions would be at the discretion of the new..."

His mind snapped back to the present as the driver turned to the west, off the main, macadamized roadway. He was also aware the graded dirt road was gradually transforming into less a motorable byway and more a well-worn, somewhat rutted track accustomed instead to the frequent commercial traffic of ox-wagons, bicycles, and the wheel-barrow like hand carts on which much of the local produce made its way to market. This was more like the Africa

Wellington had known when he first joined 1/2 Kings African Rifles as a junior subaltern during the Great War. That was when he had met RSM Juma. Only recently having completed officer training, Lieutenant Rangely had just assumed his duties with the first battalion of the second regiment, Kings African Rifles, seconded from the Northamptonshire Regiment which he had joined as a private at the start of the Great War.

The noise of the motorcar arriving hardly startled Juma, although the sight of *Amiri Likwemba* beside his bed did take the retired RSM aback. How many years had passed since they last met? Seeing his former lieutenant warmed Juma's heart. The thin moustache had turned from golden blond, like the flower of a maize stalk, to a more gentlemanly grey, but Juma thought of him by the name the *askari* had first given the young second lieutenant because of that strip of hair which adorned his upper lip. The epaulets of the dress uniform Rangely had donned for dinner, though, signified his new rank. Obviously the young lieutenant learned well under the watchful tutelage of the Regimental Sergeant Major, then only recently promoted himself.

Now that they were face to face again, it wasn't necessary to exchange many words. Rangely greeted Chotsani, Juma's new wife, who acted as an intermediary of sorts. Not that Juma could say much as it was difficult even to breathe; his open eyes and smile of recognition did much to set the tone. Rangely tried to assure the old *askari* that he would be looked after as best the battalion could. Ample supplies of food, including daily deliveries of milk, would be sent to Majowa for his family. Then the Colonel took Juma's hand in his own.

He leaned down to say goodbye to his old friend: *"Kwa heri, rafiki yangu."* Rangely spoke in *Kiswahili*, the language they had both learned, and shared, as soldiers in the KAR. Then to Chotsani, the same: "*Asigaleje*," the best *Chiyao* he could muster.

Juma tried to speak in return, but only slipped into a deep coughing fit. Both men realized it might well be the last exchange between them.

"He was … or is, rather … a legend," Lieutenant Resten Lipenga muttered quietly as he followed his commanding officer out of the small house, returning to the vehicle they had arrived in a few moments before. Once they were on the road back to Cobbe Barracks, Colonel Rangely began making good on his promise:

"See to it his needs are met, Lieutenant," he ordered his aide-de-camp. "We both know how important he has been, and not just to our regiment!"

On Assignment

"*Cisukusuku! Cisukusuku!*"

As the earthen tremors shook the bones of everyone in Majowa Village, Juma Chimwere's voice echoed a chorus of recognition heard all across Chief Chikowi's domain. Earthquakes were not unknown to the Yao, but were rare enough to be taken as a sign that something was unstable in their world. Indeed, for many the shaking ground underneath their feet conjured a very specific image, a relatively new creature in their cosmological lexicon:

"*Napolo!*"

Juma wasn't alone in believing the great snake living deep in the bowels of Zomba Mountain would shift about in his cavernous den when provoked, causing any number of disruptions in the land above. And for Chief Chikowi and his people the provocation was all too clear! *Napolo* knew as well as they it was the *Angelesi* —the Europeans who recently settled amongst them—bringing many *uti* with them. Not that the Yao were unfamiliar with such guns; still, the new weapons were scarce among them. And soon different men—*Wasanda* soldiers wearing turbans—came with more guns to enforce the will of the English upon the Africans amongst whom they now lived. Thus the sudden shaking signaled not merely the fragility of hard-won Yao hegemony; it also confirmed the tenuousness of their position vis-à-vis the new settlers, not just on Zomba Mountain, but within the territory of all the Yao chiefs.

Word quickly spread that the Europeans and their Sikh soldiers were making war on Yao chiefs living even beyond their mountain. Chief Kawinga sent news of being spared after his main village was overrun, but only by agreeing to assist the *Angelesi* in further campaigns. As the number of such reports increased, news reached Zomba that the English and Sikhs—with various allies, including Kawinga and his men—defeated other Africans far to the north and the south. Might these newcomers use their warlike methods to subdue Chikowi's people as well? Chief Chikowi realized he must take action before the *Angelesi* could force his hand.

Calling together his *ndunas* and other councilors, Chikowi sought their advice. Some, of course, simply urged preparing for war against the new threat. Others noted the accommodations Kawinga had made to forestall a worse fate. But a few—aware that individual Yao warriors from other chieftaincies had thrown in their lot with the British forces—urged another way. Why not send a few of the fittest and bravest of their mature youth to join the new *asiliakli* force being organized by the English? Those doing so would have recently passed through initiation into manhood. Glorious stories of Yao history would be fresh in their minds. Obligations to their Chief and people would be impressed into their consciousness. Could not they be trusted to remain true, despite working for the *Angelesi*?

"*E-e-ya!* That is the way!" Chief Chikowi proclaimed to the assemblage. Indeed, it was the third option which appealed to the Chief. Encouraging his young men to become *asilikali* for the British might well open a pathway to avoiding the loss of land

and influence as had befallen other Yao chiefs. "Send word to my people! Call on brave young men to volunteer!"

Juma Chimwere, after consulting his uncles, was among the first to come forward. A strapping and well-spoken young man, Juma stood out among his peers. He was the model of a warrior, despite not yet having actually proven himself in war. But he was usually the victor in the various contests held among his mates—the boys, now young men—who had completed initiation with him. Whether wrestling or running, throwing the *lipanga* or using a *cikolongwe* spear when hunting for hippo in the marshes where the Mulunguzi flowed down from the mountain, Juma almost always seemed the most adept of those who had passed their initiation tests with him. Chief Chikowi was well pleased to see Juma would be at the forefront of his new strategy.

"Go well! Stand tall!" his uncle Masamba urged him. "Never forget you are a Yao first, but be proud as an *msilikali* as well." Not that he was lacking in self-confidence, but Juma was heartened by his uncle's words.

Taking the lead, Juma set out with his best friends, Issa Bakali and Stambuli Likuleka, journeying around the mountain to the place where the British were welcoming Africans, and especially Yao, to join them as *askari*. When they reached the encampment, he took the lead in dealing with the British recruiting sergeant. After he announced their intent, a smile appeared on the face of the recruiting officer. Juma, in return, also shyly smiled.

"What is your name?"

"Juma."

"Any other name by which you are known?"

"Juma Chimwere."

"Who is your chief?"

"Chikowi," Juma replied proudly.

"Ah yes, you are not the first of this chief. And these others also?" the recruiting officer asked, gesturing to the two young men who had queued behind Juma.

Remembering what he had been told about their chief's decision in council, Juma spoke softly:

"E-e-ya. We are all of Chikowi."

"And your village, Juma?" the recruiter asked.

"Majowa." Juma thought of his mother as he answered. No longer would he be living in her house, being guided by her brothers. He was both sad, yet also thrilled to put his boyhood behind.

After a few additional questions, he was told to wait for the others to complete their interviews. Juma did not know that as a result of his answers that he was recorded as being 18 years of age, although that might have been an overestimate. Among his peers, Juma appeared by his size and confidence perhaps to be older than the rest. Nor did he know that he was registered as *askari* No. 103, indicating he was among the very first Africans enrolled in British service, forming a part of what the *Angelisi* called the Central African Rifles.

∞∞∞∞∞∞

> *"Mtu mmoja alienda,*
>
> *"Alienda kulima shamba.*
>
> *"Mtu mmoja na mbwe yake*
>
> *"Walienda kulima shamba.*
>
> *"Watu wawili walienda..."*

The recruits sang heartily as they learned to march! Though wondering why any man would take a dog with him to hoe a garden, Issa, Stambuli, and Juma sang along with the others. In the process they were learning not only to march, but also to follow commands in *Kiswahili*, a language which they had previously heard but had not yet learned to speak with any fluency. It most probably escaped their consciousness that this nonsense song about a man, his dog, and the field they were going to tend, was little more than a rough *Kiswahili* version of a traditional English childhood counting verse. Put to use by their new military instructors, they were learning not merely to march in step to the tune, but also important numbers, nouns, and their modifiers in the language of command which would dominate their lives as British *askari*.

There was certainly marching, then more marching, far more than Issa especially appreciated. But Juma seemed to excel in the demonstration of his physical prowess and so didn't mind it nearly as much.

"Pangana safu!" The words were barked out with authority, ordering them to attention in their prescribed military formation.

With that from their instructors, all the new soldiers tried to find their way into the ranks and files of a proper military formation. Too often at first, Issa found it hard to line up correctly with the others, much to the disgust of the British and Sikh drill instructors who labeled him, perhaps more than almost any other, as a hopeless raw recruit. *"Askari mchanga"* they yelled at him so frequently, poor Issa became known among his fellow soldiers, who also were just learning this new language, as *"Mchanga."* As they frequently did, the Africans seized upon anything—large or small, good or ill—as a focal point to describe their fellows as well as those in command. Issa's nickname stuck. However, none of the new *askari* could stop to worry too much about the jocularity which ensued, as once they mastered the formations required for military order and discipline there was still much more to learn.

When properly lined up, the company awaited the command *"Endeni!"* and would set out, marching in step, all heeding the call of the instructor, by the numbers:

"Moja!

"Mbili!

"Tatu!

"Nne!"

They were expected to follow the lead of a designated soldier whose gait was intended to guide their steps, first with their left foot, then their right:

"Kushoto!"

"Kuume!

So quickly did he grasp the pattern, and so rhythmic were his foot falls, Juma frequently was given pride of place in the formation as the soldier expected to set a pattern for the rest in marching exercises, even during the longer marches down the mountainside into the start of the savannah beyond. While proud to be singled out in this way, he also realized there were other important skills to learn. Among them, both Juma and Issa especially enjoyed rifle drills and soon became expert in following those commands.

"Karibu karibu!" Shoulder to shoulder, they would form a line, then turn on command so their rifles would all point toward the targets at a distance from them. They learned to concentrate on listening for the next commands, which they soon came to anticipate.

"Tayari!" The weapons readily came up to their shoulders, one hand near the trigger mechanism, the other stretched out to the hand grip along the barrel.

"Lingeni!" Their eyes focused down the sights above the trigger and at the end of the barrel, aiming at targets some distance from their firing line.

"Pigeni!" But when the order came to fire, once they pulled the trigger no bullets would actually discharge from their guns. The instructors at first only gave them wooden models of guns for practice. *"Takataka bunduki"* the recruits called them: "Toy guns good for nothing."

It was those wooden toys, however, which they used in learning how to attach and wield the bayonets they soon came to understand would sometimes be their most effective weapons. Using the long knives at the end of their rifles seemed almost second nature, much like the removable points of the *cikolongwe* spear Juma, Stambuli, and Issa had learned to wield as older boys when hunting hippo. So smiles came to their eager faces when the command, *"Choma kwa singe!"* was uttered during rifle drills. The order to "Fix bayonets!" always seemed a less enthusiastic command from the instructors, perhaps because many of them thought the new Yao soldiers were just a little too eager to jump into action. This may have been confirmed one evening in camp, after drills were completed and the *askari* had a little free time before the bugle sounded, calling them to their beds.

At first Issa pretended to affix a bayonet onto an imaginary rifle. Then he thrusted it menacingly at his friend Stambuli. As he often had when they were boys in Majowa, Stambuli eagerly played along with the pantomime. Another thrust, this more from above. Then a third, upward but to the left. And in the grand finale, a direct plunge toward the midsection of the "victim." At that point Stambuli, pretending to be hurt during the simulated attack, acted out a realistic imitation of a wounded man taking his last breathe. A throng of recruits gathered to witness the display, cheering excitedly for both victim and attacker. All the noise drew the attention of an instructor, who seemed at least mildly amused even as he chastised the two leading participants, informing both that such horseplay, however well intentioned, was not appropriate behaviour for serious *askari*.

Despite each now having a reprimand on his record, Issa and Stambuli were still able to join Juma and the others a few days later when they were finally issued fully functioning rifles. They were allowed to load bullets into the firing chambers, proceeding to complete the usual rifle drill, but now firing real bullets at their distant targets. Perhaps it was a result of their excitement, but not many of them were successful in hitting the marks. Clearly there would be more practice in store! But before that could continue, they learned how to take the weapons apart, clean, and then reassemble them, practicing those operations many times over as well. Again it seemed to Juma—who grasped such complications more quickly than most of his comrades—that their training was taking far longer than necessary. But he realized (though he told none of the others) perhaps even he needed time to make certain he could actually fire his weapon with some degree of accuracy!

∞∞∞∞∞∞

"E-e-ya! Ndiyo! E-e-e!"

Not merely happiness, but something more like ecstatic enthusiasm overcame Stambuli, Issa, Juma, and the other recruits as they were ordered to join in their first real experience as soldiers! That morning Captain Manning called the recruit company to order.

"Simama sawasawa!" he bellowed, and they quickly came to attention. Manning then told them they would join a Sikh company and three more seasoned *askari* companies in a march toward Lake Chilwa to put an end to a pattern of highway robberies in Lomwe lands near the southern lakeshore. The men were understandably excited knowing that all their efforts of the past few months would actually come to fruition. They wanted to prove themselves as soldiers and impress their Captain and the other officers. It would be a glorious opportunity, they felt certain. And it came quickly. Almost immediately they were ordered into marching formation with the other companies, followed without delay by a command that surprised many:

"Endeni upesi!" This would be a double-time march even though there was quite some distance to travel! For most of the recruits, it was a familiar sight in front of them as they marched from their encampment, one the entire company had seen during numerous training drills. However, they were now expected to traverse that same landscape as quickly as possible. The Chilwa plane stretched out from Zomba Mountain as the woodlands gradually

turned more into savannah, then grassland and eventually a swamp as it neared the lake. It was a tableau Juma and his friends had seen many times on youthful explorations, gazing east and north from atop Zomba Mountain. It was as well terrain they knew in detail from hunting trips to the Mulunguzi swamp. From their youthful vistas it had looked like an easy walk. And their pace on hunting excursions had usually been slow and deliberate. But now even Juma, who had helped to set the pace for his company in training, found the going more taxing than he'd anticipated. Like the rest, he welcomed the brief break the column received as they came upon a cluster of baobab trees. Fortunately, it was not the hottest part of the dry season, so Juma was glad that, even without most of their leaves, the *milambe* which shaded the column provided some relief.

During their short respite Juma recalled the stories he had heard about Chikowi leading his followers along this same way, though traveling in the opposite direction. He especially recalled his uncle's historical account, offered during their initiation only a year before:

"After sloshing through swamp and pushing open a path through the tall *bango* reeds, we came to a grassland clearing before making our way to a small grove of *milambe*." Could his uncle have actually stopped near these same baobabs? Looking back toward the mountain, in the direction of the route the *askari* had just marched, Juma imagined the next scene from his uncle's story:

"After resting for a bit, our Chief bade us move beyond the shade of the big trees and look to the horizon. We could see a splendid mountain rising up so high it pierced through the clouds to touch the sky! Immediately, everyone knew Chief Chikowi had led us to a new home where we would at last be safe." Now, as Juma reflected on his own position—while resting in likely that very same place—he knew his was an opportunity to ensure the dream Chief Chikowi sought for his people would remain intact. But doing so required he be the best *msilikali* he could possibly be, starting with this, his first test as a soldier. His thoughts drifted back to the present, and not a moment too soon. The column was ordered to reform and quickly resumed its fast march through the last of the dry savannah and into the swampy grasses as they approached the lake.

They passed several small villages where people were starting to prepare their rice fields in anticipation of the rains which should begin within a couple of months. Captain Manning ordered the column to slow its pace, however, as they approached the village of Chief Serumba whose people were suspected of complicity in the recent robberies. Soon two of the companies, including Juma's, where ordered into a single line. *"Karibu karibu!"* shortly followed by *"Choma kwa singe!"* and then the anticipated order *"Endeni!"* Having learned the drills well, the new *askari* acquitted themselves famously, coming into formation almost in unison with their more experienced comrades.

Bayonets protruding from their rifles, the two companies moved forward in several lines. They looked menacing—as they no doubt were supposed to!—proceeding toward and into the village. Soon Chief Serumba came out and meekly surrendered. Captain Manning ordered him bound and escorted away from the village under guard. Juma was one of those detailed to attend to the deposed chief, making certain he did not flee. Others were instructed to set fire to the village after insuring the inhabitants had scattered. Juma was sorrowful as he listened to the wailings in *Chilomwe*. Though he did not understand the language completely, the lamentations of the villagers were clear enough, mourning the loss of their chief and with him their collective identity. Juma knew it was precisely an effort to avoid such a calamity for his kinsmen and the other followers of Chief Chikowi that had brought him to his present position. This new experience only strengthened his resolve.

As they made camp after their confrontations with the Lowme villagers, the *askari* were much more at ease than they had been during their march to the Lake. While a few, such as Juma, remained on guard duty in a separate area where Serumba was confined, their commanding officer allowed the remainder to relax. A small group, including Issa, quietly found their way back toward the rice field they had passed on the march to Serumba's. There the *askari* were able to obtain several fermenting pots of a sweet liquid which had an expected effect on several of their number. In fact, some were intoxicated to the point that they attempted to "liberate" some of the few possessions the fleeing Lomwe had tried to take with them before the village was burned. The ensuing noisy confrontations grew nearly to a riot, which unfortunately required their officers' attention. Lieutenant Manwaring was ordered to defuse the disputes. Visibly angry that the *askari* had consumed so much of the intoxicating beverage, the Lieutenant harshly asked them:

"Pombe?!" trying to confirm that locally-made beer was the cause of their inebriation and, almost inevitably, escalating their bad behaviour to the point it spiraled out of control. He was looking for someone on whom to focus his ire when his eyes fell on Issa, who clearly had over-imbibed. The lieutenant's angry scowl was enough to provoke a response:

"Hapana, Bwana!" Issa tried to reassure the Lieutenant. *"Hapana pombe."* No, he had not taken any *pombe* at all he insisted, knowing any excessive consumption of that local brew by *askari* was frowned upon by CAR officers. His faculties, and inhibitions, were so compromised, though, that Issa instead smiled and, with a reassuring tone, offered a mitigating word in his native tongue:

"Utobwa!"

That local mead or honey beer was equally intoxicating, however, and this explanation of Issa's indiscretions did not relieve him from the Lieutenant's wrath. In fact, when Manwaring finally worked out the complete meaning of this claim, he seemed if anything more irate. Only recently arrived in Zomba, the new subaltern was still unsure in his command of *Kiswahili* and as yet not familiar with *Chiyao* or any other local language. So it didn't seem to matter that there were several other *askari* who were equally guilty. Soon Issa, too, was under guard with a second reprimand entered on his record. And in his condition the long march back to Zomba the next day was particularly unpleasant, having confirmed the sobriquet he'd been given in training.

∞∞∞∞∞∞

Glad to be back at the CAR camp in Zomba, Juma, Stambuli, and especially Issa were hoping they would be granted leave to go home for a least a brief visit. They had been away from Majowa now longer than ever before. However, no leave was forthcoming. The recruits were instead reassigned to several of the existing companies of the force and, shortly thereafter, ordered to prepare for moving to Fort Alston, far to the north, where they would be needed to quell a rebellion of Ngoni tribesmen whom, they were told, threatened European missionaries and settlers. The new camp was much farther away from home than any of the new recruits had previously traveled. Realizing that, they came to understand their absence would continue more than for just a few days more. But it was hard for any of them to conceive that they would remain apart from their families even longer in the future.

Juma's A Company was the first ordered to depart, joining a small detachment of Sikhs, all commanded by Captain Brake who had arrived in Zomba only a month before. Their move to Fort Alston was uneventful, as the men marched on an already established route until they reached the Shire River. They then followed well-trodden but narrower paths across the low savannah woodland until they reached their destination. The fort they found, though, was little more than a small building, not nearly large enough to accommodate the one hundred or so soldiers under Brake's command. As such, Fort Alston offered little respite, so within a day they continued on toward the reported trouble at Chief Mpezeni's on the sunset side of the watershed they traversed.

Their advance now became far more difficult. Even though there was only a gradual change in elevation, rapid deployment in rain soaked woodlands took a toll on the men. Not even the occasional tightly packed cluster of trees provided any shelter from the downpours. It was an exhausted column that relieved the worried garrison at Fort Jameson. Not one to complain, Juma nonetheless was among many of his fellow *askari* whose feet ached following nine very long days of double time marches ordered by their captain. Encouraged by some of the Sikh non-commissioned officers, a few of the seasoned *askari* searched for some familiar plants to make a kind of foot salve to ease their discomfort, but without much luck. Juma, however, did manage to gather some leaves—his mother called them *cilisya*—for reducing swelling of arms, legs, and feet. But as a very junior member of the detachment, his efforts weren't particularly appreciated. As it transpired, no search for remedies to relieve aching feet would have mattered, since Brake had his men, and the reinforcements from Zomba who soon joined them, campaigning almost every day.

Only a day after marching thirty miles to rescue a small police detachment at Luangweni, the men awoke to the sounds of a large number of Ngoni warriors gathering not far away from that village. The entire CAR force was ordered to assemble outside their camp. Juma was pleased his company was one of two selected to confront the Ngoni who could now be seen dancing, singing, and menacingly waving spears at the smaller British contingent. His attention focused on the tasks directly confronting his small group of *askari*. On command, the two companies came to formation. They released a single volley of rifle fire, aimed above the heads of their adversaries. The massed Ngoni seemed to expect such a response to their threats. But what followed almost certainly took the warrior assemblage by surprise.

On the first order, *"Choma kwa singe!"* all the *askari* attached bayonets to their rifles. That was followed by *"Endeni polepole!"* and a slow, steady, silent march toward the Ngoni. The two companies were anchored in their resolve by the discipline of their Sikh non-commissioned officers, who kept the line steady in stride, spirit, and silence. To little effect, the Ngoni threw their spears toward the *askari*, rather than holding them for close quarter combat as had been their usual practice. The Ngoni warriors then began a slow retreat as the *askari* line continued toward them. It was at that moment the tide turned. In the process Juma learned a major lesson about how armies operate in the field and why it was important to follow orders precisely. The remainder of the force, which Juma thought had remained in place after his company advanced, unexpectedly joined the fray! Lieutenant Sharpe and the remaining *askari* companies appeared on the flank, causing the Ngoni to flee in some disarray. Just then one of the 7-pound guns a Sikh unit had brought into the field broke the silence, sending further shockwaves into the Ngoni army which now seemed completely routed.

As the *askari* regrouped and began a return to Fort Jameson, another Ngoni force—which must have been dispatched not long after the first—now approached. Captain Brake immediately ordered a machine gun unit to fire on the newly advancing Ngoni, protecting the British flank. He then sent A Company forward in a full charge to contain this second threat. Despite the fact that they weren't able to catch up to and fully engage their fleeing enemies, the two responses quickly ended the immediate danger. It must have seemed to the *askari*, as it clearly was to their commander, that the Ngoni were no match for the Central African Rifles! But their campaign was far from over. The two main commanders who had organized Mpezeni's resistance were yet to be captured and Mpezeni himself personally defeated.

Nonetheless, all the *askari* appreciated being given a break of almost a day, even though Brake insisted they take much of that time to clean and prepare their weapons. As he did so, Juma wondered if the Ngoni against who he had been campaigning might have felt like his ancestors. His uncle's initiation lessons again came to his mind:

"When famine struck the coastal people, the peaceful life of all the Yao was broken. The Walolo with their guns made war on all the Yao chiefs." His uncle's account for the initiates went on to explain that this was before the Yao themselves had guns. Then he continued: "Every attempt to resist was in vain. There was no option but to flee, so the Yao scattered in every direction. Our only hope was to find a new home where we might be safe. That is why Chikowi led us to Zomba." Perhaps, thought Juma, this is merely what the Ngoni are doing now. Would his present course be sufficient to protect Chikowi and his people from the fate of Ngoni and Lomwe peoples he'd been ordered to defeat? He did not have long to ponder such questions, for early the next day Juma's company was again in action, marching directly into Ngoni territory.

After fifteen hours of skirmishing, the Ngoni commanders fled, leaving a large herd of cattle unprotected. These were herded towards the CAR camp while the Ngoni villages were burnt, though none of the unripened crops in the surrounding fields were destroyed. When he later learned that Captain Brake had not wished to create famine and provoke additional African grievances, Juma was initially impressed. However his experience of war as one of devastation inflicted on an enemy was rekindled in just a matter of days. His company, after burning Mpezeni's village, chased the chief and his dwindling band of followers into barren country. Not long after that, Issa was with Lieutenant Brogden's F Company when Mpezeni's son Singu—one of those Ngoni commanders Juma's A Company had put to flight just days before—was surrounded and captured. When Issa later described to his friend the quick trial and execution of the Ngoni heir, Juma was further discouraged by his experience as an *askari*. And the incarceration of Mpezeni following his voluntary surrender did nothing but deepen the disquiet he felt.

∞∞∞∞∞∞

As the entire CAR force slowly made its way back towards Zomba, taking the defeated Mpezeni into enforced exile at Fort Manning, Juma brooded over his continued service. The plan that led him to join the *asilikali* force now appeared fraught with difficulties. What sort of actions might incur British wrath sufficient to order him to war? Where might he be ordered next to make war on Africans who had displeased the *Angelesi*? When the troops finally returned to their home base, the news he received almost paradoxically increased his apprehensions: a promotion to Lance Corporal! Moreover, Juma received an award—the Central Africa Medal—in recognition of his service during what his officers called the Mpezeni Expedition. And he also received a second award, somewhat delayed, for his time at Lake Chilwa shortly after completing his first training course. He was proud of these recognitions for being a good *askari*, yet if he was now a favoured soldier, how could he be certain he wouldn't next be ordered to fight against his kinsmen and assist in deposing Chief Chikowi?

Thus Juma was relieved when his company was ordered to join in another patrol across the Shire River, this time toward Dedza mountain. Juma felt honoured to be entrusted with command of a small squad of three others as the *askari* searched even the smallest villages, looking for evidence of the Ngoni warriors whom they were told had been gathering in the area. Though Dedza "mountain" itself was nothing like the Zomba massif he called home, the patrols moved slowly, careful not to miss any possible hiding places in the nearby woodlands and hills. There was almost no actual combat, certainly nothing like the confrontations he had experienced before. Only once did he even fire his rifle, and only one additional time was the squad ordered to use its bayonets to impress villagers with their seriousness. Mostly the *askari* were expected to march smartly, keeping their rifles clearly visible, and simply making their presence known to the local people. For Juma it was a far cry from his two previous deployments, and he returned to Zomba in much better spirits. And when he was granted leave to return home to Majowa for several days, there was definitely a joyous spring in his step as he took the path around the mountain to his home village.

Of course his outlook may have been buoyed by thoughts of Ambikanile. She was from Majowa as well, though he had not really known her well until their meeting during a feast held at Chief Chikowi's not long before the great earthquake. She admired his poise and quiet confidence which probably was a result of having been entrusted with manly responsibilities, having so successfully completed his initiation. And though he had seen her before, the almost sudden interest she showed towards him was especially flattering. They met again several times in the following days, not really by accident. Just before he left Majowa to enlist as an *msilikali*, she had agreed to marry him. And as was customary, his uncle went to her family—not immediately revealing Ambikanile and Juma had agreed to do so—but beginning the process which would eventually lead to marriage. But as Juma was becoming a soldier and would be away from the village so long, the negotiations became far more protracted than usual.

Only through occasional messages he was able to receive and send while he was training, and later away on assignments, did Juma participate in the process. As he knew, this was most unusual. His friends didn't let him forget it either, with Stambuli and Funsani—a new *askari* friend from Chief Makanjila's—particularly sharp in their barbs. Juma tried to laugh them off, but couldn't ignore them completely. He worried: Would Ambikanile, and particularly her family, be willing to understand that he now had dual responsibilities? So just prior to leaving on the march to Fort Alston, Juma sent a sizeable portion of his accumulated army pay to his uncle and father, asking that they use the funds to construct a *nyumba* for him where he might live with his bride when he returned. Building a house, he well knew, was customarily the responsibility of an intended bridegroom. Asking his closest male relatives to do so on his behalf was the best he could manage, given the soldier's life to which he'd now committed himself. When he was back in Zomba, the message awaiting his return was that the building was underway and the marriage also agreed. In return he sent hopeful word back to arrange a marriage feast for the days after his return from Dedza, as he expected to have leave at that point. The news which awaited him when his company returned from Dedza "mountain" to *their* mountain was therefore totally welcome. Having received informal news Juma's company was marching back from Dedza, his uncle along with Ambikanile's uncle, had arranged the required feast to solemnize the marriage in just a few days.

'Sir!" Juma spoke to Lieutenant Brogden, under whose command he had marched to Dedza and back. He explained the plans for his wedding feast as soon as they reached their Zomba camp. "I am requesting leave to join my bride, sir."

"*Sina hakika nalo*," Brogden replied. It really wasn't in his hands. Juma's heart sank. While he understood the British Commissioner would need to make the final decision, he hoped for greater encouragement, even support, from his latest company commander. By being so uncertain, the Lieutenant confirmed the nickname, given him first by Issa and frequently used in private by many of the *askari*. Tall and thin himself, the lieutenant almost looked like the walking stick he carried on the march. *Mtindiso* was straight and formal in dealing with the men as well! Juma was further discouraged when he also recalled Brogden was one of the officers involved in the capture, summary trial, and subsequent execution of Mpezeni's son, Singu. So when word came back the next day that his leave had been granted, Juma was indeed pleased, all the more when *Mtindiso* himself offered congratulations.

Being told he would be a lucky soldier—*askari wa heri*—to have a wife was much more than Juma expected! It was then the lieutenant showed a much more affable side of his personality. Describing how happy he was about his own marriage, Brogden also offered advice about managing the long separations which soldiers, their wives and families often must endure. Juma smiled as he acknowledged the concern. He was glad to witness a more human side of command, and joyfully made ready to leave camp for his home around the mountain. It was an obviously jubilant Juma who finally reached Majowa with just one more evening to spend in his mother's home before he and his bride would have a home of their own. Juma hoped that at some point Ambikanile would join him as an *msilikali's* wife in a home built for them within the CAR *boma* on the other side of the mountain. He was also comforted in knowing that they would always have a home in Majowa where they could return.

Although it was, on the one hand, a solemn occasion, on the other it was joyous for both families. The uncles of the bride and groom were there as formal witnesses to the marriage, as were both their fathers. Ambikanile's mother had pounded sufficient flour that she, and Juma's mother, might each prepare a large pot of *ugali*. To serve with his mother's porridge, his aunts slaughtered and cooked a cockerel as *mboga*, while Ambikanile's aunts made a similar relish with a hen. Their families then exchanged and ate the food, in doing so symbolically signifying their joining together in the marriage. Finally, each of their uncles spoke as formal witnesses in acknowledgement of their union. Juma's uncle Masamba, however, continued at length about what this marriage meant not just to the families, but to the village and Chief Chikowi's people as well. He cautioned both the bride and groom about the promise and the perils of Juma's service as an *msilikali*, and how they each needed to bear those burdens not only for themselves but for a greater good. As important as his words were, they may have been lost for the moment on Juma and his bride as they both longed to begin their new lives together.

It was a sad departure for the couple when Juma had to return to duty less than a fortnight after their marriage. But his demeanor was much different when he arrived back in camp. Not only his friends and fellow *askari* noticed; Issa was quick to congratulate his long-time friend, while Funsani, Stambuli, and some others made good natured jocular references to his new status as a married man. Though they were less vocal, the CAR officers—led by *Mtindiso* himself—also took notice, talking among themselves about the renewed sense of confidence they sensed in the new lance corporal. Though only vaguely aware of such barracks gossip, Juma tried his best to reciprocate.

∞∞∞∞∞∞

Activity in the camp began to accelerate soon after Juma's return. At first it seemed all, or at least a large part, of the battalion would soon begin a new deployment. But only a few small groups—totaling about one full company—left the camp. Each group deployed to one of the numerous small forts established in recent years by the British. Juma had only seen about five of them, but he knew from orders given other *askari* that there were more than twice that many. Those conversations also helped him realize that the three expeditions he had been a part of were likely the most violent involving his battalion. Following the departures, activity in the headquarters camp only continued to intensify. Finally, the reason became clear: A newly recruited battalion of the Central African Rifles was to begin training. Then, when he learned he'd once again been promoted—this time to corporal—his initial thoughts were he might be expected to join the new battalion.

At first this worried him. Even when he learned his company and several others would be expected to help train the new recruits, he could only imagine that he would now be thrust into further campaigning against nearby peoples. Before his heart sank further, though, there was word the new battalion wouldn't be sent into nearby territory, but across the sea. After that he breathed a sigh of relief and was able to throw himself wholeheartedly into training activities. He most enjoyed helping the recruits on evening drills at the headquarters parade grounds and night marches on the roads nearby, especially when the moon lit up the light mist on the mountain. He thought about how many of his friends had struggled when learning the commands and formations, so he was keen to help the new *askari* through similar difficulties. He was surprised when the new battalion received orders to join the British garrison in Mauritius. They were just as uncertain and underequipped as he, Issa, Funsani, and Stambuli had been when they started training. Yet these latest recruits were thrust into duty far sooner than he had been. Juma could not imagine how they might fare on what he understood was an island in the middle of the great sea. He was almost visibly relieved he had not been ordered to join them!

To Juma it seemed a reward for his efforts in helping the recruits of the new battalion when he was promoted yet again. He was now a sergeant! He knew well this meant a great deal more responsibility. And it might mean more concerns and self-doubts such as those which plagued him before his marriage. But his latest promotion also meant Ambikanile could join him at a home of their own in a dedicated non-commissioned officers' section of the headquarters camp. This was all the more important as she was now expecting their first child! He was truly a man now, with a family and the attendant duties of any full established Yao man as well. Those thoughts made him proud, and he knew this new status was, in part at least, due to his decision to become an *askari*. He was grateful for a brief leave from his duties so that he could escort Ambikanile from Majowa to their new home.

When Juma arrived at the home he had built—well, actually, that his uncles and father had built in Majowa—for his wife, it seemed as though Ambikanile had done virtually nothing to prepare for their journey, even though it would be a short one.

"Why aren't you ready to move to our new home? I've asked relatives to be here to help us, and now you have not done as I've asked and made ready!" His tone was noticeably sharp, as it might have been were he scolding some of the askari under his command, and he could see that she was offended by his manner.

"But this is our home," she replied, but not quite so sharply. Ambikanile's voice became softer as she continued to speak. "I would really prefer to stay here, where I can be close to my mother, just as she was to her mother when she first married." The customs of their people were very strong in her heart. But so was her caring for this man whose child she was carrying. The conflicting emotions were extremely difficult at that moment. Her eyes teared up ever so slightly, even as she looked down toward the floor. He struggled to compose himself, realizing this could be an important moment in their life together. He thought first of the words his uncle had spoken at their wedding, emphasizing the duties they both shared to affirm his role as an *msilikali*. His mind then turned to the unexpected advice from Lieutenant Brogden. After considering both, Juma sat down beside his wife.

"We must make our home whenever we are able to be together!" he suggested reassuringly. "The life of an *msilikali* is the one I have chosen; and now you have chosen it as well. With it comes…uh…uncertainty, it is true." He chose the word carefully: *kusingalilwa*, which carried a suggestion not only of anxiousness, but also the potential for trouble. "Especially at times when I am ordered to face that uncertainty directly, there will be separation and loneliness. But there are also times when we can be together. So we must take advantage of *all* those times, to wipe away that uncertainty from our minds! And to help senior *asilikali* do so, there is a *lijumba* at the *boma* just for us." Again he chose the word carefully, so his wife would understand this was more than just an ordinary village house, such as the *nyumba* his uncles and father built for them in Majowa, but a larger and more substantial dwelling instead. "Please, let us go and make this our home. We will be more fortunate than most," he added, attempting to reassure her. "We will also have our original *nyumba* here in Majowa where we may easily return to visit our families."

Despite her reluctance, Ambikanile accompanied her husband around the mountain to the camp. Though he had made attempts to transform the stark army quarters into a livable family home before their arrival, when she saw it there was much she also asked him to do. He was willing, and did so as his military duties allowed. And when she asked to go back to their home in Majowa to await the birth of their child, he was again grateful to his superiors for allowing him to accompany her. Just after she was settled, most of Juma's company was ordered far up the shore of the big lake and beyond on a new expedition to settle another problem for the British. Even though his soldier-mentality led him to believe his place was with those fellow *askari*, his father-to-be-mentality was happy his squad was not one of those selected on this occasion. He was sure Apesile (and her mother) were happy too, as he was thus able to visit his daughter shortly after she was born at their home around the mountain.

Juma took his new family back to their home at the battalion headquarters before the remainder of his company returned from their exhausting march of what he was told was more than a thousand miles. Now his job became helping the tired returning *askari* readjust to life in camp by day, then helping his almost as tired wife with their new child by night. Juma later would recall this brief period of his life as one the most demanding he had experienced. Yet he would also recall that in many ways it was a time of calm before a trying, if extremely rewarding, period of almost two years spent mostly away from Zomba.

∞∞∞∞∞∞

Apesile was only seven months old when Juma said goodbye to her and her mother on his way to a place he knew only as Asante, said to be in a far distant part of Africa. He—and most of the *askari* of what then was the 1st Battalion, Central African Rifles—were ordered to help in putting down a full scale rebellion against British rule in their Gold Coast colony. A smaller number, including Issa and Stambuli, would remain behind for garrison duty. All the details of these assignments were largely unknown to Juma, but he was coming to put more trust in what his officers told him. He also realized they had an increasing confidence in *his* abilities. As a result, he felt a duty and an obligation to be a part of bringing some stability to this far-off land, just as he was beginning to find around his beloved mountain. Once his battalion reached the sea by river steamer, the great challenge for him was boarding the immense *ngalawa* which awaited them. The ship, far larger than any he had seen before, was to transport most of his battalion, their maxim and field guns, as well as considerable quantities of supplies, across the sea to the place called Asante. A few of his fellows expressed considerable apprehension about the prospects for the voyage, and one or two flatly refused. The price for doing so was dismissal from the ranks. As for Juma, no matter his apprehensions, that would have been going too far. Besides, now that he was a non-commissioned officer and had much greater standing in the regiment, he understood his obligation to lead by example.

Once they were at sea, Juma wasn't alone in feeling sick as the ship rolled first to one side, then to the other during much of their passage. His friend Funsani suffered perhaps even more than most. Concerned, Juma asked him about the obvious discomfort he displayed.

"*Ligogo*," Funsani replied meekly while holding his stomach. "As if I had eaten very bad food."

Juma could sympathize. Between occasional bouts of *njofu*—fewer than Funsani and the many *askari* who seemed almost permanently slumped over the ship's rail—Juma managed to maintain a degree of decorum, earning the respect of both the officers and African other ranks. After rounding the Cape of Good Hope, sailing north along the African coast, the seas calmed a bit. But as the vessel entered the waters of the Gulf of Guinea, a large waterspout was spotted not far off the ship's starboard bow, nearly causing a panic among the still queasy *askari*. Although he, too, was amazed as the tower of spinning water seemed to approach the ship, Juma kept his composure. His was one of the few voices among the *askari* cautioning against the assumption that they would be consumed by the wet whirlwind. Major Cobbe, who was in command of the battalion's force sent to West Africa, commended his fortitude in remaining clam amid, almost literally, a storm!

Nonetheless, all were relieved when soon thereafter they disembarked at Cape Coast and began a march overland north into Asante territory. As they began, the savannah woodlands seemed at least somewhat familiar, though it was not long until they came into a rainforest unlike any they had experienced. Even the rains, which the *askari* understood limited operations, were different, more insistent than any they had known. The torrents seemed to be filling streams and swamps all around them even beyond their normal capacity. There were few clearings, though each appeared to encompass an entire village. And the paths between those habitable spots were exceedingly narrow, almost never permitting more than a single person to pass at a time. So much for the linear attack formations they had learned in drill after drill and had used in previous engagements!

Once the battalion began actual military operations, almost two months after they departed Zomba, the reality of their task proved far more difficult than even the most optimistic among them—including the now supremely confident Sgt. Juma—had imagined. Ordered to clear the forestland to the north and east of the British garrison's base at Kumasi, Major Cobbe and his men encountered what seemed a massive stockade, one that fully blocked the main path they had taken out of Kumasi. Although Juma was not in the initial group attacking the stockade, he was among the rear guard which struggled to avoid rifle fire from snipers who were seemingly all around them. Replying with their machine gun, 1/CAR was unable to deter the Asante warriors. The fighting was far fiercer than any he had seen before, so Juma considered himself fortunate not to be among the many of his fellow *askari* who were wounded.

As their situation appeared increasingly dire, the *askari* expected a call to retreat. Instead Major Cobbe ordered a general advance, from the flanks as well as another frontal assault. The ferocity of the *askari* attack, led by their wounded commander, finally dislodged their enemy. The Asante warriors just melted into the bush, abandoning their war camp and the stockade they had just been defending. Juma could hardly believe the extraordinary extent of the massive fortification when he saw it! More than five feet high and just as thick, it extended into the heavy forest a further fifty paces or more on either side of the path. It was so well disguised, none of the *askari* realized it was a formidable stockade until the Asante opened fire on them. Few of the Central

Africans had ever seen a redoubt quite like it! On reflection, though, Juma believed it might be the equal of the coastal stone forts he had heard about in his youth from relatives who had traveled to the sea engaging in trade.

As it turned out, that engagement was the most memorable military action to occupy Juma's battalion during their Asante campaign. Their fellow *askari* of the second battalion arrived from service in Mauritius and Somaliland within the month, and the entire Central African Rifles contingent enjoyed a few weeks rest and recuperation with minimal campaign duties save a few patrols outside of Kumasi. Having suffered very high casualties—nearly 10% of their total strength—1/CAR played a lesser part in actual combat operations as the expedition managed to defeat and arrest most of the Asante chiefs. Juma, however, did play a significant role as he was given command of squad charged with bridging the River Ofin, swollen by torrential rains. His experience in the forests on Zomba Mountain served him well, directing *askari* in first selecting and felling the tallest tress, then stripping each one of unnecessary limbs, and carefully setting the long trunks across the river to make an effective if rudimentary bridge. In just five hours his efforts and those of his men made it possible for a column of nearly 800 to cross in pursuit of the last significant Asante force.

Once their duties in the mopping-up operations were concluded, the *askari* of 1/CAR happily cleaned and polished their weapons, packed their gear, and prepared for the journey back to Zomba. It was amazing how much more quickly time seemed to pass as they made their way homeward! Even their experiences aboard ship didn't appear to induce nearly as much seasickness as they had experienced on their way to the assignment in the Gold Coast. Juma, like so many others, longed for a return to family.

He was almost beyond joy when the final march of their return journey took the men into Zomba, where his wife and daughter were waiting for him. Ambikanile, and even the young Apesile smiled and tugged at him once the men were able to break their formation.

The family's blissful homecoming continued for several weeks as Juma first had leave—enabling all of them to visit Majowa—and then his duties were confined to small tasks at regimental headquarters. As if there could be too much euphoria, their familial happiness was broken when Juma received word that he was assigned to a special detachment which was once again headed to sea, this time to Britain itself. At first Juma was disappointed, as he knew Ambikanile would be as well.

"I've been ordered to Britain," he quietly told his wife after arriving home the day he received his new orders. She was crestfallen; her face quickly changed, revealing not just worry but an underlying fear. Not wishing to alarm her with his news, Juma began to explain further: "There will be only 20 of us, and this will not be for war!"

"But you are an *msilikali*," she interrupted. "Why else would you be ordered to leave us again?"

"We're going to meet the King!" he proudly told her!

∞∞∞∞∞∞

Much of the journey from Chinde, where the Zambezi river steamers met the much larger ocean-going ships, was more relaxed than the *askari* remembered from their hurried deployment to Asante. Captain Percival, in command of the small detachment, tried to busy the men with many talks about their trip. He explained they would traverse what he called a modern marvel, the Suez Canal, on their way to London. He was also at pains to explain that the King was, in fact, the son of the previous Queen who they had sworn to serve. For Juma and, many of the others, this was a difficult concept. As long as he had been a soldier, the Queen was the distant authority his commanders always mentioned as the touchstone for their actions. Only after they returned from Asante did the *askari* hear them speak instead about the King. As did the rest, Juma wondered why there suddenly was a King, even if the revered Queen was now dead. And now they were being taken to meet this mysterious fellow. That a son should suddenly assume the position of respect once accorded his mother seemed very odd indeed.

Captain Percival's explanation of English royal succession did little to resolve their questions, but that did not deter him from offering many other shipboard "entertainments" in any effort to prepare the select group of *askari* for what they would find on their arrival. They were flattered to be singled out as representatives of their regiment in paying respects to the new ruler. In that spirit, perhaps, Juma and the rest tolerated their commander's incessant talks. Yet when he was out of earshot they referred to him as a persistent talker, *Mkaŋwa*; even those who weren't native *Chiyao* speakers knew that was a less than complimentary reference to his incessant explanations. Indeed, much of what he said seemed mere fantasy to the select group of otherwise well-traveled Africans who comprised his audience

London, or *mji mkubwa mno* as Captain *Mkaŋwa* usually described it, was indeed a huge city almost beyond their imagination. Even those who had seen the larger European settlements of Blantyre or Cape Coast, found the prospects of this place hard to fathom: a multitude of buildings, crisscrossed by roads, plus unlimited shops and market stalls—not to mention what seemed to them must be almost countless people—clustered in one massive village. And the incredibly extensive official building where he said they were to meet the King—*boma mkubwa*—certainly would dwarf the Cape Coast Castle Juma recalled seeing on the way to Asante or even the costal stone forts he envisioned from stories he heard as a youth. The gardens their commander described certainly did not sound like the *mashamba* they associated with agricultural pursuits in their villages. No doubt a good deal of the confusion was born out of the fact their Captain was trying to communicate with his *askari* in a second language—*Kiswahili*—that all of them had learned primarily to facilitate their military endeavors.

After their otherwise pleasant journey finally brought the 1/CAR detachment to London, the reality they found was, indeed, well beyond anything they had imagined from Captain *Mkaŋwa*'s attempts to prepare them. Debarking their steamer at the London docks late on the day of their arrival, the men were ordered to clamour aboard an army goods wagon for a short journey to their temporary quarters. In the diminishing daylight, this city was utterly different not only from any they knew, but also from that they imagined listening to Captain *Mkaŋwa*'s descriptions. Their accommodations—St. Georges Barracks, they were told it was called—were far grander than any they'd ever been housed in previously. It was difficult to think about resting in such a place. But told they would meet the King in just over a day's time, Juma did his best by trying to think of it as no different than sleeping in the forest between engagements with Asante warriors. It wasn't the same, though, as there was a cacophony of unfamiliar sounds all about.

Juma was determined to remain as calm and professional as he possibly could be when the detachment was ordered into formation for their march, through city streets, to meet the King. Along with soldiers from the Coldstream Guards and a similar detachment from 2/CAR which had arrived in London directly from West Africa only a day before them, Juma and his fellow *askari* donned their best dress uniforms and then marched out of the Barracks grounds on to Orange Street, turned down Haymarket, continuing on toward The Mall. He wanted to look at each person and every building along the route, but also knew he was expected to display only exemplary military bearing as an example to the younger and less experienced members of his detachment. However, when they turned on to Waterloo Place and came down the steps past the Duke of York's Monument he gasped: ahead was a grassy woodland lake that was St. James Park. At that point he broke his concentration to stare, if ever so briefly, at the awesome sights all around him. Only then did he realize there were many people looking back in awe at the sight of African soldiers formally making their way through the streets of the city.

The entire party continued their march uninterrupted along the edge of the Park toward two very large structures, one straight ahead and another to their right. Before reaching them, however, they stopped at Marlborough House, which seemed to the *askari* a much lesser structure than the other two. Here they were ordered unto two columns and then marched into the surrounding gardens.

"Pangana safu!" Captain Percival ordered the men to attention, then to remain at attention for inspection. At that point a very large man in an elaborate uniform, much more splendid than any Juma had ever seen his officers wear, passed in front of them,

pausing ever so slightly to look at each *askari* individually. After viewing the entire group, the man spoke to them all in what seemed to be English, which of course Juma did not fully understand. Captain Percival soon made clear this was, indeed, King Edward VII, expressing his approval of their appearance and formation, thanking them for their service in Asante. Assisted by several other officers, the King then presented each *askari* separately a medal in recognition of that service. Then they were all ordered to repeat a salutation after their Captain:

"God Save the King!" Though they all had heard—and most had spoken—those English words before, the two *askari* detachments were glad they were bolstered in their response by the Coldstream Guards and others in the company, as such enthusiasm was not in their usual repertoire. The resulting hearty cry seemed indeed to please the King. As they continued to stand at attention, the King bid farewell and retreated back into the house. After a respectful interval the command *"Endeni polepole!"* and the entire group slowly marched from the Marlborough House gardens along Carleton House Terrace, back to Wellington Place, and thence along Pall Mall to the front of what, they were told, was the War Office. There they were inspected once again, this time by the Commander-in-Chief of the British Army, Lord Roberts. After other spoken words—which meant little to any of them—they then began their march back toward St. George's Barracks to the continued astonishment of onlookers.

∞∞∞∞∞∞

The entire day was exhausting. Juma had previously marched much further. He'd also stood for inspections many times before.

This experience was decidedly different. Captain Percival emphasized many times over how important this was, and Juma felt that tension as well. But above all, the setting in which they marched, and the places where they were inspected, were outside of any experience he had ever known. Moreover, the streets were so hard his feet hurt even more than they had after the difficult marches during the Mpezeni Expedition! That evening he was glad of his little wooden bed, just the same as those provided for each of the British soldiers. As he attempted to drift off to sleep, thoughts of his experiences that day rushed through his mind. Why was the *boma* where they met the King not one of the much larger ones just beyond it? Surely a man so important should have one of those. Why were so many people in the streets watching the *askari* so intently? And what about the woodland lake they had seen? Why was it seemingly surrounded by so many huge buildings?

A question from Havildar Major Jaimal Singh, senior NCO with the two Central African Rifles detachments, startled him, even though he wasn't asleep. The Havildar Major was simply making his final rounds of the barracks rooms where the CAR *askari* were housed. Juma tried to reply: Though he certainly was tired, he had been unable to sleep. Both men struggled a little with *Kiswahili* when discussing matters that weren't strictly military, but the Havildar Major wanted to ease the mind of a man under his charge who'd clearly been unable to gain comfort in slumber. So he was actually not able to answer Juma's questions very well, instead attempting to reassure the sergeant that the experiences of the day were nothing that should worry him. The next morning when the *askari* assembled in the barracks courtyard that message was resoundingly re-emphasized for all to hear.

"Bravo!" That was the cheer the officers had for the *askari*.

"That was the word Lord Roberts used to congratulate all of you. The Commander-in-Chief was very pleased all round, the way you acquitted yourselves with the King, and the wonderful presence you displayed to the people of London! In fact, he was so pleased that he has arranged a special event for you! We will all be going to visit the Military Exhibition at the Earl's Court." Captain Johnson-Stewart, who was in command of the 2/CAR detachment, spoke to the *askari* as the senior officer of the group.

The men were as puzzled as they were pleased. But just two days later they discovered what the Captain was trying to convey, as the entire company marched to Charing Cross Station. Though they could see trains inside the station and many tracks coming into the covered platform building, they were directed to board a horse-drawn London Omnibus. It was reserved just for their use, for a journey through the streets of London. As one of the more senior men, Juma claimed a place on the upper deck, and was glad he did so. From his higher perch above the street, he was eager to take in all he could see. After first journeying down Pall Mall, where they in fact had marched just days before, they turned up Regent Street to Piccadilly Circus. There Juma could better see the London which Captain *Mkaŋwa* had obviously been trying to describe. Vehicles crowded all about. Goods wagons and Ominbuses jostled for position while trying to avoid smaller carriages, bicycles, and groups of people merely walking about. He was fascinated by the many flower-sellers and others, mostly women, who took up convenient spots on the edges of the street, close enough to sell their wares but sufficiently removed from the traffic hoping to remain safe in the hustle and bustle. Their numbers seemed to dwindle as the Ominbus continued on down Sloane Street into Brompton Road, but the numbers of anxious goods sellers increased again when they came to Kensington

Station, as did the crush of vehicles. At the station there were also men with hand carts about, and Juma thought he caught sight of one—a wagon was it?—which seemed to move all on its own without either man or beast propelling or dragging it!

Escaping the station throng, the great confusion diminished as the Omnibus traversed Lillie Road and finally came to a stop amidst yet another smush of traffic. They had arrived at Earl's Court. Clambering down from the Ominbus, the *askari* were marshalled into small groups and led first into an exhibit featuring a tableau that was supposed to represent the entire British military. There were figures who, indeed, looked as though they might have been their officers, and one or two who clearly looked like the Coldstream Guards who had accompanied them to meet the King. And, as Juma pointed out to his group, there was one who bore a striking resemblance to Havildar Major Jaimal Singh! But nowhere were there any figures looking at all like the *askari* of the Central African Rifles. There was one black soldier, but his uniform was quite different. A West Indian regiment, they were told, though that did not mean very much to any of them. There continued to be some obvious disquiet among the *askari*. "Lord Roberts hoped you would see that you are part of a much larger military establishment," Captain Johnson-Stewart explained to them. Somehow Juma, at least, wasn't very reassured.

What most impressed Juma were not the other military exhibits, such as the various types of weapons available to a modern military, nor the extensive displays of scenes from supposedly exotic places such as China. For him, it was The Great Wheel! Erected in 1895, it was not actually part of the Military Exhibition. Extending 300 feet above the ground, however, it dominated the Earl's Court landscape and drew great attention from the *askari*. When Captain Johnson-Stewart announced that as their final stop all who desired might ascend the wheel, Juma was delighted. He realized that from its great height he would be able to see far more than even from the upper deck of the Omnibus! He and a number of his companions—including their two commanding officers—nearly filled one of the forty gondolas; the Havildar Major, at his own request, remained behind with the few men who opted not to ride. The entire *askari* party were the only passengers on a single car, prompting their constant chatter of amazement as they looked over the city from the Wheel, particularly as they approached the apex of their excursion. Some claimed never to have seen such vistas, though his view of the Thames reminded Juma of times as a youth when he and Issa would hike to the top of Zomba Mountain and look back from Chingwe's Hole toward the Shire River.

Two other outings, one to look at industrial establishments elsewhere in the city and a final excursion to view a fireworks display at the Crystal Palace were also *askari* favourites. The day before their departure for home a Coldstream Guards officer, accompanied by an interpreter, interviewed the *askari* of both detachments, asking each one of them what he thought was the most amazing thing he had seen on this special journey from their homes in Africa. As Juma listened to other interviews while awaiting his turn, he realized everything that stood out in his mind—The Great Wheel, a woodland lake within the city, throngs of traffic, even the Omnibus—had already been mentioned by others. When his turn came, Juma searched his brain for something else to say, believing the expectation was something making his memory unique. After hesitating for a few moments, he made a reluctant suggestion: "A waterspout on the sea." Though greeted with skepticism, his response was duly recorded and actually remained in his mind as an official utterance.

∞∞∞∞∞

He wanted to tell Ambikanile about all he had seen and share every detail of his experiences, but Juma found, just as had been the case when he returned from Asante, he was not really able to do so. The worlds he was now a part of were so very foreign to anything she knew. Even if he could find individual words to describe them, she would most likely be unable to truly comprehend his experiences. So he settled for just a few superlatives as a means of conveying the great differences between them, reassuring her that his preference was for her reality rather than the world beyond of which he was now a part. Proud of her husband, she did not question further, even his mentioning of *lipundugulu* as the most amazing thing he had seen. Of course she knew that was the morning mist they had both seen many times before on Zomba Mountain. But she could not know that in struggling to find words for his experiences, Juma happened upon one which in *Chiyao* was amazingly imprecise, at best!

For both of them the joy of their reunion and the opportunity to be a family again was far more important than the details of his most recent adventure. However, Juma was concerned that there were many changes taking place within the Central African Rifles, with numerous reassignments of personnel, including *askari*, both between and within the two battalions. Even the name of the regiment changed—now they were The King's African Rifles—and his would be the first battalion. Could it have been, he wondered, that not just the Commander-in Chief, Lord Roberts, but the King himself was impressed in his brief dealings with the *askari* that he was now willing to include them within his British military establishment? Maybe a new Military Exhibition in London would now have to include the King's own regiment! Despite the affirmation he felt when thinking about the new name, many of the other changes troubled him. Yet when Lieutenant Colonel Cobbe took command of 1/KAR, Juma breathed a sigh of relief. He well remembered the decisive command decisions in Asante, after which many Yao askari began to call him Major *Cipandu* in recognition of his fearlessness. Only later did they learn Cobbe was actually awarded the Victoria Cross for his battlefield bravery in Asante.

Not that everything about Juma's position within the battalion suddenly turned joyous. When he was not one of the six *askari* chosen to represent 1/KAR at King Edward VII's formal coronation, Juma worried to Ambikanile that he was now less favoured than he had been just months before. Had he allowed his disappointment to seep into his performance of his duties? Did the officers, especially Lieutenant Colonel *Cipandu*, sense he had become dispirited and had lost his usual enthusiasm? As if almost to confront any such self-doubts, it was not long before Cobbe took him aside to deliver the news: henceforward he would be Colour Sergeant Juma. Despite his previous anxieties, Juma took the news precisely as it was intended: an affirmation of his good standing. And when it soon officially became time to re-enlist, he willing agreed to continue his service, especially as he knew 1/KAR would remain in Nyasaland for several more years while 2/KAR—his friend Issa's battalion—would be away from home.

Those next few years were in no way consequential to his life as an *askari*. As the second ranking NCO in his company, Juma often led road-building crews, supervised recruiting parties, sometimes spending a few days away from Zomba. He also served one, three-month tour with B Company on garrison duty in Karonga, which though unpleasant due to the isolation he felt, was thankfully short. He was always pleased he could return to Zomba and his modest home near the battalion *boma*. His personal life during those years was a much different matter, as he welcomed another child—a son!—into his family. As before, Ambikanile wanted to return to Majowa to prepare for the birth, and Juma was glad she did so. As it happened, the birth was not an easy one. Juma was urgently summoned to attend his wife one evening shortly after returning from Karonga and was readily granted leave to do so. He felt as though he was on his own double time march around the mountain, worrying all the way to the village. But on his arrival, he was greeted not only by Ambikanile, her mother, and a host of other family, but also his son—Juma and Ambikanile previously agreed should be named Mtindiso—who arrived only minutes before his father.

"No!" his mother's eldest brother Masamba protested when he heard their decision. "That's no name for a child!"

"But *akwelume*," Juma took issue with his uncle. "You must understand our thoughts. It was the man we *asilikali* call *Mtindiso* whose advice convinced us both that together we might survive my soldier's life. We merely wish to honour him."

"Fine and good." Juma's father entered the family conversation as murmurs of discontent began to grow. "But … but … it is unlucky for a child to have such a name," he continued. "Suggesting that he may be lame and will need an aid to walk is no way for your son to begin his life!"

"E-e-e! Elo! E-e-e!" Mumblings of agreement came from several others.

Sensing a growing disaffection, Juma determined he must interject a calming note. As he had left for Majowa so quickly, he was still wearing his uniform, so when he raised both arms to quiet the gathering, he was indeed an imposing figure. "Please. Please!" He began. "Look at the boy. His legs are straight and true. He will not be lame. As his parents we shall protect him well. His name will be no curse. It is instead an honour—not just to his namesake—but also to me, his father, that I am able to lead an *msilikali's* life. So you should see his name as a call to a straight and upright life. It is nothing to fear at all!"

Looking now at his wife, Juma could see her pride in him. Indeed, the entire family seemed ready to accept his reassurances and moved to embrace both father and son. Without any other means to recall the happy picture, the entire extended family clung to that image as a major turning point in their lives.

∞∞∞∞∞∞

The family returned to their home in the regimental "lines," as the homes for the *askari* were coming to be called. Apesile doted on her younger brother, as older sisters do. The boy grew stronger and, vindicating his father's predictions, began walking—well, toddling about—sooner than anyone expected. Those days and weeks passed all too quickly and, before any of them expected, it was time for Juma's regiment to leave Nyasaland and take up duties in eastern Africa. The tearful goodbyes said, the regiment marched out of Zomba on the way, eventually, to an encampment near the coastal town of Mombasa. As their ship came into the port city, Juma was astounded to see the massive Fort Jesus, which he decided must be one of the stone forts he had heard about as a youngster. As massive as it was, though, it was nothing so grand as the—was it castles, that Captain *Mkaŋwa* had called them?—he had seen in London. Despite its decidedly military appearance, 1/KAR eschewed that Fort for its initial headquarters in favor of Mazeras, which nonetheless proved to have an entirely insufficient water supply for so many soldiers. Thus Juma and his fellow *askari* had to set up a new camp, much further inland on the outskirts of Nairobi, where the battalion completed its three years of "overseas" service.

Soon enough another local problem for British settlers interrupted the battalion's otherwise mundane duties, and Juma's B Company joined about half the battalion rushing to the Island of Zanzibar to put down a police mutiny. The KAR *askari* were much more than a match for the poorly trained Zanzibar gendarmes, whose rebellion was quickly quashed. With no real police force to replace them, A & B companies of the battalion were ordered to remain on Zanzibar where not merely British colonists but the rest of local population embraced them whole heartedly. Their welcome no doubt was due, at least in part, to their familiarity with *Kiswahili*, which all the *askari* were taught during training and continued to learn during service. Many of them, including if not especially Juma, relished the chance to become more proficient in that local Zanzibari language, conversing with the populace at every conceivable opportunity.

"*Jambo! Habari gani?*" With the traditional *Kiswahili* greeting, Juma attempted to begin a conversation with nearly every resident he met on his patrols, hoping to engage them in more than just idle conversation. His effervescent personality thus opened many doors, and led to many invitations as well. One that particular intrigued him came on a sunny afternoon when he was patrolling in Old Town. He could hear the voice of a *muezzin* sounding out from a nearby minaret which, while not the tallest in the city, was easily visible above the rooftops of all the nearby houses. He assumed it was a call to prayer. He couldn't understand the words, but recognized the sound as he had heard it before in Zomba, when some of the Muslim *askari* gathered for a weekly worship service.

"Won't you join us for prayers?" was the response to his greeting from the gateway of a nearby house. A man identifying himself as Taria Karumi was about to enter the Mnara Mosque adjacent to his home.

"*Asante sana, Bwana* Karumi,*"* Juma replied in thanks. "As you can see, I am on duty and unable to join you. I must continue on my regular patrol."

"Perhaps another time? Several of your *askari* come to worship with us from time to time. You are welcome to do so as well."

He didn't want to reject such a well-meaning offer, but explained to *Bwana* Karumi that he had declined to join in worship, both in Nairobi where the battalion was now headquartered, and in Zomba, his home. In fact, though he did not tell the man this directly, he was uncomfortable with both Islam *and* Christianity—the religion of most of his officers, if they actually practiced any religion—preferring the solace of his Yao beliefs and the sense of an all-encompassing deity which they referred to as *mlungu*. He accepted that others among the *askari* had embraced Islam. And he knew that even among Chief Chikowi's people Islam had an increasing number of adherents, though he didn't feel the need to seek refuge in any foreign belief system.

"*Kwa heri, bwana!*" Juma bid farewell to Karumi with what he hoped was a friendly smile. It was never good to leave a sour impression when the job was to help people feel safe in their own home towns!

Soon after this encounter Juma became part of a 1/KAR effort to train an entirely new police force for service in Zanzibar. When that task was successfully completed, Juma returned to Nairobi with B Company, though he only spent a small amount of his time in their Nairobi compound. B Company frequently moved about the countryside, on garrison duty in Mombasa or Kisumu, and on road-building detail between Nakuru and Nairobi itself. Occasionally the company might also participate in a tax-collecting march further afield from established outposts. As he came to understand it, such fatigues were the stuff of peacetime soldiering: maintaining order, showing the flag, and keeping the wheels of British government moving in its colonial territories. There was little danger in this work, and though he missed his family, he knew they were safe in Zomba. He was certain it was better his wife and children were near home and family rather than staying with him in a far-off post as did the wives of some *askari*. When word came that the regiment would soon be returning home, Juma thought he might indeed re-enlist for another tour, but put off doing so until he was safely back in Zomba.

The *askari*—as well as the British officers—of 1/KAR highly anticipated their return to Zomba. The plan for the two Zomba-based KAR battalions to alternate service in British East Africa every three years may have appealed to London officials, perhaps even to financial planners in Nairobi, but was not nearly as popular among the troops. So as they embarked on the British-India steamer *Dwarka* in Mombasa for the passage south through the Mozambique Channel to Chinde, and thence Nyasaland, their spirits once again were high. All ahead of them seemed rosy. That is, until they encountered a huge Indian Ocean storm only a day out of port. All of them, officers and *askari* alike, had been at sea before, many even on the *Dwarka*. But this voyage was a nightmare compared to all the seafaring experiences any of them had previously known, dwarfing even the impressive waterspout in the Gulf of Guinea. The first signs of this tropical cyclone—that's what their officers called it—came with bands of rain squalls so strong almost all the *askari* abandoned the outer decks of their transport vessel. Then rising ocean swells, some of them fifty feet or more tossed the ship severely. Those not in beds or hammocks could only lurch precariously to find safe handholds; any of their equipment not safely in tied-down containers slid widely on the decks of even the smallest compartments. The steamer, thankfully, did not take on much water and thus remained seaworthy, even if the soldiers were not. When the winds and seas subsided and the sandy channels that formed the Zambezi river delta came into view, everyone was over-joyed, even though the journey from the makeshift port at Chinde to Zomba would take longer than the dreadful voyage thus far. Still, it seemed as though they were almost home!

∞∞∞∞∞∞∞

Juma, as well as his fellow *askari*, especially welcomed the four months leave which was their reward for three years of service away from home. His reunion with Mtindiso, Apesile, and of course their mother was perhaps the most gratifying, although being able to return to their original home in Majowa was almost equally special. His mother and father were both getting much older and he worried about them as well. Fortunately, his other siblings were still either in the village or nearby and could care for them as he could not. Another difficulty of an *msilikali's* lot, he told himself, even as he tried yet again to reconcile the disadvantages of the life he had chosen with the greater good he had hoped to accomplish when he had enlisted. It was that latter purpose which led him to seek out Chief Chikowi to discuss what appeared to be a major development he learned about only on his return.

"You knew, of course, that Jonstoni is gone from Zomba now," Juma began, referring to Sir Harry Johnston who had been the chief administrator of British Central Africa when he had first enlisted at the Chief's behest.

"*Etu!*" The Chief was exasperated as he took it to be common knowledge that it had been many years, at least a decade, since Johnston built and occupied the Residency around the mountain which was the heart of the British *boma* complex.

"Yes, many others have come and gone, but now I am concerned that things may change, perhaps not for the better." Juma wasn't referring merely to the many alterations in his regiment, but to a fundamental reordering of the British approach to governing their land and the territories both north and south of Zomba. "Captain Northingham told me that while we were away the British have decided to say this is now Nyasaland, the land of the great lake. Moreover, they have decided to change how they govern over us. From what the Captain told me, I fear our situation may be more difficult indeed!"

The chief pondered for only a moment, then replied. "Our lake? The one where my cousins Makanjila, Jalasi, and Mponda hold sway? If that is the focus of the *Angelesi*, maybe our plan shall work! I am well pleased that you are so important to them as an *msilikali*." He referred to the increasing stature Juma had achieved within the regiment. "You have done well, and I hope you will continue." Although his concerns weren't entirely eased following the conversation, Juma knew at least that his steady path was pleasing to his chief. His family had also come to accept this life. So when his most recent enlistment expired, Juma again agreed to continue his service, having been informed by his officers that plans were in place for their battalion to remain stationed in Zomba for several years.

∞∞∞∞∞∞

That assumption was quickly shattered, though, when most of 1/KAR were ordered to Somaliland to help quell yet another rebellion. What Juma did not know was that shortly after his re-enlistment, both British Somaliland and Nyasaland had passed to control of the British Colonial Office, resulting in two consequences for him. The first was that his services were even more likely to be required in some other British possessions. The second was an urgent mission to British Somaliland: to aid in suppressing the rebellion of Muhammad ʿAbd Allāh al-Hasan, whom the KAR officers referred to as "the Mad Mullah." Only a fortnight after re-enlisting, his company and two others were away again. After apologizing to Ambikanile and the children, and bidding them goodbye yet again, Juma joined the battalion's march to Port Hearld, steamed down the Zambezi to Chinde, and soon was cruising north through the Mozambique Channel. On this trip they avoided any ocean storms but also bypassed Mombasa heading northeast around the eastern tip of Africa into the Gulf of Aden. The ship docked at Berbera, a much better port than Chinde, which made their debarking that much easier.

The men were soon ordered into formation and, despite the heat and humidity, Lieutenant Colonel H. A. Walker took the lead as they began the march to Wadamago, which would be the battalion's temporary headquarters. The three day march up the escarpment to the grassy plain above wore everyone out. Though they arrived in Somalia's cool season, excessive moisture in the air made the ambient temperature feel hotter than it actually was. All in all, their station itself was about as unpleasant as any Juma could recall. The hot air was moist, yet it seldom rained. As their deployment continued into a much hotter time of year, he longed for the frequent afternoon rains of the wet season in Zomba. Uncomfortable as he was, it seemed to Juma some members of the battalion suffered much more than others. Actually, Colonel Walker may have been one of those most ill-suited to the climate and conditions. He also always appeared to be perspiring far more than nearly all his men, frequently removing his pith helmet to wipe his brow and thinning hair. His apparent distress led many of the *askari*, Juma included, to refer to him as *Amiri Noni-noni*, indicating he always seemed to be sticky with sweat. One of the young subalterns, Lieutenant Rolland—in an apparent attempt to ingratiate himself with the *askari*—began referring to the Colonel by that same nickname when speaking to his men, as if other officers were not in earshot.

A few days after this began Juma, as one of the senior NCOs, inquired directly of Rolland, "What do you think the *askari* call *you*?"

"Why *Afisa Mzuri*, of course!" the Lieutenant replied without the slightest hesitation.

Good officer? Stifling a nearly overwhelming urge to smile, Juma nodded and turned away, as he knew this gross misapprehension would be greeted with guffaws by his fellow *askari*. Far from his pretentious view of himself, the Lieutenant was seen as very hard taskmaster to those under his command. That was why, as Juma well knew, Roland was frequently called exactly that in *Kiswahili—afisa msimamizi—*by the *askari*. And indeed when Juma shared this story at a campfire later that evening, his company did convulse in laughter, some of them literally rolling on the ground. The exact nature of this episode of hilarity remained unknown to the battalion's officers, but it was a welcome change of pace for the *askari* of 1/KAR.

Although reports filtered into Wadamago of raids by the Mullah's forces on a few isolated outposts or the occasional goods caravan, there was little actual military activity to occupy the troops. Occasionally, small squads patrolled the paths that passed for roads in the parched grasslands. More frequently, larger groups escorted caravans of traders to or from the port in an effort to build up the economy of the British administered territory. It must have been a nearly futile effort. Juma thought he overheard Colonel Walker, speaking to some other officers about going to meet with a *Bwana* Winston Churchill in Berbera, only to be told by the British Colonial Under-Secretary of State that Somalia was a hopeless drain on the empire's resources. Without a doubt, that was how Juma felt. A little patrol and escort duty plus a few other meaningless fatigues were the only duties that occupied the battalion for an entire year. Not one shot fired from their rifles, nor even a single sighting of "dervishes"—that's what *Amiri Noni-noni* had called the supposedly "Mad" Mullah's rebels. Those were the seemingly empty results of yet another year away from Zomba. How might this make him valuable to the British?

For Juma it was a riddle without a solution, and it troubled him during their entire return journey.

∞∞∞∞∞

An additional two months leave were the result of this latest absence from his family. While it was welcome—especially as it came at a time that he could help with funeral preparations for his father—Juma wanted to return to soldiering. He was in his element on the firing range and leading the men through drills on the parade ground. Now that the battalion armoury finally was fully stocked with new standard issue Martini-Enfield rifles, he was overjoyed when ordered to supervise additional training for the men in their use. His mood was tempered, however, when his company was ordered to Thyolo district for road and bridge building. He understood the need, now that the railroad from Port Herald to Blantyre was nearly complete: the route took the tracks through Luchenza bypassing established tea plantations on Mulanje Mountain and new ones just beginning near Thyolo. His contribution would be to improve the roads so tea could be taken to the railway and sent elsewhere for sale. Someone—he did not have any idea who—remembered his good work in Asante where he directed efforts to bridge the rushing Ofin River so his column might continue their successful pursuit of the last rebel holdouts. As a result he was now tasked with constructing or repairing several small bridges on the roads from the new railhead in Limbe to Thyolo and on to Luchenza.

When the road-building company reached Limbe, Juma was impressed to see the new railway depot, though it dwarfed the one he had seen at Charing Cross in London. He was a little disappointed that the company would not get to ride the train, though many of his fellow *askari* were actually relieved they would march on to Thyolo by road. Once they reached the small *Wasungu* settlement—with its small but varied population of Italian, British, Irish, and even American settlers—Captain Northingham took Juma to meet a Mr. Cox, whom he introduced as *Bwana Chai*, owner of the new Bandanga Tea Estate.

"Jambo! Habari gani?" Juma greeted him, only to discover the man spoke only very limited *Kiswahili*. As the Captain had previously explained his task would be to help construct several bridges near the estate to improve the road to Luchenza, Juma worried how he would communicate with *Bwana Chai* about the work. As he soon discovered, one of the newer *askari* in his company, Useni Makuta, was from a nearby village and able to make himself understood in conversation with Mr. Cox. Juma immediately assigned Useni to the bridge crew, thereby greatly facilitating the work. For his part, Useni was very pleased. He was well acquainted with the nearby woodlands and much preferred working on bridges rather than shoveling and scraping dirt and rock for the roads as most of the company were doing. The two *askari* made a good team—insofar as a senior NCO and a lance corporal could be seen as a team—and formed a bond which both men anticipated would continue long after their bridge-building efforts were completed. Nonetheless, Juma again found this latest assignment somewhat less than what he expected was appropriate for a decorated *askari*.

Despite those misgivings, when the company returned to Zomba Juma received yet another award. In a battalion ceremony, all of those who deployed to Somalia were awarded a medal honouring their contributions in fighting the "mad" Mullah. This, too, seemed foolishness to Juma, who had already confessed to his family that his previous year of service was nothing special, merely time spent without any significant results. Now he told them he was contemplating leaving the KAR when his enlistment was up in just a few months' time. He did feel obligated to discuss this with Chief Chikowi, just as he had done following his return from British East Africa. Taking the opportunity of a short leave, he made his way around the mountain to the Chief's village.

∞∞∞∞∞∞

"I am convinced it is time to end my service as an *msilikali*," Juma began, after sitting down in the chief's compound.

"Cici?" The Chief wanted to know why he reached this decision which seemed to reveal a change of heart.

The conversation followed much the same trajectory as their previous talk on the same subject, with Juma now expanding his disappointments to include more recent experiences, in Somalia and Thyolo. On further questioning, Juma revealed a little more about his work in Thyolo and his impressions. The roads his company were working on there were now, he confidently believed, at least the equal of those he had seen in the East African highlands around Nairobi. He was less impressed with the tea plantings:

"*Bwana Chai* purchased land not far from Thyolo settlement, then forbade anyone who had once lived on that land to again plant their gardens. He has made workers take out most of the trees and grass. But the tea bushes he planted..." he paused and contemplated his words. "They look scrawny and weak, almost like thorn scrub where grazing animals have destroyed the land. I fear the people who have lived there, like my friend Useni, will suffer without gardens or any new land in which to plant again."

"Who is this Useni?" the Chief wanted to know.

Juma casually explained a little about the relationship he had developed with the young lance corporal.

"*That's it!*" Chief Chikowi suddenly interjected. "You have built a connection with another who has also seen how the *Angelesi* have come into our lands to enrich themselves! Useni may not be Yao, but he, too, knows well the troubles we face. Being his friend may well be an opening to our future. Challenges faced by warriors in the past, or now by *asilikali* like yourself, often must be dealt with immediately as they are matters of life and death. But those faced by the rest of us can only be confronted over time, although they, too, may turn out to involve life and death. What I have asked of you is to prepare for making both kinds of decisions. That is difficult, I know. But I leave it to you. You must choose your future based on what is best for your family."

To say he was stunned probably understates Juma's reaction. As he departed and began his trek—slowly this time—around the mountain he was unsure what he might do. Even after telling Ambikanile about the conversation he remained uncertain, as she clearly did not want to advise any action which her husband might reject. As dear as she was to him, Juma knew that providing advice at times like this was not her greatest quality. He hoped that he might find, if not advice, then inspiration from some other quarter.

For some weeks there was nothing which inspired him to make a final decision. He did receive a startling impetus, though, as news reached the KAR *boma* in Zomba that many of the *askari* would *not* be asked to renew their enlistments. Issa's 2/KAR was to be disbanded altogether, so when he returned from his rotation in British East Africa he would simply go back to Majowa. Two of the companies of 1/KAR were likewise going to be discharged. Only two regular companies—as well as a headquarters detachment—would remain. Juma's was one of the two companies to remain at full strength. His former commander, Captain Manning himself, spoke to him about these decisions:

"You have been a loyal *askari*," Manning told him. Newly appointed Governor of Nyasaland, Manning wanted to preserve the very best of his old forces to serve in his new, leaner military establishment. "Did you know, Juma, that you are now the second-longest serving *askari* in the force! Your service has been exemplary. I cannot afford to lose you. Won't you please agree to re-enlist for another three years?"

Juma didn't immediately agree, but was impressed to learn his longevity as an *askari* was important to his former commander. Certainly that was a fitting compliment to the wisdom of Chief Chikowi! Yes, he was now convinced, remaining with the KAR would be the best choice.

So he agreed to re-enlist, but also made another momentous decision: he would marry again! Once his continued service with the KAR was confirmed, he took his small re-enlistment bonus and went back to Majowa, this time leaving Ambikanile and their children in their home at the *boma*. First he went to see his old friend, Issa, now a former *askari*, telling him of both decisions:

"Bwana Manning himself asked that I remain with KAR, as did Chief Chikowi. How could I refuse when both wanted me to remain?"

Though disappointed this would mean his friend would not be returning to his village, Issa could do little but display his feelings by shrugging his shoulders while also saying, simply, "I understand." But the next news left Issa far happier.

"I have decided to take another wife!" Juma announced. With that Issa's countenance changed completely. He was aware that as much as Juma cared for Ambikanile, he sometimes felt she was not the complete partner in life Juma needed. Although he'd not confided this directly to Issa, Juma indeed was disappointed that Ambikanile at times didn't seem to understand his *msilikali* life and how it affected his family situation; quite frankly, he hoped for more sympathetic understanding from his wife.

"I hope taking another wife will make you even happier, my friend!" Issa said. And now his countenance reflected an entirely different outlook. "Who will you seek to be your second wife?"

"Today I will ask Kuliraga," Juma replied assuredly. The name did not surprise Issa in the least. Not too much younger than Ambikanile, she had married even before her. But she was soon widowed, without children. Kuliraga was well known as an extremely outgoing and forthright woman. Issa thought she might be an ideal complement to Juma's life. "Wonderful! If she agrees, please let me help you build a second home in Majowa," Issa offered, knowing that would be an important next step before a formal wedding.

As Juma was considered an amazingly successful and also desirable man, Kuliraga eagerly agreed to his proposal. Many women might not have been pleased to be a second wife in Juma's family, but she also understood that no matter whom she might marry, as a widow she would always be a second wife. Juma immediately purchased the necessary materials, but again left the details of building his second home to others, this time with Issa in charge. Juma had taken as much time as he could away from his duties with the battalion, and he also accepted he had a responsibility to inform Ambikanile of his decision.

"You will always be my first wife, the most important in my family," Juma reassured her.

"That is what I would expect," she replied firmly. "That is as it has always been among our people. You are a good man and have always been a caring husband and fine father. I would expect no less from you." Her face expressed resolve, but her eyes revealed the same slight sense of disappointment as Issa had shown when informed that Juma was to remain a *msilikali*. Ambikanile was determined that Juma would remain her husband no matter what.

She didn't accompany him when Juma made his way back to Majowa a fortnight later, however. News had reached them that the arrangements had been made for Juma and Kuliraga to be wed, and he returned for the ceremony which would formalize their union. It was not as elaborate a celebration has had charcterized either of their first marriages. The relatives of the bride and groom made the exchanges to solemnize their families coming together. Juma regretted he only had his uncle Masamba to represent him, now that his father had passed away. Once their marriage was formalized, the couple retired to the new house which Issa had built for them, and where Kuliraga remained when Juma made his way back around the mountain to rejoin Mtindiso, Apesile, and their mother. To his dismay, Juma also discovered unexpected transformations awaited him with 1/KAR.

∞∞∞∞∞∞∞

Though he wasn't aware of the coming changes before deciding to re-enlist, Juma's battalion was not to remain at its reduced strength for long. Twice in the next few months recruitment began again, with the goal of creating two additional companies for 1/KAR. It was a shame *askari* like his old friend Issa were now lost to the battalion, but Juma accepted he wasn't involved in retention and recruitment, as he had explained to his friend less than month before the wedding. Juma was himself reassigned to the re-formed A company. In fact, it was not long before both the veteran companies were unexpectedly ordered to foreign duty once again. The irony of their difficult situation wasn't lost on the *askari* nor their officers. They were off to British East Africa again, but this time to Jubaland, far to the northeast of Nairobi.

"Almost to Somaliland," Captain Soames explained to them. All Juma could think about was the wasted year he had recently spent in that place. But when their transport steamer docked in Mombasa and didn't continue to Berbera, he realized this must not be the same. Once disembarked, the company learned they were to join a patrol operation, apparently to coerce people known as Marehan and their allies to accept British control of their territory. It was not the sort of duty which most appealed to Juma, but he decided to make the most of it. Might the Marehan be anything like the Yao? Why, he wondered, did they dislike British governance so much they were willing to rebel? In campaigning against them might he gain any insights into dealing with the troubles facing Chikowi's people?

A coastal steamer took the company to Kismayo, then a smaller vessel transported them more than 300 miles from the mouth of the Juba River to Bardera. Just beyond the few buildings in the small settlement the dry savannah reached almost, but not quite, to the river's edge. The Captain directed all the company's baggage be loaded onto pack camels, and then the 1/KAR contingent began a relatively short march to Serenli where other units of the KAR, from Uganda it turned out, had established a camp. This suggested to Juma their deployment would be another long one, and his heart sank. He had only been able to send word to Kuliraga that he was ordered away. This was not an ideal start to a new marriage, he knew. However, before departing, he had reassured Ambikanile this wouldn't be like his most recent absence, or even the nearly three years he had spent before in British East Africa. He knew the children would miss him as well, a further weight on his mind. This was among a soldier's misfortunes and he bore them, and his responsibilities, with confidence even if he had a heavy heart.

The regiment's baggage only included temporary tents, designed for sleeping while on patrol. Juma's A Company soon discovered that much of their "patrolling" would be by flat-bottomed boat on the Juba River, so the small tents became their principal quarters at the Serenli base camp. The *askari* spent most of their time on the little river steamer by day, demonstrating a British presence to the Africans who lived on either the eastern—Italian—or western—British—bank of the agreed riverine boundary recognized by the two colonial powers. As Juma quickly discovered, the people who lived there didn't understand that separation. Neither did they appreciate the constant presence of *askari* among them. That displeasure was occasionally made know by gunshots aimed in the direction of the patrol craft. Rarely did the bullets do any damage, but often the captain would put in at the bank on the British side of the river and parties of KAR *askari* would investigate the origin of the rifle fire.

On one such occasion, Juma was senior NCO of a landing party led by Lieutenant Maciver. The local guide, who was with the party, warned them they had happened upon the village of a local wizard who was regarded as a sort of king of all the river crocodiles. Wizards, as most of the *askari* knew, could have special powers. So Juma was determined to warn the Lieutenant who didn't appear at all impressed with that piece of local intelligence:

"*Msawi!*" Juma first blurted out the word describing a wizard in *Chiyao*, but it made no impression on his commander. Then Juma tried again, recalling the *Kiswahili*, enunciating it forcefully: "*MCHAWI!*" Perhaps it was his apparent insistence that made the greatest impact.

"Hogwash!" That was a reaction, of sorts, from Maciver, though not the one Juma intended. Instead the Lieutenant turned to the local headman, Ali Sungura, seeking information about the two old carbines they could see discarded on the ground. "Who belongs to those weapons?" the Lieutenant wanted to know.

"They have run away, across that little creek," Ali Sunguru replied, pointing toward a small stream away from where the steamer had put ashore. It was obvious to the entire KAR landing party that was highly unlikely, as all could see any number of crocodiles in that stream, many with only their sinister eye-knobs alone peering out from the water.

"How can that be?" the Lieutenant shot back. "The *ngwena* over there would surely have stopped them!" He thought a moment, then decided on what was undoubtedly a more sarcastic approach: "Perhaps they were *eaten* after firing their guns at our boat!"

"Haw-ha-ha" many of the *askari* laughed at their clever commander, only to be shushed by their sergeant, who in turn offered an alternative opinion.

"No." Juma said, "*mchawi* need not fear any animal. Neither *simba*, *ngwena* nor any other beast will attack a *mchawi* or any of his adherents." That he would equate the dangers from lions and crocodiles seemed to annoy the Lieutenant, but the *askari* well knew wily crocs were perhaps more to be feared.

"Indeed, that is so," Ali Sunguru was quick to agree. "The king of the crocodiles has forbidden his subjects around this village from harming any person who comes into the water! So those men were able merely to swim away after firing their weapons."

"If that is so, you will prove it to me," the Lieutenant demanded sharply. "Swim across that little creek to the other side....*NOW*!" Ali Sunguru did not hesitate for even a moment. He gathered his white robe about his body and walked directly into the creek. None of the crocodiles seemed to take any notice. Juma lifted his rifle, ready to deter any threats to the headman, but Lieutenant Maciver pushed the weapon aside. As the headman began to swim in slightly deeper water, the crocodiles moved apart to let him pass; not one threatened him in any way. Pulling himself upright on the far shore, Ali Sunguru spread his arms out triumphantly and bowed his head toward the astonished KAR party.

Although his insistence had provoked this demonstration, Juma was as amazed at the result as any of the others. What might he learn from this fearless display? Did it require the power of a *mchawi* to defy the *Waingereza*? Or was there something more in Ali Sunguru's display of bravado in the face a direct challenge that might be worthy of emulation? His contemplations were interrupted by an order from the disgusted Lieutenant that the landing party re-board the steamer and return to Serenli.

∞∞∞∞∞∞

The quiet on their return voyage was broken only by the "chooga-a-chooga chooga-a-chooga" sounds made by the steam engine of their small craft and the lapping of river water on the bow. None of the men dared speak, least of all Juma, who feared once they returned to camp he would be chastised, perhaps even sanctioned, for impertinence. After they disembarked and were making their way to the tent encampment, the entire party was ordered to assemble at once on a make-shift parade ground in the middle of the KAR basecamp. Though he feared the worst, Juma followed orders and joined the rest of the assembled 1/KAR *askari*. Captain Soames strode stiffly to the front of the formal group and began to speak, slowly and loudly, making sure his words were clearly heard—and understood—by all of the *askari*:

"Men, we are at war!" He stopped, expecting a reaction. None came. The *askari* instead kept their ranks in silence. "A messenger just arrived from Bardera…bringing news of a wireless received from London. …Britain—and the entire British Empire—are at war with Germany. Fighting has begun in Europe. The war will likely come to Africa…and thus to us as well. We must move at once…and help defend Mombasa from attack…which is expected from German East Africa."

As he stopped and looked around at the officers gathered beside him, a soft murmer began within the ranks. A strangely relieved Juma spoke softly to those nearby:

"This is what we have trained for," he said reassuringly. "We must do our duty."

After Captain Soames's speech to his troops, the men were dismissed to their tents with orders to clean and prepare their weapons, anticipating they would quickly be transported to Mombasa. However, it was soon apparent their departure was not imminent. The existing river and ocean transport was insufficient to transfer all of the KAR units at Serenli to Mombasa as quickly as colonial officials had hoped. Since news of the declaration of war actually reached the base before Juma's river patrol returned from Ali Sunguru's village, units of 3/KAR at their base camp had already made their preparations and disembarked for the journey downriver to Kismayo. And while they were on their way, B Company 1/KAR also had to march from outstations in Yonti and Gobwen to join the rest of the regiment. Only then could they, too, be transported to Kismayo, followed by still more waiting for the small ocean steamer to return so that A Company, 1/KAR might actually participate in the defense of British East Africa.

Waiting was hard on the *askari*. They talked among themselves and rumors were rife. Juma listened intently as members of his A Company, almost all of them Yao, tried to discern what might have caused the Europeans to fight among themselves. All were familiar with the *Waingereza*, but few knew much about the *Wajerumani*, not having had occasion to deal with Germans. Lance-corporal Twaambo, a Tonga who had transferred into the company, previously dealt with Germans as a deckhand on the lake steamer *Hermann von Wissmann* before enlisting in the KAR. He had not been impressed, and much preferred his KAR officers. But because of his experience, the men gravitated to his explanation:

"The *Wazungu*, both the *Waingereza* and the *Wajerumani,* are too proud," he asserted firmly. "That is the cause of this war; I'm sure of it."

"It is true." Juma was quick to agree, his affirmation seconded by a number of the other *askari.*

"So, here is what happened." Twaambo continued his explanation of how the war began: "The sons of both great sultans of these peoples started the conflict. One had a white horse. The other had a black horse. Each believed theirs was the best. They argued about this, but could not agree on how to resolve their dispute. Eventually they came to blows, each rallying many friends to his defense."

"*Ehee!*" "*Ebu!*" Expressions of agreement came from several of the *askari* as they listened intently.

With such acceptance ringing in his ears, Twaambo came to his conclusion: "Finally the two sultans decided there should be a way to resolve the disagreement between their sons. Both then decided they should go to war! That is why we are now ordered…" Just as Twaambo was about to complete his explanation, Juma interrupted:

"*Hapana farasi!!*" Not horses! Juma could hardly contain his exasperation. "All the *wazungu* may be proud, but this war has nothing to do with who had the best horse!" Juma insisted. He wanted to explain further, but didn't have an opportunity as the steamer came into view on the horizon. They were immediately ordered to form up for boarding. But the steamer couldn't accommodate all the *askari* waiting for transport. As a result only half of those waiting were on the ship as it edged out of its dock and headed southwest paralleling the coast. The rest of A Company was forced to wait for the steamer to return. In the confusion of such rapid redeployments, however, the captain thought he was to land these men at the mouth of the Tana River, returning to Kismayo for the remainder of 1/KAR. Rather than remain idle, those troops began an overland march toward Bura, expecting to join the rest of the battalion later at Voi. When the steamer ultimately returned to Kismayo, it took the remainder of the *askari* on board, delivering them directly to Mombasa. Thus Juma and his A Company comrades were unexpectedly delayed in joining the defense of British East Africa.

∞∞∞∞∞∞

Book Two

Growing up on the Althorp Estate, Wellington Rangely was very familiar with guns, as his father was assistant gamekeeper for the estate. The usual expectation for a boy of his standing was that he would follow in his father's footsteps. But soon after his birth, Wellington seemed—not merely to his parents but all who met the child—an exceptionally bright boy. His parents sent him to a nearby junior school where the headmaster and teachers quickly recognized his abilities. Their intervention with the Earl resulted in a scholarship for the promising lad to attend Wellborough School. Although he excelled in his studies there, what most captured the attention of young Rangely were the school's sports teams and Cadet Corps. His familiarity with weapons both attracted him to the latter and also helped account for his success as a junior corpsman.

As were most of their countrymen, students at Wellborough were surprised by the outbreak of war in 1914. Wellington was just beginning his final year of studies, and his parents fondly hoped he might be sponsored for study at university. But their country was ill prepared for another war so soon after the South African conflict. Thus, it was no surprise that, like so many other young Englishmen, their son was quick to enlist in the army. Wellington joined the Northamptonshire regiment and was soon in training, which consisted primarily of drill and route march, followed by more drilling and marching. There simply were no rifles available for shooting practice. When the recruits finally did receive rifles, they were only able to fire less than twenty rounds, all on the coast and into the sea, before being ordered to join British forces already fighting in France. Some of his comrades bemoaned their inadequate rifle training, but for Wellington that was not a concern given his fortuitous upbringing.

Posted to the 1st battalion of the regiment, Wellington's voyage across the channel to La Harve on a cold and rainy December day was most uncomfortable. Yet the freezing and miserable conditions did little to dampen his considerably elevated spirts. The deflation came when he and more than forty of his fellow soldiers were almost literally herded into a railway cattle truck for transport to their bivouac area at Etaples. Only a few days later, another cattle truck excursion saw them to Givenchy where his company joined the rest of the 1st Northants in the front line.

"Blimey, you'd think we're nothin' better than some stinkin' cows!" It was Eddie Matthews, his mate from recruit training once again complaining, just as he'd been doing since they'd left Southampton bound for France. Disgusted by Matthews' continuing bellyaching, young Rangely immediately shot back:

"You'd rather be marchin' in this muck?" His query met by a responding "NO," Wellington addressed the entire group: "Just be thankful for havin' a ride at all!" As unpleasant as their journey was, they continued in silence only to disembark into an even more troublesome quagmire. Hardly the organized fortifications they were led to expect, the men found little more than a series of shell-holes, most nearly filled with water. Real trenches were impossible in the low lying land. Instead of trying to dig deeper, they anxiously filled bags with sand from another railcar and built parapets above the shell-holes, hoping for a modicum of protection from possible enemy fire.

During several periods of rest between a series of front line deployments, Wellington's company underwent additional training. During one drill, instructors were impressed by his athletic abilities, especially being able to throw heavy objects a great distance. That skill earned him a place as a bomb thrower when the regiment was sent to Aubers Ridge. So when they attacked the German lines, he was one of the first over the top into no man's land leading a small bombing unit toward the enemy trenches. Under withering machine gun fire, the attack achieved little; Rangely, however, was seriously wounded. He simply lay quietly until darkness began to fall, when a corporal from the Sherwood Foresters, whose unit followed the Northants in the attack, helped him back to the relative safety of the British trenches. For that and several similar acts of bravery on the day, Corporal James Upton was later awarded the Victoria Cross. It was an example Rangely would not soon forget, especially as it came during an action in which his regiment sustained extraordinarily high casualties

Recovering in a field hospital, Wellington received word of his promotion to sergeant, and then the even more exciting news that he was granted "Blighty" leave. In addition to visiting his parents, he made courtesy calls on the headmaster and cadet commandant at Wellborough, and even briefly spoke to the Earl. Just as his leave expired, he received orders to report to an Officer Candidate Unit for several months of training. He was uncertain if those visitations had anything to do with his selection, although he knew as a former Wellborough cadet—and an experienced survivor from the western front—he joined a few select men from the other ranks deemed worthy of elevation to the officer corps. Yet having seen his own company commander, Captain Dickson, and so many other junior officers cut down in futile attacks, he was uncertain if this was truly such an honour!

After completing his training and joining the ranks of the army's new subalterns, Rangely was therefore somewhat relieved when asked if he would agree to being seconded to the King's African Rifles, now gearing up for what suddenly seemed was going to be a longer than expected campaign in East Africa. He accepted immediately; perhaps only his parents were more delighted than he at the news! Determined to seize this new opportunity, he stopped briefly in London before going on to Southampton, where he was to board ship for Cape Town and on to Mombasa. Specifically referred to Foyles Bookstore—"the most comprehensive educational bookshop in London" his former headmaster called it—to acquire reading materials which might help prepare him for the new assignment.

"How may I help you?" were the first words the smartly uniformed lieutenant heard from William Foyle as he came in the door.

"Well, uh...I need to prepare for my new assignment with the King's African Rifles."

"Certainly, sir! We have what you need." The proprietor of the shop had assisted other outbound officers before. He took Rangely into another room of the shop. "Bishop Creighton's *English Primer for Swahili Scholars* has been helpful to many other new KAR officers." He spoke as he reached up, taking the small volume from a shelf at the top of a bookcase.

"Yes, but..." Rangely hesitated, sensing the man knew more than he had imagined about what lay ahead of him. "I've been told in addition to Swahili, I might instead be dealing with Nyasaland soldiers."

Hesitating for only a moment as he scanned his memory, Foyle thought of a solution. "Nyanja, then, though I'd advise sticking with the Swahili as well," he said, looking down the bookshelf. "Ah, yes, here it is!" On a bottom shelf he located Alexander Riddel's *A Grammar of the Chinyanja Language*. "I believe this has an English-Nyanja vocabulary as well." He stopped to leaf through the book. "Indeed! Perhaps this in addition to the Swahili *Primer*, sir?"

Rangely was persuaded to purchase both, in addition to Heinrich Brode's *Britain and German East Africa* which Foyle assured him offered "the most up-to-date, pre-war information" on the region, and Harry Johnston's *British Central Africa*, a title suggested by his former headmaster. Though he felt somewhat overwhelmed as he left the shop, the new KAR subaltern had more than he needed as a diversion on the long sea voyage which awaited him once he arrived in Southampton. Although a good student while at Wellborough, he found the language study, especially, offered a new challenge in addition to the many other trials which lay ahead in his first command. Nonetheless, he did his best to learn as much of the languages as he could with no native speakers on board ship until he reached Durban, where his ship docked after being diverted following a U-boat scare approaching Cape Town. His voyage to Mombasa was thus delayed, but before departing he did meet an African gentleman who spoke a little Swahili. This enabled him to get at least some practice during the penultimate stage of the journey to join his new regiment.

Mombasa looked much as he pictured it from Heinrich Brode's book, but was no longer a sleepy Indian Ocean port. Rather, there were more ships and certainly more people than he'd imagined, most likely due to the war. After the delay in South Africa, he rushed to locate transport to his assigned battalion, 1/2 KAR. He had been meant to join the battalion in Nairobi where they'd been in training following their formation just a few months before. His delayed arrival disrupted that plan, and he learned the battalion had been advanced to Morogoro, inland from the former administrative center of German East Africa at Dar es Salaam. So Rangely was directed instead to motor transport bound for Tanga—which he knew had been the site of a major British defeat earlier in the war—to meet his battalion there before they would be deployed to Kilwa. His arrival coincided with frenzied activity at the Tanga seaport with ships unloading and others preparing to ferry units elsewhere as ordered, so on reporting to the adjutant he was most unceremoniously taken to the assembly point of A Company with nothing more than the briefest introduction to Company Sergeant Major Juma.

"*Kwa hairy, sarginti,*" the lieutenant nervously mangled the traditional Swahili greeting he had been practicing for days.

"*Habari gani*, sir!" Juma saluted smartly as he replied in almost perfect *Kiswahili*, while trying to suppress the smile which started forming on his lips. He surmised his new company commander, while well-intentioned, would require careful tutelage if he were to become an effective KAR officer.

At War

When A Company at last reached Mombasa, they were almost immediately ordered to a temporary defensive outpost at Gazi, twenty-five miles south of the port. There, a small garrison under the command of Captain George Hawthorn defending approaches to the city was under attack; he took care to explain the grave situation facing them to all the officers and NCOs now under his command. Most of the NCOs, including Juma, wondered if they would be going into battle facing the German army which they somehow understood was opposing British forces in Europe.

"No," Hawthorn assured them. *"Askari Wajerumani."* African soldiers like themselves, but who joined the German *Schutztruppe* (comparable to their own KAR) fighting to defend the nearby German colony. Their captain did not dwell on this explanation, however, as he hastily began organizing his men for a new transport experience: *"Garimoto!"* he explained, "carts with engines. It will be the fastest way to relieve the outpost. There won't be space for every *askari* to sit or even stand. Some will need to grab hold of the roof or sides. But by all means keep your feet off the ground and on the cart somewhere."

"*Cici*?" Several of the *askari* wondered at once exactly what the Captain was trying to explain. Juma, as had a few of the others, recalled seeing such self-propelled vehicles before—his first near

Kensington Station in London—and two or three later in Nairobi, but like the rest he'd never ridden in one. Hawthorn decided it would be best to explain that local military authorities had seized several of the vehicles which had recently arrived in Mombasa, thinking they would be of use since the fort at Gazi was at the end of the only motorable road outside the city center. The idea was simple: when the remaining KAR forces from Kismayo docked, they might be rushed to relieve the small garrison at Gazi. Although speed was the motiving factor in this instance, Captain Hawthorn also was concerned about the reactions of the *askari* to being ordered into the automobiles! That is why he'd convened a meeting with just his officers and NCOs to explain. With their cooperation in calming the men, he hoped the plan just might work.

Juma was assigned to organize the group of soldiers assigned to one of the twenty or so assorted vehicles commandeered for the operation. He stood up, next to the driver, an Indian shopkeeper who had volunteered to go with his vehicle. Several other *askari* clamoured into the seats, two had their feet in the luggage compartment, several others were planted on the running boards or standing on the rear bumper (such as it was). Juma, quite frankly, did not know if all their weight could be moved down the road or—even if it could—whether the speed of travel would throw some of them off! Their journey was, amazingly, without incident. Most of the other vehicles were also successful. As they climbed off, the men wanted first to inspect the conveyances which had delivered them to the battlefront, but none of the officers or NCOs would let them. After being certain each *askari* had his rifle and other equipment, the focus was squarely on Captain Hawthorn who issued orders for them to engage the German force.

With reinforcements and the original garrison co-mingled in the defense, there was a great deal of confusion. A lull in the German attack allowed Captain Hawthorn to take decisive action, ordering C Company to attack again, with Juma's A Company in support. Captain Hawthorn soon fell wounded, and Juma saw Captain Stoner shot as well. But he heard a voice trying to rally the original defenders of C Company: it was Colour Sergeant Sumani! With the officers unable effectively to command, he was trying to inspire his company to keep on the attack. Juma's A Company joined in following up the initial attack; together their efforts were successful in driving off the German force. As twilight fell over the field, all the KAR *askari* realized they had carried the day; now they could care for their wounded. It was a difficult duty for Juma, as he was one of the *askari* detailed to carry their severely wounded commander back to a vehicle for transport into Mombasa where he could receive medical care. Men had been wounded in his presence before, even Major Cobbe in Asante, but Juma just knew Captain Hawthorne deserved a better fate! Having taken special care to ensure his *askari* remained confident riding in their *garimoto* convoy into battle, it seemed especially unfortunate that he would be wounded on this day.

∞∞∞∞∞∞

Following their successful defense of the garrison at Gazi, Juma and the rest of his battalion were ordered to Nairobi where they could be organized for deployments defending the Uganda Railway. When not patrolling, much of their time was spent in drills, not unlike those Juma had known in Zomba. But when word reached battalion headquarters of the disastrous invasion attempt by British forces at Tanga in German East Africa, the pace of training intensified. Even though the officers didn't speak directly about it, all the *askari* soon knew something of the military setback to British forces. They now practiced close order attack in areas of thick bush, where each company would be divided into smaller sections to practice attacking under a layer of live fire from local European reservists. Usually Juma was given command of one such section, welcoming the opportunity to calm his fellow *askari* who unlike himself, had seldom been under enemy fire. All of them knew, however, they would soon have an opportunity to test their resolve in actual combat situations. That was confirmed when Lieutenant Colonel Graham spoke to them about their specific task:

"Mafia Island is defended by only a small German garrison," he was at pains to reassure them. "But it is essential we take this outpost from them to protect our approaches to the Rufiji River. Major Soames has prepared you well…" As the colonel went on, *askari* glanced at each other noting that their commander had indeed been promoted. Juma did hear Graham conclude: "I have every confidence you will succeed in this task!"

They then assembled for a photograph of the four companies which comprised this half battalion; finally they marched to the railway station for the journey to Mombasa. Quickly detraining, again they marched, this time to the docks. There they boarded an armed merchant cruiser, the *Kinfauns Castle* and, following the Royal Navy cruiser *HMS Fox*, headed out to sea, south past Pemba and Zanzibar toward Mafia Island. Theirs was an uneventful passage during which they practiced rapid deployment on deck, anticipating a landing from small surf boats on the island. When Mafia came into view shortly after dawn on their second morning aboard, the *Fox* began shelling the westernmost point on the island's coast. The *askari* quickly boarded the boats and were ferried ashore during gaps in the nearly deafening fusillade on either side of their landing point. As they were heading ashore, Juma took special notice of the turned and twisted roots of the mangroves which lined sections of the beach, extending in places to well over the height of two men. Only occasionally were there openings in the tangled wall of roots, not of all of which had been made by the Fox's guns. Anticipating finding more such natural obstacles when they advanced inland, he turned to Lieutenant Joyce, who had only recently taken command of A Company:

"It is just as the forest stockades we faced in Asante," he observed. "We'll need to take care avoiding snipers on our flanks, hiding behind those trees," Juma further advised his inexperienced commanding officer. Their landing, however, was unopposed and the entire KAR force was able to move off the beach and beyond the mangroves. Major Soames set up a temporary encampment with pickets at several distances away from the main cluster of KAR tents, anticipating an advance the next day on Ngombeni Village about two miles inland. After purchasing the island from the Sultan of Zanzibar, the Germans had selected Ngombeni as a site for plantation research, building a small station around a nearby hill. Once the British shelling of the island began, the small German police force retreated, establishing a defensive position on that hill. It did not take KAR scouts long to identify the German positions, and the entire force was deployed to attack, with Lieutenant Joyce's company at first held in reserve.

The lieutenant appeared to have taken special note of his Colour Sergeant's experience. This became clear when, as the frontal attack seemed to stall, their Company was ordered to press forward on the German right flank.

"Sergeant!" Joyce called to Juma. "We're to attack that tree lined section of the German defenses." He pointed to his right. "Bring up your squad and we'll lead the attack." While not the same mangrove tangle he had originally noticed, Juma recognized the danger the company faced as it advanced. The tree line was dotted with a number of large mango trees which could well provide ideal vantage points for snipers. Lieutenant Joyce tried to position himself near the center of the small squad, itself in the center of company's attack. Perhaps out of willful exuberance coupled with his lack of combat experience, Joyce failed to seek out sufficient cover as he led the company forward. He was soon badly wounded. Juma rushed to the Lieutenant, carrying him to safety behind a small outbuilding, motioning another *askari* to care for the Lieutenant. He then hurried back to the men:

"*Tsogolani!*" He commanded the men to move forward, much as he recalled Colour Sergeant Sumani had done at Gazi. "Be careful! Take cover," he also shouted to them. Going from one to another, he pointed out likely sniper positions first to one man, then another. Avoiding the most open places, Juma placed his *askari* at key points behind trees. He spotted a something else:

"Corporal Katapoli, you and Private Bomali," he shouted to the two *askari*, pointing to a small plantation shed. "*Jengo!* Behind there."

Fortunately, the entire German force was incredibly small, less than thirty in all, with no more than six or eight on the tree-lined flank his company was attacking. Juma continued to move steadfastly between his men. He directed their fire, urging them to move ahead carefully. At last the return fire seemed to cease.

Pressed on all fronts, the German force retreated into a small valley, only to be raked with *askari* gunfire. The KAR fared better, routing the German defenders and retaking the island, confirming Colonel Graham's confidence that they would. And despite losing their commanding officer to sniper fire, A Company took no additional casualties.

"*Asilikali wotchuka!*" You are a hero, some of Juma's fellow soldiers called out to him in *Chichewa* as they returned to their temporary camp. While he appreciated their accolades, it was the words of Johnson Kwayera, one of the younger Yao soldiers of his company, which touched him most.

"*Nanyula*," he called Juma. "You are like the knob thorn tree—strong, firm, and everlasting." They had not, at least not yet, seen any such tree on the island, but they were widespread it the forest lands around Zomba where the wood was valued as sturdy building material. Johnson intended it as a compliment, Juma knew, and he was grateful when it heard it used to describe him. As long as he had been an *askari* it was as close to a nickname anyone ever had for him! The *askari* frequently had such sobriquets—not always complimentary—especially for their officers and NCOs, though they mainly used them in private conversations. But *Nanyula* was of another order, so he did nothing to suppress its use. He may have even encouraged it!—at least at first. Perhaps that's why the name stuck in the minds of many *askari* who came to use it even when speaking directly to their sergeant.

When all his company were safely in camp, Juma immediately sought out Lieutenant Joyce. He found a young *Mjeremani* woman tending to the officer's wounds. He also found Captain Giffard there too. He had a very minor wound, suffered as he assumed command of the KAR contingent after Major Soames himself was severely wound. All of them appreciated the kind efforts of the German woman, actually the wife of *Schutztruppe* Lieutenant Erich Schiller who had led the defense of the island. Giffard quickly explained all this to Juma, but wanted to say much more to the Sergeant:

"What you did today will not be forgotten," he assured Juma.

"*Asante sana*, sir." Juma expressed his thanks, but also added confidently, "That is what I must do as an *askari*, sir, nothing less."

"The lieutenant tells me that you did much more than save his life. You returned to the men and kept the attack moving forward. He believes, and I agree, that you were an essential part of our success today. That will not be forgotten," the captain repeated. While Juma did indeed appreciate what he took as kindness, he didn't understand precisely what the words meant. He could not know that his name and achievements would be recorded in the official report Captain Giffard filed concerning the KAR's action at Mafia Island. Even if he had, the idea that he had "been mentioned in dispatches" would have had little impact on his consciousness. He was, after all, merely an *askari* doing his duty as he had agreed to do.

∞∞∞∞∞∞

The entire Mafia Island operation lasted less than three full days. Juma never had a chance to see if there were actually any knob thorn trees on the small island. Instead, along with the entire KAR half battalion, he embarked on the transport SS *Barjora* for a return to Mombasa. They soon discovered the situation on the mainland was, if nothing else, fluid. Instead of Mombasa, they were ordered to disembark at Vanga to relieve 3/KAR *askari* who had been defending a British outpost at Jasin, just across the border in German East Africa. At least that's what Captain Giffard told the officers and NCOs before they began disembarking to begin their latest assignment. No sooner had the entire contingent been put ashore, Giffard began issuing orders:

"Form up your squads! Concentrate the companies!" were Giffard's first commands. Juma recalled the next order involved collecting all their spare equipment and ammunition for assignment to the local porters who were to follow them with the supplies. They were to dislodge a sizeable German force which threatened the small British outpost at Jasin. As he worked to help A Company get ready for their own orders to advance, Juma could hear the sound of battle not far distant; he also saw several signal rockets explode in the sky to the south. Then Captain Giffard's voice boomed out again:

"The fort is under attack! We must move at once to their aid." But B Company alone was ready. Exasperated, Captain Giffard therefore ordered them forward before the rest of the contingent. Juma regretted his assistance had been insufficient for Lieutenant Richmond, A Company's newly appointed commanding officer. Juma saw it as his failure to have the men ready. Nonetheless, they were soon marching south, into the fray. The men waded across the shallow Suba River. Then they established defensive positions in thick bush. Just beyond, they could see a large building which Juma had been told was a sisal factory. It was their intended destination for a later surge forward. But they were pinned down by continuous firing from the German lines.

"Return fire!" Juma ordered his men. He hoped to discourage the German *askari*. Not merely fruitless, the effort seemed to embolden their enemies. If anything the intensity of the incoming rounds increased. Machine guns joined in opposing their efforts. Suddenly the sound of bugles. Then cheers from across the field near the factory. The German *askari* were charging toward them! Though Juma saw several attacking German soldiers—including one or two *Wasungu*—fall during the ensuing melee of hand-to-hand combat, he also knew A Company had by then expended much of their ammunition. They had to fall back across the swampy river. As soon as Captain Giffard ordered the retreat, Juma turned his attention to his wounded men, ensuring that they too were brought to the northern bank and then attended to by the stretcher bearers who had followed them to the river.

As the company reorganized and replenished its depleted ammunition supply, two small field guns opened an intense barrage on the other side of the Suba. Juma could see the explosions of the shells and hear the shouts from the German lines. The enemy's attack was blunted! It didn't surprise him that Captain Giffard ordered another assault across the Suba. This time A Company was assigned a place on the extreme right of the line. It was late afternoon when the order to advance came. By then the sun was bright in their eyes from the west. Juma and his men reached the southern bank of the river. They were experienced *askari* now, so glaring sun in their eyes did little to deter them. But again they met withering German fire along their entire line. Though A Company appeared to be meeting less opposition than others, Lieutenant Richmond told Juma and his other NCOs not to press their attack *too* quickly:

"We must not become isolated!" he shouted to them just before the attack began. "Hold back with the rest!" While his instincts were to continue pressing forward with even the small advantage they seemed to have, Juma did not want his men to be vulnerable. He followed the Lieutenant's orders. It was perhaps best he did so! Suddenly there was increasing German resistance. Captain Giffard then ordered another retreat to the north bank of the river. As casualties were low after this latest assault, Juma wondered if they might be ordered to regroup and perhaps make another attempt to reclaim the Jasin fort. He was almost disappointed when that never happened. Only much later did he learn that though the Germans had won the day, it had been a pyrrhic victory; the losses the KAR had inflicted on the *Schutztruppe* at Jasin significantly changed, and prolonged, their campaign.

∞∞∞∞∞

As 1/KAR moved further north to a temporary base camp near the Umba River, not far from where they had come ashore following their victory on Mafia Island, Juma was feeling far less steadfast and almost resented being called *Nanyula* by his men. But as the entire battalion assumed defense positions to prevent the Germans following up their victory at Jasin with an incursion toward Mombasa, he managed to put that thought out of his mind. He was a soldier and had a new job to do. He—and his fellow *askari*—were to stand tall against a potential enemy advance! But any solace he might have had from that realization did not last long. After a few short weeks, three companies of 1/KAR, including Juma's, marched back to Vanga, boarded first a coastal freighter for Mombasa, and then the train to Voi. They bivouacked at what was a quickly becoming an expansive military encampment. This wasn't a rest stop, however! A Company was headed toward Saliata Hill, nearer the border between British and German territory, riding the first few miles on what they called the "crazy train"—so-named because its hasty construction left riders uneasily rolling and rocking as their carriages wound along on its bumpy rails.

When they detrained, Juma noticed the wind started to pick up from the south, but didn't have time to reflect on the sudden change in the weather. The entire company was ordered to board twelve motor transport vehicles which were lined up near the end of the improvised tracks. Intended to become a link to Taveta, further construction could only be assured if German raiding camps such as the one they were to attack were eliminated.

"You will be the first *askari* to travel into battle riding in a *garimoto*!" Lieutenant Richmond proudly told his company.

"*Lakin...*" Juma started to contradict him, but caught himself before finishing his first word. Recalling his first experience riding in a motorcar at Gazi only a few months before, he knew better. It was true these were new vehicles lined up before them, with drivers in smart, crisp uniforms of the East African Motor Transport Company; his previous experience had been a decidedly different, ad hoc affair. Moreover this was only a minor detail and not worth the risk of provoking his company commander's ire. Instead he focused on getting the *askari* on board the transport and on their way to Saliata Hill.

They had only traveled about a mile into the bush when the rain came! The deluge was typical of the *kusi* monsoon season in east Africa, though perhaps earlier than usual. The timing couldn't have been worse for their advance. Despite the nearly full moon, they did not see how rapidly the dust was turning to mud. It was only a matter of minutes before the tires were virtually entombed in mire.

"Out of the vehicles!" came the order. "We will proceed on foot." What followed must have seemed some sort of comeuppance for his thoughts and words, almost uttered, just before climbing into the cars:

"Sergeant Juma!"

"Sir?" He replied surely and swiftly, but the order he received was unexpected and out of the ordinary.

"Your squad will help the drivers extricate these vehicles." As the remainder of the company moved out with the Lieutenant on foot, Juma and a few *askari* set to manhandling the cars back toward the vehicle track which paralleled the crazy railroad.

The task was a bit easier than he first imagined, once the cars were emptied of their passengers. Yet *Nanyula* with his men—pushing, prodding, and eventually pulling the vehicles through the thick mud—was not an image which gave him any joy. Though he followed the orders without hesitation, for Juma it was yet another setback in his service as an *askari*. Had Lieutenant Richmond—and perhaps even Captain Giffard—lost confidence in him? If so, he wondered, how much confidence he should vest in his KAR commanders? His growing despondency nearly turned to utter gloom when the mud-covered vehicle convoy at last met the main body of A Company, stumbling through the bush following their own precipitous retreat under fire, having lost not only three *askari* killed and three more wounded, but also one of their machine guns and thousands of rounds of ammunition. Even learning that a member of his company, Corporal Disi Katita, had nearly saved the life of the Somali interpreter assigned to Lieutenant Richmond, failed to cheer him. Only his determination to repay the confidence so many had previously displayed sustained him as 1/KAR regrouped and returned to their field camp near Voi.

The next few weeks were hardly quiet ones for the battalion. Many of the men were sick, Juma himself feeling feverish for several days following the return from the Saliata Hill disaster. The rain continued, with heavy downpours most afternoons. As often as every other day one group of *askari* or another would march out on patrol, seeking to prevent any further German attacks on the railroad, either the mainline which ran through Voi or the ramshackle spur which was slowly creeping towards Taveta. Seldom actually confronting *Schutztruppe* raiders whom they were intended to intercept, the patrols were not without excitement and occasional dangers. More often than not the difficulties were posed not so much by German *askari*, but by a few of the indigenous inhabitants of the region: lion, elephant, giraffe, and—at least in Juma's experience—rhino.

On one occasion, while leading a small patrol south of Maktao, through some of the bush so thick it was nearly impossible to see more than ten or fifteen feet ahead, the *askari* marching at the point of the small column heard rustling noises ahead. Raising his hand to signal a stop in their advance:

"*Wajeremani*," he whispered to the man behind him, who in turn quietly passed the word back to CSM Juma who was marching near the rear. Again remembering his experience in Asante, Juma signaled to the men to spread out slightly before continuing forward. He did not order them the fix bayonets, however, fearing any sunlight which might glare off one of the blades could reveal their position. Just as he motioned the men to begin an advance they all heard an extremely loud snort:

"Brruhaa! BRRUHAA!" It was, in fact, an enormous bellow, accompanied by sounds of obvious disruption in the bush.

"Chipembere!" shouted Lance Corporal Johnson Kwayera just as he dove to his right, out of the way of a charging black rhino. The animal, a large one even for the species, was unable to shift direction once beginning its charge toward the KAR party and continued on past the entire patrol. Juma quickly shouldered his rife, and as he turned took a single shot at the rhino, apparently in vain. The rest of the *askari* dissolved into what was a nervous laughter, not at their sergeant's failure to hit his unexpected target, but at their close encounter with yet another "enemy" in their otherwise tedious wait for any meaningful advance on their principal adversaries, the Germans.

A fortnight after encountering the rhino Juma, was called to a meeting with Lieutenant Richmond and the other NCOs of the company.

"Our little railway"—the lieutenant used a diminutive in reference to the "crazy line," rather than referring to it as did his men—"has now been completed to Maktau. And we have word the Germans have moved closer with a base near the large baobab grove, at Mbuyuni. The General" (as he referred to Brigadier Wilfrid Malleson) "has decided we should mount an offensive against the new enemy camp." It was welcome news after so many weeks of little meaningful soldiering. Merely fighting rhinos wasn't Juma's idea of what he, or the KAR, should be doing!

∞∞∞∞∞∞

When at last two companies of 1/KAR joined a similar number from 4/KAR and the 29th Punjabis, plus some British scouts heading west from Maktau, the *askari* were delighted and it showed. They were a picture of confidence, marching smartly in perfect rhythm, singing cheerfully even as they began a journey into battle. Though their spirit was joyous, their song revealed a much deeper understanding of the situation in which they now found themselves:

"*Sole! Sole! Sole!*" they sang, a corruption of the English word "sorry" which they took to include "sorrows" as well.

"*Sole! Sole! Sole!*

"We don't know where we're going

"But we're going anyway!

"Because it is the war!

"*Sole! Sole! Sole!*

"We men are going to war

"Because the enemy is near!

"It is a time of trouble!

"*Sole! Sole! Sole!*

"Time of trouble"

The entire column advanced about eight miles west and then camped for the night, under strict orders not to fire their weapons unless absolutely necessary. But once a nervous Punjabi machine gunner fired at a sound in the bush he thought was an enemy patrol, any hope for a surprise attack in the morning was undone.

What none in the British forced realized was that not only was surprise lost, but the Germans were able to reinforce their positions on Mbuyuni ridge. Nonetheless, the attack proceeded, with the Punjabi battalion ordered to advance on the right before dawn in an effort to get behind the entrenched German defenses, well-situated at the top of the small hill. Both 1/KAR companies prepared to make a frontal attack, across a shallow valley toward the base of the hill and a large grove of baobab trees, *mbuyuni*, which gave the entire area its name.

"Uhha!.......Uhha!......Uhha!...Uhha!" A rhythmic chant began in the KAR ranks as the sun rose. The *askari* advanced, rapidly at first. In response there was steady fire from the German positions. Juma directed his squad toward a clump of small trees. Next to them A Company's machine gun began firing. But the gun's position quickly drew increased attention from their enemies. Glancing to his right, Juma saw some of the Punjabis on a crest. They were attempting to engage the German lines. That seemed to lessen incoming fire on his men. Yet supporting fire from his left flank suddenly ceased. In fact, the attack appeared to stall along the entire front. Juma tried to lead his men into a more advantageous position. None seemed available. Machine gun fire raked the bush everywhere. Then German small arms fire increased as well. They were attacking! Juma suddenly felt a bullet hit his right shoulder. His arm went numb. He was stunned. But he also knew this was a time for action. He rallied all the nearby men. Then he ordered those still upright to carry wounded companions. He aided Lieutenant Richmond, his wounded company commander, himself. All the while he continued to direct the men in firing at their enemies as they withdrew.

Ignoring his pain, Juma actually led his fellow *askari* back across the valley and towards Maktau. Word soon spread in the temporary camp that 1/KAR were back with their wounded, carrying their dead, some from other regiments, and all the machine guns they could find. One of the Punjabis, who had only shortly before returned to camp, passed a message of their return to Brigadier Malleson. The commander acknowledged receipt of the news, but he didn't move to welcome the *askari* even though they had been under his command for the assault. Perhaps he didn't want to admit that he had trusted his own, in this case *bad*, judgement. Intelligence officers told him Mbuyuni would be defended by more than 2,000 well entrenched German troops.

"Hogwash!" he had replied to Colonel Meinertzhagen, the intelligence officer who made the estimate of the enemy he would face at Mbuyuni.

"There can't be more than 300 over there! I'll march more than a thousand against them. Even if half of mine are Punjabis and Africans, we'll mop up the entire German force on that ridge!"

Such disparaging opinions of their value as fighting troops had, of course, been heard before by the KAR *askari*. They also knew well the reputation—ill-prepared and uninspired—of the *Wahindi*, *Baluchi*, and *Banyani* soldiers whom they joined in this campaign; stories of their failures at Tanga just a few months before were well known to the Nyasaland *askari*. They were justifiably proud, especially the veterans like Juma, of their own service, and they were determined to put any scornful opinions of their own value to rest.

Yes, they had been unable to advance against the well prepared machine guns of the German force. But they had managed to find spots in the bush in which to conceal themselves. They did not retreat or run in disarray! Rather they waited for their officers to lead them out of the firestorm in which they had found themselves. But it was Colour Sergeant Juma who had rallied the men of the two KAR companies. First ordering them to protect the retreat, Juma made sure all the men—dead and wounded included—were accounted for and took inventory of the KAR equipment. Finally, ignoring the danger to himself, he personally led the *askari* back toward Maktau, leaving nobody and nothing of value to their enemies behind. With most of their officers dead or wounded, and Brigadier Malleson having voluntarily absented himself, it was only Colonel Price of the 29th Punjabis who greeted the valiant *askari*. The Colonel was appreciative; his troops had accomplished no more, and in fact withdrew in disarray, sometimes leaving guns and equipment on the battlefield as they did so.

"Well done, men!" was all he could manage. It was certainly a true, if anemic sentiment. Despite not speaking *Kiswahili*, nor any other African language, the colonel still made clear his appreciation for their service and sacrifice. He also managed to find Juma who was now being attended to by an Indian stretcher bearer, who served as a translator.

"I saw you from the flank. It was impossible to press on!"

"E-e-ye! *Chiwaya* (machine guns) all around. *Mtolanje*......." Juma's voice tapered off, as he slipped into a state of only half consciousness. Colonel Price could not know he was trying to describe, in his native *Chiyao*, withering fire which disrupted the KAR retreat and also took its toll on Juma himself. Badly wounded in the right shoulder, he was weak. But his men were safe now. About his own fate he was less certain.

∞∞∞∞∞∞∞

Juma remembered little of his time in the casualty clearing station in Maktau, nor his short ride on the hospital train from Maktau to Voi. When he finally awakened on a mat in the makeshift hospital, he only barely realized he was lying in a railway transfer shed near the Voi depot. Once semi-awake, though, he was troubled by the amount of time that passed before an African orderly, walking between patients, noticed he had roused himself.

"*Utotou*," the exasperated Juma almost shouted at the man, though his voice was much softer than it might have been. He was trying, as best he might, to explain in *Chiyao* that he was in considerable pain.

The orderly look puzzled. "*Sifahamu*? The quizzical look helped Juma recognize he should have spoken in *Kiswahili*.

He tried again, but in a softer tone: "*Inauma*."

"*Ewaa! sajini*." The orderly suddenly realized the wounded sergeant, his military superior, was in considerable pain.

"Yours is a severe shoulder wound, and your arm is broken," came the brief explanation. The orderly then scurried off without any further words or attention to the patient. However, it was not long before first a nurse, then a doctor appeared, and Juma was soon resting more comfortably under the influence of a liberal dose of morphine.

He didn't know how long he was asleep, or indeed how long he had been at the field hospital in Voi. He was distressed at first not to find many of his *askari* companions nearby, as he could recall that many of them had been wounded at—where was it? Mbuyuni ridge?—the place his company had been ordered to attack did not immediately come to mind. His memory instead focused on the machine guns and sniper fire which had claimed so many of his company, including himself. He had faced bullets many times before. That was a part of being an *askari*. Yet never before had any of those bullets found its target in his body. Why was that? He was, at least at first, at a loss for an explanation of his ill fortune. As if from another dimension, a voice, much softer than he had heard before, interrupted his thoughts.

"Rest well, *sajini*!" He recognized it was yet another orderly encouraging him back to sleep. And he was happy to take refuge from his thoughts in that happier place.

In fact, Juma rested, or more precisely remained in a morphine-induced sleep for several days, going on perhaps for a week or so. He could not know the very limited and greatly over-worked medical staff at the Voi field hospital had little else to offer. Their supervising doctor, in fact, prescribed the continued use of morphine as a substitute of last resort for the intensive nursing care they could not provide. While in some cases that was a paltry replacement for nursing care, for many of the strongest patients—men such as CSM Juma—just the time to heal was important and greatly appreciated. Juma soon enough was able to sit up a little despite being bandaged from his neck all along his right arm to just above his fingertips, which he could only barely move. His movement was further restricted because the brace from his back to his wrist was elevated in an iron hoop itself held in place by rope fastened to a pole mounted next to his mat. He assumed it must be a piece of wood which so restricted his movement, though it was instead a thin piece of steel—cut from a bit of salvaged corrugated roofing—and fashioned just to fit his body. Despite such restrictions on his movements, Juma begin to assess his surroundings. Some of his 1/2 KAR companions were also in the hospital unit, if one could call the floor of the railway transfer shed anything so grand! Several were soon able, for short periods, to engage in limited conversations.

Among the first Juma recalled were exchanges with Corporal Saidi Dabi, whose major injuries came as a result of machine gun fire at Mbuyuni. Only the determined efforts of the Army surgeon at the field hospital, Captain McClower, saved his life, but not his leg. Despite the amputation and all that implied about his future, the Corporal would, and frequently did, tell anyone who would listen how grateful he was for the doctor's efforts. As a sergeant in Saidi's company, and confined to a nearby hospital mat, Juma was more or less a captive ear. Saidi mentioned his gratitude so often, Juma at last challenged the younger corporal to take some positive action instead of merely talking incessantly about the matter.

"How can I?" Saudi offered. "It's the doctor who should bring me my present!"

"*Lipo gani*?" Stunned, Juma wondered what sort of gift the young *askari* expected. What payment could he possibly expect from the doctor whose determined efforts had already saved his life? Undeterred, Saudi persisted. Finally, after several days of his continued insistence, the Corporal explained:

"Such an effort must surely indicate my value to the doctor! Why else would he have tried so hard to save me? And now that I've survived, he surely must want to bring a present of thanks." Saidi made it sound as though there could be no room for disagreement with his logic. But even the experienced Juma could not condone such a convoluted presumption held by one of his men, especially of an officer, and a committed medical officer at that! So Juma simply, yet very directly *ordered* Saidi never to mention the matter again.

"Yes, *sajini*!" came the sad reply. Corporal Saudi saluted the CSM; and he never discussed his wound with Juma, or the doctor, again.

∞∞∞∞∞∞

There was, however, another matter which Juma did want to discuss, but not with just anyone. It was only when his old friend Issa Bakali, who had also taken up Chief Chikowi's challenge to became an *askari*, appeared beside him that Juma did so. Though Issa had been discharged when 2/KAR was disbanded, he returned to the *askari* ranks when an appeal went out for old soldiers as the force was expanded rapidly when the war began.

"*Mwino*!" Issa addressed him as an old friend, setting aside the usual protocols of military rank. "I have come to see for myself that you are recovering!" Among the new *askari* sent to British East Africa, Issa had heard a rumor that his friend had been wounded. But Issa had little time. His company was merely passing Voi as 1/KAR moved to its new posting, at Longido.

Surprised, and quite frankly shocked to see his old friend—who he thought had left the *askari* life behind several years before—Juma was nonetheless overjoyed to unburden himself of a concern that had bothered him every time he was able to think about the wound he'd recently received.

"Tell me, Issa, why did I have this misfortune now, after so many years of being a soldier? What did I do that this misery should befall me now? Isn't it true that calamities such as mine are the result of misdeeds?"

Issa did not disagree, as both knew from their boyhood that everything had both a cause and a consequence, even if there might not at first be a readily observable connection.

"Whose misbehaviour might have been the cause, then?" Juma didn't allow his friend time to answer. "It must have been Kuliraga," he blurted, mentioning his second wife. "Her misbehaviour with other men is most assuredly the cause of my pain!"

Having known the woman since before Juma had taken her as a wife, Issa did not doubt the possibility that Juma might be correct. He also knew Juma had left for Jubaland only a short time after their marriage. But only their long friendship permitted him to caution the man who now out-ranked him:

"Do not be hasty, my old friend. You will have time enough to deal with this matter after you are healed and we have returned to Majowa."

They didn't discuss it further, as Issa quickly left his friend's bedside to fall in with his company for the march to Longido. And Juma nodded off to sleep again.

∞∞∞∞∞

When he awoke, Juma recalled the song he and his fellow *askari* had been singing on their way to Mbuyuni. It was, indeed, a "time of troubles." Though he knew a German bullet was the immediate cause of his wound, he had convinced himself the blame fell squarely on Kuliraga. Such reasoning was all he had known since he was a small boy. But he was also coming to understand—especially when the effects of his pain medication subsided—his recovery would not be easy. The doctors were clear that he would be moved to Nairobi as soon as possible, but would not be able to return to Nyasaland for perhaps months. Oh to return home! He longed to see Ambikanile again; this new war had already extended his time away from her. And his children! He worried they might not recognize him, or they might not remember him. Apesile would almost be a young woman! And Mtindiso—he must be such a big boy by now! How would he be able to deal with them if he were still recovering from his ... his misfortune? Then he felt—or at least almost felt—guilty he had not thought much at all about his family since leaving Jubaland, at least until he began worrying about his "troubles." That surely was a *"sole"* situation as described in the *askari* song!

For two long weeks he continued to mull all these matters over in his mind as he waited in Voi for transport to Nairobi. When finally boarding the train west, he began to feel somewhat better about the future, and his arrival at the Nairobi Military Hospital—much larger, and clearly better equipped—actually brought a smile to his face. On his arrival, doctors told Juma his arm would only be of use if he tried to help it work again. Although he was a bit uncertain what that would entail, the possibility that it could happen in this facility seemed much better than if he were still on his mat in the Voi railway transfer shed. As the pain eased, he gradually was able to move his fingers a little more. But his arm continued to tingle as it was still wrapped up around the corrugated iron splint. Juma longed to be free of that encumbrance!

News from Nyasaland did arrive in Nairobi, even if it still took a while to filter through to the hospital. His wound gratuity had already been paid, as he had requested, directly to Ambikanile. Other news from home was much more distressing, however, concerning a violent uprising against the *Wasungu* in Chiradzulu, not at all far from Majowa. Some of the *askari* who had remained in Zomba had been mobilized against the rebels, chasing the leader—John Chilembwe, as he understood it from several somewhat vague reports—toward Portuguese East Africa, where he was killed.

"Who is this John Chilembwe? Why has he caused our people to be in trouble?" Juma asked a 1/KAR *askari* whom he met in the hospital. Ndasala Chiputula was not a fellow Yao, but a member of E Company. His legs were severely mangled by machine gun fire near Tsavo. But his home was near Chiradzulu, so Juma hoped he might know more.

"A Watch Tower man," Ndasala told him. "He went to America and came back to build a church, one with a big bell! I'm told he's been preaching against this war and tells people not to do as the *Angerezi* order them. Then he organized an army…"

"That was playing with fire!" Juma struggled to comprehend the story Ndasala offered, but once the gist of it was clear, he abruptly interrupted him, almost yelling at the Corporal.

"Inde ndithudi!" Absolutely, Ndasala immediately agreed, but clearly in *Chichewa*—a language Juma did not know as well as *Chiyao* or *Kiswahili*. This sudden response helped Juma realize Corporal Ndasala was a more recent recruit assigned to his battalion, one who might not completely embrace the philosophy of service which had grown in Juma's mind over the years. As they continued to discuss the uprising, he only cautiously indicated why he longed to have been one of the *askari* called upon to help restore order and preserve the peace. Juma had no doubt Chilembwe's actions were misguided and indeed much more troubling than those of Chief Serumba who had been the

object of his first campaign, at Lake Chilwa, or even Mpezeni. Seeking a middle way, as Chief Chikowi had explained it to him so long ago, was one of the reasons he had joined British service in the first place. Now he found himself fighting in a big war, far away from his beloved mountain. He longed to go home even more!

That was undoubtedly why Juma felt his days in the hospital passed slowly. When at last the bandages and splint were removed, though, he despaired further: his arm seemed useless. He could move the fingers a little more than before and grasp objects, even bend his elbow to move those objects about. But he seemed to have little strength in his wounded arm; his shoulder continued to ache as well. Of what use could he be in such a state? Men whose recovery appeared to parallel his own were released and sent home, with no mention of returning to their units. It wasn't a fate he welcomed. After fifteen years as an *askari*, what else could he do? How might he complete the mission which had brought him to the Central—now King's—African Rifles? Even the repeated assurances of nurses and doctors that he could recover the lost function in his arm didn't seem to improve his spirits.

"We need you to do all you can to get back to being as you were so you can join us again!" Those first words, spoken during an unexpected visit from his former commander did more than any other to improve his spirits.

"Jambo, Kapteni! Habari gani?" Juma was all smiles as he greeted his visitor, inquiring if he was well.

"Actually, it's Major now," George Giffard replied softly with no reproach evident in his tone. "You have been one of our outstanding *askari* for some time now, and you proved that again at Mbuyuni. The Brigader," he went on, referring to Malleson, "thinks so too. He's mentioned you in his dispatches—and recommended you for a medal honouring your brave devotion to duty. Perhaps even the Victoria Cross!"

So completely stunned by this news, Juma didn't immediately reply. His mouth agape, he just listened as Major Giffard continued.

"We will need you in the KAR now, especially as we're about to form a new battalion. We hope you'll return to Nyasaland and help recruit new *askari*. And, if you agree to re-enlist, I believe there will be a promotion to Sergeant Major in the new 2/KAR."

More than any medal, this was the encouragement Juma so needed. He quickly reassured Major Giffard that he would welcome returning—first to Zomba and then, as he continued to regain his strength—to a new position in 2/KAR. Indeed he was a happy man! The time passed much more quickly now, until finally he took the train to Mombasa. He could see a future much more to his liking as he once again returned from an assignment that had taken him far from home.

∞∞∞∞∞

Juma was uncertain which welcome pleased him most: The cheers and accolades from his fellow *askari* as he stepped onto the parade ground at KAR headquarters in Zomba? Or the somewhat more subdued, but equally sincere celebrations as he came around the mountain to Majowa? In both places he was truly and clearly *home*! Both homecomings were joyous, yet each offered challenges. After the initial excitement at KAR headquarters, where he was now temporarily posted, the new commandant, Lieutenant Colonel Soames, granted Juma leave, allowing him to return to his village for a few weeks. So it was an easy decision for him to begin dealing with family issues. First, he wanted to reassure Ambikanile that he was well, reiterating this message over and over by demonstrating his determination to regain fully the strength a German bullet had taken from him—not only in his injured arm but also the ability to work at a prodigious pace, a characteristic she had always admired in him.

Working to improve his general fitness also allowed him to establish a more mature relationship with Mtindiso. The boy was now nearly twelve and Juma wanted to help prepare him to be a man. It would not be long before he would face the initiation tests which his father has passed not long before beginning his journey as an *asilikali*. In an effort to ensure both goals could be met, father and son first walked, and then began running, the many paths around the mountain and up to the top of Zomba plateau. As they did, Juma took care to explain to his son many of the notable features found in those familiar environments, including the flora and fauna. He took pains to point out the *nanyula* trees on the mountainside, although he was equally careful not to mention how his fellow *askari* had come to associate their sergeant with that valuable species! But he did want his son to learn about other complicated legends associated with his home. On one of their walks, Juma deliberately led his son toward a spot on the top of the mountain overlooking the Shire River:

"Osati ano!" Not there, Mtindiso objected, not wanting to approach the large depression clearly visible near the edge of the massif. Juma wondered why the boy would object in *Chichewa* rather than in *Chiyao*. But the response contained a clue:

"*Mizimu yamakolo,*" Mtindiso replied softly. He seemed afraid, which Juma understood from the words themselves: spirits of the ancestors. He had heard many Chewa *asilikali* speak with awe of the power such spirits had in their lives. Then he remembered that this place, Chingwe's Hole, was one the original inhabitants of what were now Yao lands had venerated as drawing the unwary to their deaths. Like a rope—for that was the name of the place—it would pull any inattentive visitors to their deaths down a seemingly endless opening in the earth.

"How did you learn this tale, son?" Juma wanted to know. It took some time for the boy to divulge the source of his knowledge, but the essential elements he seemed to have gleaned from playmates he had meet, not at Majowa, but rather when he had been at their home at the KAR base. Those mostly *Chichewa*-speaking boys had passed on the stories of the mystical Chingwe's Hole, as well as the injunctions that no one should approach that place.

Juma too had heard these stories before, and much more: Enemies of an ancient king had been thrown into that abyss and their bodies had never been seen again. The depression in the earth extended down to the valley below, and the remains were washed away in the river. Alternatively, so many bodies had disappeared into the hole that its base was now filled with bones! The latter account so fascinated two *Angelesi* officers—both of whom he had met during his early service with the Central African Rifles—that they had actually attempted to climb down into the cave-like cavity to see for themselves! But they had descended only about a hundred feet or so before abandoning their expedition without finding any bones at all. At least that's the story which filtered through to the *askari* after the curious young officers returned from their adventure.

Leading his son right up to the edge, Juma directed him to throw several rocks, one at a time, into the cavern, each time listening for the sound of the rock hitting the bottom. They could hear the faint echo of a single *"thud"* after every rock was thrown. This certainly did not seem to be a bottomless pit! Nor were there clattering echoes as if one of the stones might have fallen upon a pile of brittle bones. Neither did either of them feel as if they were about to be drawn into a vortex which might cause them to fall into the hole.

"You must not fear the unknown, my son," he told Mtindiso. He didn't want to scold the boy, but rather hoped to drive home a lesson: "It is always wise to hear what others say about what they believe, but it is best to test their ideas for yourself, if you can!"

However sure he was about making an impact on his son's life, Juma was equally uncertain that he had been—or even could be—a significant influence on Apesile. After she was born, he had doted on his daughter, but the teenager he met once he came home was almost unrecognizable, as if she were a completely different person. Even before he had left for Jubaland she had completed her *msondo* ceremony and learned the expectations her father—indeed all of Yao society—would have of her as woman. And now that he was back from this latest extended deployment, she greeted him with a proud pronouncement:

"I have now grown up!" As her father, Juma understood this could only mean that, with her grandmother's guidance, she had completed *nadakula*, her second and final initiation. He had missed all those important passages in his daughter's life; now all that lay ahead for her would be marriage and motherhood. Would he be able to be a part of those important events? He was frustrated that he could not know. Soon he would return to his

KAR duties in Zomba and then expected to join the new battalion in East Africa. His only consolation was that for those steps in her life, Juma knew it was Apesile's mother, his first, dearest wife, who might offer the best guidance in any case.

One other family matter also needed resolution before he could return to duty: Kuliraga. In addition to Ambikanile and their children, ever since his conversation with Issa in the hospital at Voi he'd been turning over the matter of Kuliraga in his mind. Nothing he could imagine changed his conclusion: her misbehaviour must have been the reason behind his injury. Nonetheless, he did not want to subject her—nor his children, let alone himself—to a long proceeding in the chief's court which would result if he publically accused her of adultery. So he decided to approach her directly:

"Kuliraga, I do not think our marriage has a future. I'm asking that we find a way to dissolve this union." As he finished he handed her a bullet, though he did not mention his wound, he was certain she had learned about it. "This is our *mpamba*," he told her. Both of them knew it wasn't literally the arrow a husband usually gave to his wife when seeking a divorce; but it was a potent symbol. He did tell her, however: "If I come back, it will kill me," the traditional divorce injunction.

"We shall arrange it," she assured him, setting in motion the negotiations between their relatives which would seal their divorce. She clutched the bullet in her hand knowing that, too, was her future. Should she wish, that bullet would be a signal to a new husband that she indeed was free to marry again. All they needed now was for their relatives to agree on the dissolution of their union; then it would be done. Juma, though, took it upon himself to take one more step:

"I have decided to divorce my wife," he told the now elderly Chief Chikowi.

"*Ambikanile?*" was his incredulous response.

"No. NO! *Kuliraga.*" Explaining his reasoning—including his certainty that her infidelity was the cause of his misfortune at Mbuyuni—Juma apologized for not seeking a resolution through the Chief's court, a choice which denied the Chief a share of any compensation.

"Oh yes, I believe I'd heard something like that," the Chief replied wisely. "Fear not, my son. You have become one of the savers, a brave *asilikali* who helps cement our people's place in the new state created by the *Angelesi*." The royal reassurance warmed Juma's heart, leaving him better prepared to return to KAR headquarters in Zomba to once again enter his *askari* world.

∞∞∞∞∞∞

He was glad to don his uniform and once again make his way around the mountain. He had business to settle at headquarters as well, then he expected his children and their mother would join him at their home in the *askari* lines. He walked quickly along the familiar path, though perhaps not quite as speedily as he had those many—was it really almost twenty now?—years ago. He was able to swing his arms as he walked now, showing little effect from his wound. Once at the KAR camp he reported straight away to Lieutenant Colonel Soames.

"You are looking quite well, Sergeant Major!" The greeting took him a bit by surprise. While Major Giffard had mentioned a promotion, Juma did not realize that it was now confirmed. "We shall need to get these new chevrons sown on your uniform," the Lieutenant Colonel continued. "You will want to look your best as we complete some training for the new regiment. I believe you will be Company Sergeant Major for A Company once 1/2 KAR is at full strength and is mustered for duty in East Africa."

"*Asante sana*, sir!" A grateful Juma saluted. There still were the formalities of re-enlistment, much as he had done on six previous occasions. This time, however, he agreed not to a fixed term of service, but instead "until the end of hostilities." He understood this meant until the Germans were defeated, which his officers seemed to think was the most likely outcome of the "hosilities." He wanted to share their optimism, although most of his encounters with the *Schutztruppe* and its *askari* had thus far done little to encourage him. With this new regiment soon to join the British forces—and the numerous others he was told would also be deployed shortly—perhaps the prospects were indeed better. He certainly hoped so! Once the details were arranged and he had, yet again, sworn allegiance to the British crown, Lieutenant Colonel Soames surprised him further:

"There is another matter I want to discuss with you, Sergeant Major. I believe you can help me resolve a dispute involving some of our *askari* here at headquarters." Juma knew that as a sergeant major the officers of the regiment would turn to him concerning all manner of issues involving the men, not just of his regiment but of the whole Nyasaland battalion. So he assured the commandant that he would do his best to assist.

"Are you a Christian or a Muslim?" He was startled by the bluntness of Soames question.

"I have pledged myself to neither." Juma had heard appeals from advocates for both beliefs, yet he had always preferred the ways of his Yao people. Their explanations of life seemed to make the most sense to him. That was the way he had dealt with Kuliraga and, he thought, was the way he lived. The commandant seemed to have some difficulty understanding as Juma tried to elucidate, as best he could, the basis of his convictions.

"I still believe you are the very person to help me," Soames concluded, and began explaining a dispute which had arisen at the barracks shortly after the Chilembwe uprising. Both Muslim and Christian *askari* wanted to have places where they might worship within their encampment, but because some of them asked a *Wazungu* priest to speak for them rather than approaching their officers directly, the men had been punished. It was a complicated issue, certainly much more convoluted than he expected as the first test of his ability to help resolve matters concerning the soldiers.

"I shall inquire, sir," Juma promised, and saluted the commandant, despite being unenthusiastic about delving into the controversy. Aware that the new, younger *askari*—unlike himself—were frequently drifting away from the ways of their grandfathers, he wasn't certain his own beliefs would offer much leverage in brokering a resolution. But after making extensive inquiries, it seemed to him the matter had been largely a result of a considerable exaggeration by the Reverend A. M. Anderson, a Church of Scotland missionary, presenting a request in the name of some *askari*: The men had wanted a private place to pray together; Anderson, claiming a mosque was provided for Muslims, had asked for a Christian school. The latter was clearly contrary to well-established military policy, provoking punishments for the soldiers he represented since they had bypassed the military chain of command. As Juma understood the original Muslim request—a small venue for prayers during

Ramadan, because Zomba had no mosque—was roughly equivalent to what the Christian *askari* had actually been seeking, even though there presently were several Christian establishments in and near the town.

"Sir, I believe there is a solution that will improve morale among the troops," Juma reported to the Commandant a fortnight later. Then finished with a smile: "However, it may not please the missionaries, sir!" His suggestion—that each group be given a small hut for prayer meetings, but that no Christian missionary nor Muslim *mwalimu* (or other teacher) be given access to those places—provided a face-saving answer for the KAR. The Commandant agreed. Once in place, the new policy may have appeared to some in the local European community as providing an unacceptable accommodation to Islam; nonetheless, the *askari* seemed generally happy their spiritual wellbeing had the attention of the officers, as well as the new sergeant major.

The busy atmosphere of the expanding headquarters detachment pleased Juma. He enjoyed dealing with the new recruits, especially the orientation sessions, which often were his responsibility. The rifle range was also an important part of his duties. He had feared his arm and shoulder wound might hamper his marksmanship, so welcomed any chance to practice as well as teach new *askari* about using their weapons. Leading them in bayonet drills was a special joy, as he always affectionately remembered the hilarious pantomime of Issa and Stambuli during his own training, though he was disinclined to mention the details since that performance had landed both of his friends on report. Other stories from his service did offer opportunities for Juma to make further positive impressions on the young *askari* likely to be joining his battalion in Nairobi.

The story of his exploits at Mbuyuni were not among those he offered the recruits, but somehow accounts of his actions gradually were whispered throughout the camp, in the officers' mess, and ultimately the *askari* lines as well. That Juma was a genuine hero among them became abundantly clear once the entire headquarters detachment and all the recruits were ordered to a special dress parade: His Excellency the Governor, Sir George Smith was to present military awards. All the troops assembled at the KAR parade ground and proceeded to the more expansive Zomba Gymkhana Club sports field for the occasion. The clubhouse terrace, just above the cricket pitch, offered a preferred viewing area for the many government officials and other important civilians who were in attendance. Having been told in advance about the occasion, Ambikanile, Mtindiso, and Apesile joined a large number of other Africans under the trees on the outer edges of the sports field to witness the proceedings. Their presence seemed to add a decidedly festive atmosphere to what otherwise might have been a starchier, formal occasion.

As the entire headquarters detachment—including the regimental band and the training battalion—marched into the ground, there was a hush at first, followed by a stir in the crowd gathered at the edges.

"Shhh!" Ambikanile cautioned her children. "That's what your father would expect. And that's the way to be respectful." Both of them followed their mother's lead, as those around them also turned quiet. The entire *askari* company marched by the official viewing area, and then turned back toward the center of the field, finally coming to attention facing the clubhouse terrace. Governor Smith—wearing the full regalia he was due as the King's representative in Nyasaland—marched stiffly down the stairway from the clubhouse, flanked by Lieutenant Colonial

Soames and the headquarters detachment adjutant. They paraded slowly past the entire assemblage, inspecting the troops, then returning front and center. As the names of several *askari* were called, each quickly marched to face the Governor who pinned good conduct medals on their uniforms. Then Juma's name was announced. As he came forward it was clear he already had a breast full of medals, more than any of the others preceding him.

"Sergeant Major Juma…number one hundred three," the Governor began speaking slowly and loudly, reading the formal citation. "For gallant leading of the vanguard … under heavy machine-gun and rifle fire … during the action at Mbuyuni … on July fourteenth, nineteen fifteen … and though severely wounded … steadfastly continuing to rally your men … commanding them during a disciplined withdrawal … you are hereby awarded the medal …for Distinguished Conduct in the Field." With that, Governor Smith pinned yet another medal on his uniform, then stepped back. Acknowledging Juma's salute, he spoke again: "God Save the King!" The KAR band followed suit with their own rousing rendition of that tune, accompanied by singing, mostly from the Europeans in the crowd on the clubhouse balcony.

Though the presentation of the Distinguished Conduct Medal— not the Victoria Cross Major Giffard had hinted at—was the climax of the entire parade ceremony, it seemed more an anti- climax to Juma. Still, he remained at attention until the music ended, then executed a well-practiced right-face turn and marched smartly back to his place in formation. As the KAR band played one of the battalion's marching songs, the men remained in formation while making their way back to headquarters. Juma caught a glimpse of a smiling Mtindiso watching from beneath a eucalyptus tree opposite the clubhouse.

Once dismissed, Lieutenant Colonel Soames sought out the proud father to explain that, in accordance with the King's African Rifles Ordinance of the Protectorate, after being awarded the medal for Distinguished Conduct in the Field he would now be exempt from paying the usual hut tax for his home at Majowa during the remainder of his life.

"Had it been a Victoria Cross instead," Soames added with a slight, almost apologetic smile, "it would be three huts!" The ironies struck Juma at once, especially as at present he had just one home on which he would not pay tax each year.

∞∞∞∞∞∞

"I must return to the war tomorrow!" Juma's news, even if expected soon, still was a great disappointment to his family, coming just days after his big public moment. Apesile and Ambikanile were openly distraught. How could someone who had just been honoured by the Governor, no less, be sent so soon back to the fighting? Mtindiso, though less demonstrative, expressed his sorrow in a pointed question:

"Who will teach me to be a man if you are gone?"

Juma's reply was swift and certain: "Your uncles, of course!" He managed to disguise his own uncertainty about that idea, borne not only out of questions about his in-laws but also thoughts about the military actions which he knew were ahead. He couldn't allow any such anxieties to overtake his preparations, however, as Lieutenant Colonial Soames and the entire recruit contingent would the next day begin the long journey to British East Africa. Since some of their new officers were only to meet them on arrival, the expectations placed on senior NCOs would be particularly demanding.

The young *askari* were predictably excited as they began the journey—first on the march, then by train and river steamer—to the seaport at Chinde. The prospect of several days on the ocean tempered their enthusiasm, so Juma was grateful the passage north was a relatively smooth one, unlike the storm-tossed voyages he remembered from his previous ocean transport deployments. For several of his young charges, though, it was the first time at sea requiring Juma to nurse them through several trips to the ship's rail. But for most of the new recruits his reassurances were thankfully proven true, which he knew would enhance their trust in his leadership during challenges ahead. The first of these was coping with a sudden change of plans: putting ashore at Tanga rather than Mombasa. Only recently abandoned by the Germans after an intense naval bombardment, the port facilities weren't completely destroyed. Nonetheless, the considerable damage to the docks and piers made disembarking the *askari*, all their weapons and gear, as well as supplies, very difficult. Once the improvised lighters had finished ferrying A Company and all of its *katundu* to the beach, Juma organized his men and the locally recruited carriers in moving to an inland field where they set up a temporary camp. No sooner had they pitched their tents than the regimental Adjutant, Captain Murray, appeared at the edge of the company area:

"Sergeant Major!" he called out, hailing Juma who could see another young officer following immediately behind.

"This is Lieutenant Rangely who is your company commander. He is seconded from the Northamptonshire Regiment, and only just arrived to join our battalion. Make him welcome." Captain

Murray nodded to each of them, stepped back, and with a salute disappeared into the confusion nearer to the port.

It was at best an awkward introduction for the two who shared, almost literally, the task of transforming their company into an efficient military unit. After his service in France, Rangely knew he would need to lean on the Sergeant Major—who was probably at least fifteen years older than himself—if he was to be successful in his first command. Juma could sense his new commander was, despite any deficiencies in experience, nonetheless eager to become an integral part of the regiment. So he called the company together:

"Pangani safu!" The men were soon in formation in front of their tents. Rangely stood at attention next to their Sergeant Major, quietly proud of himself for understanding the command that brought them together. But then Juma, unexpectedly, led the Lieutenant on an inspection of the ranks, going *askari* by *askari* introducing them to their company commander. Juma didn't really expect Rangely to remember their names, but was pleasantly surprised how well he did in repeating each man's name as he looked directly into their eyes. The technique, the Lieutenant confessed later to his Sergeant Major, was one he learned when a cadet commandant at school. When the next morning he was able to speak directly by name to many of his *askari*, Juma was suitably impressed! The entire company was almost immediately engaged in repacking their gear for transport south, in the coastal channel past Zanzibar and Mafia Islands to Kilwa, were they expected to join in a new British offensive.

When the company landed at Kilwa Kisiwani and then set up camp, Lieutenant Rangely alone among them realized this couldn't be their true destination. He understood from reading

Heinreich Brode's book that there were two Kilwa settlements: One on the island where they now found themselves, and a second on the mainland—Kilwa Kivinje—several miles north on the peninsula opposite the island. The latter, however, had no natural port, so they would certainly need to move again by sea before they could begin any campaigning. As he tried to explain this to Juma, his Sergeant Major could only think how grateful he was that they now had practiced ocean to coast transfers twice in less than a month! For Juma these practical considerations seemed much more important than the finer points of coastal geography, as he was the one who actually oversaw the deployments. Indeed, that final move to Kilwa Kivinje needed to be a smooth operation; two days after landing, the entire battalion was on the march inland toward the Mtumbei hills.

On the second day of their trek, the advance guard encountered a well defended German position at Kimbarambara. The entire column worked around to the south of the hilltop entrenchments; an enveloping attack was ordered. A Company advanced over the more open ground east of the German position. Juma took care directing his men. He chose the most concealed positions in the torn scrub. They confronted a spirited German defense. Only rifle fire opposed their progress. The lone German machine gun faced the western approach. There B Company had greater cover in full savannah woodland. Yet the entire 1/2KAR force pressed forward in attack. The KAR rifles were effective. As a result, their outnumbered enemy withdrew into the protective dense bush north of the hill. Unable to effectively begin a pursuit, the entire column halted. When Lieutenant Rangely ordered his men to pitch camp, Juma heaped praise on his largely inexperienced *askari*, hoping to bolster their confidence. Led by one of the most seasoned, Sergeant Anusa, they suddenly began singing:

"We are the lions.

"We're the lions of the whitemen!

"Nyasas are the lions, eh!

"Nyasas are the lions of the Wazungu!"

The Lieutenant attempted to sing along, though Juma had to help him, explaining the full import of the words only after the impromptu chorus faded when the men eagerly began consuming coconuts found at a plantation nearby. It was encouraging to both their commanding officer and senior NCO that the morale of the company seemed lifted by the success of their first actual combat.

Rangely took the moment to ask Juma about what he'd heard from his men about their Sergeant Major:

"Why do they call you *Sajini Nanyula*? How did you come by that name?" The Lieutenant was very curious to know; however, his Sergeant Major was almost equally reticent in explaining. Finally, Juma pointed out one of the knob thorn trees nearby, and then reluctantly recounted his experiences on Mafia Island when *askari* first began using his nickname. Rangely's broad smile of recognition revealed his great pleasure in knowing Juma was so well respected by the *askari*. Nor was he upset to learn from Juma his own *askari* nickname: *Amiri Likwemba*—the officer with the maize silk mustache—as he understood it conferred a sort of respected status.

∞∞∞∞∞

The full column reached Kibata fort three days later, only to discover its German defenders had withdrawn, leaving a white flag flying. One KAR detachment was left to shore up the defenses while others patrolled nearby to ensure no German force remained. Most of 1/2 KAR then moved southwest to establish a temporary headquarters base, where Lieutenant Colonel Giffard assumed command of the regiment. Juma ordered the men to dig a trench as their company latrine, though the location he chose was unfortunately downwind from the temporary redoubt they had constructed, prompting pointed reactions:

"*Sajini*, the stinking smell is horrible!" complained several of the young *askari* who seemed to expect their sergeant major to solve any problem and to put right any inconvenience despite the rigours of campaigning in the bush. Taking several of the most vocal complainers aside, Juma admonished them quietly. When he explained the matter to Lieutenant Rangely—without offering any names—the commander only chortled, explaining the far greater discomforts he had endured in Flanders. In fact, two weeks of relative quiet at Kibata allowed Juma to get to know his company commander a little better. Not only were they both combat veterans, they also shared a boyhood spent largely outdoors, exploring the woods and grasslands near their homes. They also again discussed the nicknames *askari* had for each of them, enjoying the fact that both were references to the natural world.

The brief respite was soon broken when A and C Companies were dispatched to forestall a German advance attempting to retake Kibata. After a strenuous forced march, both companies had to dig in under withering German fire. Their quick action deterred the Germans, who withdrew. But Lieutenant Colonel Giffard ordered a full scale improvement of the defenses at Kibata. Thus Juma again found himself a combat engineer, but the tasks were much different than any he had faced before, either in Asante or on Mafia.

"This is becoming more like the war in France," Rangely confided to Juma, explaining about the trenches, dugouts, and tunnels—and especially the mud—he had known there.

"*Eeh, matope!*" Juma commiserated with the Lieutenant. Mud was, indeed, a major factor as 1/2 KAR worked on extending and improving the perimeter defenses around Kibata fort. The *kaskazi* or warmer monsoons were well underway, but they weren't quite as overwhelming as those he had encountered near Saliata just before being wounded. Nevertheless, maintaining their defensive positions in and around Kibata was discouraging to the *askari* because they seemingly did little while being bombarded by German artillery shells every day. Occasional KAR assaults on nearby German positions, even when temporarily successful, seemed unable to break the ongoing siege. After reinforcements finally arrived—and 1/2 KAR was at last resupplied—Juma hoped *askari* morale might be lifted again. When at last A Company was ordered into the attack, the men were eager. And from the company's forward trenches, Rangely showed Juma a new technique for scouting the bush ahead.

"What is this device?" Juma wanted to know. "Is what I'm seeing actually the field ahead where we will attack?"

"It's a periscope," Rangely explained, "and yes, you can see over the top of our trench to the field ahead."

"Where did this come from? How did you get it?" Juma wanted to know everything about this magical device. But he also understood this was not the time for detailed explanations, so merely accepted his Lieutenant's brief reply:

"I used one in France, and was happy this arrived with our new supplies." Taking back the periscope, Rangely scanned the field they were to attack. He and Juma had already selected several of their strongest *askari* for a special assignment. He now ordered that select squad to advance as close as possible to the German lines on Mbiriki Hill, where they were to throw smoke bombs toward the enemy. The tactic was successful, and the artillery at Kibata—using the smoke to find the range—began a barrage of fire successfully directed at the enemy positions. Once the firing ceased, both A and B Company rushed the hill, only to find the Germans fleeing in disarray. Colonel Giffard ordered them to press their advantage. They advanced over a slight rise. They then managed to seize yet another German defensive position. Moreover, their casualties overall were minimal. Yet RSM Chibwana, who had been with B Company during the attack, was badly wounded.

Juma had known Chibwana for some time, as he had joined the CAR shortly after Juma's own enlistment. They had served together at Mpezeni's and in Asante; it was Chibwana—rather than Juma—chosen to attend the formal coronation of King Edward VII. But Juma also knew that he, not Chibwana, was the first to actually see the new King! Certainly they were colleagues, and treated each other as such, although there always was a competitive edge to their friendship. Despite not being the closest of friends, Juma's first reaction when he learned of Chibwana's wounds was one of regret. He sought out the RSM just as his colleague was being transferred from a field dispensary to the battalion's casualty clearing station. Leaning down to speak with the obviously weakened RSM, Juma wanted to reassure him:

"Be strong, *rafiki yangu*," he addressed his friend. He started to explain his own path to recovery from his own wounds, hoping to reassure his fellow *askari*.

"You, too, must remain strong, *sajini*. You will now be our Regimental Sergeant Major! The *askari* must look up to you, as they have to me." Only then did Juma fully realize, with Chibwana's wounds, the position would most likely pass to him, especially with Lieutenant Colonial Giffard in command.

"*Ndiyo*," he agreed, quietly at first. Then more firmly: "*Ndiyo*! I will make our regiment proud ... as have you." Once confirmed, the hardest part of adjusting to his new responsibilities was saying goodbye to the men of A Company and especially to Rangely. He had genuinely come to respect *Amiri Likwemba*, as his *askari* had nicknamed the Lieutenant with the thin, blonde mustache. Juma felt certain his leadership—drawing on his experiences with the Northants on the front lines in France—was especially important for their recent successes around Kibata fort. His assessment was confirmed shortly thereafter when, in his first action as RSM, 1/2 KAR outflanked the German rearguard attempting to make another stand, causing the *Schutztruppe* to abandon all operations in the Mtumbei Hills.

Juma's first real test as RSM came a few days later as he was ordered to join a force of nearly half the regiment, including his former A Company, marching northward to attack the German base at Utete, set on a hill next to a bend in the Rufiji River. Their target was a fort more impressive and formidable than its counterpart at Kibata in the Mtumbei Hills. Initially rebuffed by a German sortie, the column was first supported by *askari* of 1/3 KAR and then by a British airplane sent to bomb the fort. Unfortunately, given the rudimentary aerial support available in

East Africa, the first bombs landed not on the fort, but on the entrenched positions of 1/2 KAR. The young *askari* of his regiment were frantic, not so much afraid of the airplane itself, but rather that its bombs seemed to target them, not the enemy.

"Will the Germans send another bird to attack us?" Or, "How can we fight this bird that drops powerful eggs on us?" Juma fielded many such questions as best he could. He recognized the markings on the planes and knew they were British, not German. And he had been the victim of friendly fire before. It was hard, nonetheless for him to convince the new recruits that they should not be afraid:

"*Nkhondo ndi gehena!*" he told them, repeating the phrase he'd heard former SGM Chibwana use so often. But he also knew merely saying "war is hell," as had his predecessor, would do little to calm their fears. He went on to explain, first, that it was a British airplane, and second, when it returned, the bombs would land in the fort and on their enemies. Then, as calmly as possible, he reassured them:

"War is messy and confusing. I too have been fired on by both my friends, and my enemies. But it is the enemy and not our fellow *askari* who should concern us. We need instead to depend on each other to survive the confusions of combat. I will also support you, and I am counting on all of you to protect me. Can you remain calm and join me in helping each other?" Unsure that his words were at all what was called for, Juma was relieved when Lieutenant Rangely, who had overheard his speech, later assured him that the appeal seemed to have indeed mollified the worries and fears of the *askari*. At least when they were called upon—twice in the next two days—to attack *Schutztruppe* patrols from the fort, the *askari* acquitted themselves well, despite taking some casualties.

∞∞∞∞∞

The entire regiment welcomed withdrawal from active combat for rest and resupply in Kilwa, although several months of construction duties—on an airfield, storage sheds, and even a short light railway—didn't seem as restful as most of them might have liked. And Juma was not nearly as happy again being a construction foreman; he much preferred leading his troops in the field. All were pleased to receive new combat kit, including new webbed belts and pouches. As the RSM, Juma also received a pair of leather boots of a type usually only issued to officers. Having never before campaigned in boots, they felt strange to him. Some of the *askari* envied their RSM, though; many of them saw one of the principal distinctions between themselves and their officers was that they alone weren't issued boots. He'd never shared this particular complaint, perhaps because he had since boyhood walked through the thickest bush in only his bare feet. However, Lieutenant Colonel Giffard noticed when his new Sergeant Major was not breaking in his new boots:

"Where are your new boots, Sergeant Major?" Juma was surprised his regimental commander spotted their absence from his feet.

"I have never worn any boots, sir. And I see no reason to do so now. Since I was a small boy I've run through the bush—savannah and forest—and my feet are hard." Juma explained, while also assuring the commanding officer he did welcome the wrapped leggings which were now part of his *askari* uniform;

they served to protect his calves from thorny scrub, such as that in which they'd recently been campaigning.

"But the battalion medical officer tells me many of the men complain they have nothing to protect their feet from thorns, rock, scorpions and other dangers. I don't want my Sergeant Major unable to march should his feet be injured!"

"Yes, sir. I shall not allow that to happen, sir." Juma thought of his first major campaign at Mpezeni's, when many *askari* couldn't continue because of sore feet. Though he'd not been one of them, neither were the Sikh NCOs who, like the *askari*, wore no boots. "I would prefer the men see me as one of their own, sir. I would ask your leave to forego the boots."

The Lieutenant Colonel paused for a brief moment. He had not expected this argument, although he admired the leadership instincts shown by the new RSM. "Yes, you have my permission, Juma, at least for the time being."

"Yes, sir!" he replied, coming to attention and saluting smartly. Later he gave the boots to the porter who carried his kit and happily continued without wearing them. Nothing further was said of the encounter, yet the men of the battalion took notice. His bare feet merely confirmed what they already knew about *Sajini Nanyula*, and helped convince the 120 young recruits who soon joined them that indeed their Sergeant Major was one of them. It was not long, however, before they—and their new Sergeant Major's bare feet—were put to the test!

Deployed to Lindi, a smaller settlement further south along the coast, 1/2 KAR joined other units preparing to push into the interior of the German colony. Although the battalion's journey by coastal steamers was short, Colonel Giffard insisted on being among the first ashore so he might make a reconnaissance flight to assess the terrain inland from the small port. Glad he had not been asked to accompany his commander, when the seaplane touched down in the estuary mouth and coasted on the water to the dock, Juma was anxious to learn of the experience:

"Did you feel like a bird?" he wanted to know.

"Not really." Giffard confessed. "We were unable to fly below even the tallest branches, as do the birds. So we actually could see very little. A few paths, some farm houses and outbuildings, but no fortifications. We still have work to do if we are to proceed inland."

"Then what did you learn, sir?"

"Not to fear the airplane, Sergeant Major!" Juma smiled, still glad that he had not also been required to make the flight.

The battalion spent two months shifting outposts on either side of the Lindi estuary, hoping the rainy season would soon abate. It did not. In fact—though none of them really understood it at the time—they arrived in Lindi just as the worst rains in several years were beginning. Intelligence officers continued to make reconnaissance flights when weather permitted. Even occasional patrols provided minimal additional intelligence about the region. As Sergeant Major, Juma seldom joined those patrols. But aware of the strategic plan, he was frustrated idling away time waiting for a break in the weather. So when Lieutenant Colonel Giffard at last gave the order to advance northwest toward Namembo, Juma was elated.

After a fast march through largely agricultural plantation lands, the battalion stopped to organize for an advance on Yangweni, a key German outpost. Their nighttime attack in the persistent rain took the Germans by surprise. Not long after dawn, they withdrew avoiding combat with the KAR. Giffard chose not to follow immediately, sending Juma with scouting parties to locate where their adversaries had chosen to encamp. It was the next afternoon before he reported they had moved southeast to Lutende.

At nightfall 1/2 KAR mounted an assault on entrenchments surrounding that small village. The Germans weren't surprised a second time. Two companies pushing forward centrally were repulsed. The Germans counter-attacked. The *askari* stood firm. Serious fighting continued all day. Two officers were wounded and evacuated. B Company's commander went missing. Many of soldiers didn't know precisely what to do. The battalion was not fighting as a unit. Lieutenant Colonial Giffard tried to rally the men, but he couldn't be heard. He ordered Juma to command B Company. He went from squad to squad steadying the *askari*. At dusk, the bugler sounded retreat. All the NCOs managed to prevent a rout. In the rainy darkness the fatigued *askari* gradually managed to make their way back to camp at Namembo. Though they had given no ground, neither had they managed to push the Germans further inland.

Another lull in the campaign allowed the battalion time to welcome replacements for their recent casualties, and Juma busied himself organizing training for new *askari* and assisting in orientations for the new officers. Meanwhile, Brigadier O'Grady—in command of the forces concentrated around Lindi—was planning an operation against the local *Schutztruppe* headquarters. Intelligence officers believed it was at Schaeffer's Farm, only about five miles inland from the British advance base at Matonga. With additional reconnaissance of the area, O'Grady concocted a scheme for a three pronged night advance, with 1/2 KAR marching south overland from Namembo as the right flank in a coordinated attack. What seemed brilliant to staff officers on paper, however, as too frequently happened, turned out to be vastly different in the African countryside!

The battalion's night march began using compass bearings alone, supplied by Lieutenant Colonel Giffard from notes made during his previous seaplane reconnaissance flight. The unfarmed bush was thick as they started out, and further obscured by tall grass, though this wasn't clear at first to Juma. He was near the rear with the reserve force, on this occasion Lieutenant Rangely's A Company. Although his specific task was to ensure there were no stragglers, as the battalion set out he took the opportunity to engage in a conversation with the Lieutenant:

"It's almost a new moon tonight," Juma observed, "so we'll have little to illuminate the path ahead."

Rangely agreed. "At least we're not blazing the trail for our attack tonight. I'm glad that Captain Brodie has that task."

They exchanged a few more words, but as the evening went on they spoke less. Theirs wasn't expected to be a surprise attack, but there was no point in contributing any unnecessary noise as they approached. Knowing a simultaneous attack at dawn by all three columns was expected, Juma began to worry as he could see the first rays of sun from the east through the tall grass. Soon he could hear the faint sounds of guns firing in the distance. No, their arrival at Schaeffer's Farm wouldn't be a surprise! And when at last the lead companies began to engage the German defenders, machine gun fire halted any general advance. Then the harsh "bratatatatat" stopped. Only sounds of a few rifle shots remained. Suddenly a loud cheer went up: "Arragh! Arragh! Arragh!" The *Schutztruppe*—Europeans and *askari*—were counter-attacking. Juma worried. Then a shout: *"Singe!"* A bayonet charge. KAR *askari* fell back on their reserves. Rangely ordered A Company forward. Juma went with them. They charged past retreating comrades. Hand to hand combat ensued. But the German surge was spent.

Juma knew the battle was not over. A bugle sounded retreat. He gathered a few old soldiers around him. Rangely and Captain Brodie motioned to them. The groups merged, holding a firing line. They protected the retreat. Insulated from further German fire, Giffard and his other officers managed to re-form the fleeing *askari*. A full scale rout was avoided. And 1/2 KAR's reserve ammunition kept out of enemy hands. Realizing his perhaps too complex plan failed, Brigadier O'Grady ordered his troops to retire. Giffard then led the battalion back to the Matanga post, where the other two columns soon joined them. Juma made the rounds, visiting each company in its billet. He made sure to stop at the casualty clearing station as well. One thing was clear to him: *askari* morale was dipping lower once again.

∞∞∞∞∞∞

"Our Lindi force is like one claw of a scorpion," Lieutenant Colonel Giffard explained. He had beckoned Juma to join him in his tent after receiving the Sergeant Major's report of his informal inspection of the battalion. "Another claw is coming from west. We will trap the Germans between us! Then a central column will be the stinger, striking down from the north and eliminating them. Our claw will sometimes move slowly, only occasionally driving our enemy back." While he understood battlefield tactics—and also how a scorpion struck its prey—Juma was much less certain about his commander's explanation of campaign strategy. But the

Colonel was asking that Juma explain to the battalion *askari* why their part in the campaign was important. Juma, however, was uncertain that was possible.

"*Ushindi…ama upotevu.* That's all the *askari* know." The dichotomy of victory or defeat, Juma knew, best explained the morale of the battalion. "If we attack and are driven back, even if our enemy withdraws to new defenses, and we simply attack again, perhaps to be once again stopped—how can the men feel as though they've achieved a victory?"

"If it is our enemy—not us—falling back to a new defensive perimeter, it is a victory!" The Colonel was insistent. He tried another approach, drawing a very rough map of sorts in the dirt, in an attempt to demonstrate the strategy. "If the Germans continue to move away from us, we can push them toward a trap!"

"And our friends will then strike them? That will be our victory? How will we know? Must we wait long for such a celebration?" It seemed to Juma a less than satisfactory approach; he was certain the men needed some sense of real achievement as they campaigned. "When might we know something to measure our success in this greater effort?"

"If I have news of other victories, I will tell you, Sergeant Major. And I will expect you to inform the *askari*. But it is very difficult to know when we might have something obvious to celebrate as a battalion. Soon, I hope." Giffard paused, looking down at his map scratchings. "Soon."

The battalion's respite was relatively short-lived, just over a fortnight, before they were again in action, pressing the *Schutztruppe* south and east. This time they again began marching west in yet another flanking operation, but with

Lieutenant Colonel Giffard himself in command of the advance guard. Departing Matanga at midday, they marched through the night but were able to easily overwhelm a small force at one German encampment. Continuing on without further opposition, they approached a German outpost at Schaedel's Farm, only to find that the main *Schutztruppe* force had withdrawn. 1/2 KAR entrenched for the night, observing considerable enemy patrol activity, saving their attack for morning. When dawn came, however, they faced no significant opposition, the Germans having once again slipped away. At least not another defeat, Juma thought to himself. He was disappointed, though, when another unit was assigned to occupy the farm complex 1/2 KAR had liberated from German control.

Instead the battalion was ordered north to occupy Mingoyo, a small dhow port on an inlet of the Lindi estuary which they'd bypassed on their march the day before. Though despoiled by the obviously hasty German withdrawal, the *askari* were delighted once they entered the hamlet. For the first time in weeks they were able to sleep in buildings with roofs to protect them from the rains! They weren't bothered by the disorder they found all around: goods—mostly broken—from nearby shops scattered about; once neat stacks of export products broken up, including several elephant tusks shattered into bits; even three dhows—probably sunk by machine gun fire—listing on the bottom of the little harbour.

"*Washenzi!* That's what our enemies are." A frustrated Giffard exclaimed to Juma after reviewing the damage. Indeed the scene did look like a band of savages had ransacked the small town.

"Yes, desperate men at war take desperate measures." Juma recalled some of his previous encounters with the aftermath left by fleeing enemies. "They do not want to leave anything useful behind. But of what good would much of this be to us in any case?" He gestured toward a bent baby carriage and several broken typewriters in the rubble. "For the *askari* it feels like a victory! They are happy tonight in their warm and mostly dry huts. I am happy for them!"

"Don't let the men remain too grateful or complacent, Sergeant Major," the commander cautioned.

As it happened, those wise words proved almost prophetic. The *askari* "victory" lasted only a little more than a week before German artillery bombarded Mingoyo, forcing Juma once again to help supervise entrenchment of the battalion at a more secure location. And within two weeks came another move, this time to occupy the farm which had been the site of their previous actual "victory." All the while, they were subjected to intermittent shelling. Shortly after setting up defenses around the farm, an exceptionally large shell struck the farmhouse, detonating in the middle of the battalion headquarters. Juma felt fortunate that neither he, nor the Lieutenant Colonel, were injured, with just one *askari* clerk wounded on that occasion.

"This doesn't really seem much like *ushindi*, after all!" The complaint of Lance Corporal James, who himself had just survived during a recent patrol by hiding in an ant-bear hole, summed up Juma's feelings as well. Their recent results didn't feel like a victory! Though the Lance Corporal obviously intended it as just a passing comment, Juma stopped him to respond:

"These Germans will not easily be defeated." He wanted to reassure the resourceful and brave *askari*. "We must be willing to stay the course if we're to reap the rewards of a full and complete victory." Could such assurances serve at all to sustain battalion morale? He wasn't entirely sure they could. Had he known what challenges awaited 1/2 KAR a mere two months later he likely wouldn't have even have tried.

Their column, as Lieutenant Colonel Giffard had tried to explain, continued to force the *Schutztruppe* inland, if ever so slowly, down the Likuledi River valley. The Germans showed no willingness to engage in a decisive battle, preferring instead short, sharp engagements followed by strategic retreats. Almost as frustrating as their opponents' tactics, though, were the continuing rains which seemed, if anything, heavier and more insistent. That problem exacerbated another: Expected convoys of porters bringing food, water, and other supplies to the troops were continually delayed. Many *askari* grew hungry and some were further weakened by disease after drinking from suspect pools and puddles. Blankets, which might have comforted many of them, were also in short supply. After several weeks 1/2 KAR were replaced in the front lines. Juma was glad, not just for the men, but for himself as well, especially having at least a few more substantial meals and clean water to drink.

Soon enough they were on the march again, into a changing landscape along the north bank of the Likuledi. They left behind the thorny scrub woodlands where they had been campaigning for four months, finding instead a more open savannah grassland of rolling hills with precious few clumps of trees breaking up the terrain.

"I wouldn't like to fight in this country," Juma said really to no one, although several *askari* heard him. "There is little cover to be had." Nonetheless, the ease with which they were now advancing made him cautious, expecting they might soon be thrust into battle again. Just then the sudden "brrraapp, brrraapp" of a motorcycle startled him, and he watched as a dispatch rider handed a message to Lieutenant Colonel Giffard. As he and the other *askari* had come to expect, that was a sign they were likely to be fighting again soon.

That afternoon they reached Nyanago, where a Nigerian brigade was assaulting German trenches which had been protected by barbed wire. A and B Companies were the first committed to battle. A German counter-attack drove them back. Then C Company made a bayonet rush through them. Lieutenant Colonel Giffard himself led the charge. Another German counter-attack stalled that advance. Then they, too, fell back. Juma joined D Company as 1/2 KAR made another attack. Sergeant Saidi led a bomb squad forward. They disabled a German machine gun. 3/2 KAR arrived in support. They were met by a third German counter-attack. Both KAR units dug in. Firing continued until dusk. At sunset the *Schutztruppe* withdrew. Juma then began attending to the many wounded, directing stretcher bearers and dressers to care for them. But there were far more casualties than the battalion had suffered in any previous engagement. At one point, he noticed Lieutenant Rangely ministering to one of A Company's fallen *askari*:

"A dresser will soon see to the corporal," he shouted to the Lieutenant.

"When?" came the disgusted reply. He knew there were too few available. So he took a flask from a tunic pocket and handed it to the corporal. *"Kunyawa!"* Observing a hesitation, he ordered to corporal to drink. A big swallow left the *askari* coughing. Expecting water, the whisky took him by surprise. "I have no other medicine. That will have to do until a dresser can help you."

Watching the scene, Juma wanted to stop and thank the Lieutenant, but could not. There was much more to be done. Bodies of fallen *askari* needed to be removed for burial later. Defensive fortifications were needed as surely the Germans would be back in the morning. Just after dawn a substantial artillery barrage announced that indeed another attack was imminent. When it came, 1/2 KAR was soon removed to the rear. Juma's task was helping the commander reorganize the battalion as a reserve, should they be needed. They were not. After the horrible losses the day before, Juma was relieved, not merely for the lull in combat, but also that he was not again a casualty. He felt no shame in thinking about his own good fortune—that he would once again return to his family—as he was equally certain there was much more he had to accomplish.

∞∞∞∞∞∞

This latest engagement was another, similar German victory. But somehow it seemed different. An increasing number of *Schutztruppe askari* deserters found their way to the 1/2 KAR lines where it was Juma's duty to interrogate them. His spoken *Kiswahili*—or *Kiregiment*, as some of the officers called their military argot—was just barely sufficient for the task. Though the *askari* of the *Schutztruppe* also spoke *Kiswahili*, the influence of *Kijeremani* words in their speech made Juma's task more difficult than he had expected. He did learn that the enemy's losses were also great, not so much in manpower but certainly in supplies spent with little further reserves. The deserters, now prisoners, believed their commander, *Bwana Oberst,* would soon be forced to surrender. Juma explained this to Lieutenant Colonel Giffard, who seemed to understand:

"A pyrrhic victory for Colonel von Lettow," he called it, without explanation. "It should not be long now before we can have that celebration!" he assured the Sergeant Major.

Juma quietly wondered to himself what there would be left to celebrate. The battalion he joined just over a year before was now at less than half strength. In addition to the many wounded, perhaps as many as one hundred *askari* had been killed in action. Others were missing, presumed captured rather than deserters, as they were so far from their homes. He thought about all the families who would be devastated by the losses just his battalion had suffered. And there were now other battalions, not only from Nyasaland but from much farther afield, even some the prisoners with whom he had recently been speaking might be asked to join! What could there be to celebrate? He didn't have long to contemplate that question. The desperate nature of their current situation came starkly into focus when 1/2 KAR and 3/2 KAR—which had a similarly high number of casualties—were united into a single battalion with Lieutenant Colonel Giffard in command. As senior NCO of the combined unit, Juma became RSM, continuing in that capacity after the arrival of two new British NCOs. It was a new experience for him, serving as a military superior to Europeans in the same battalion. Though he did outrank them, they were not directly under his command as they were sergeants, squad leaders in two of the newly formed companies.

More quickly than any of the veteran *askari* would have liked, the new battalion was on the march, following the German withdrawal in a column with the Cape Corps, from South Africa, in the lead. Though he had known people of mixed race before, this was another new experience for Juma and one that made an impression on him. Some of the *askari*—following the lead of the frequently shrill and surly South African Cape Corps officers—referred to these latest allied troops as Bushmen. It didn't seem to Juma a flattering or even fitting word to describe soldiers who proved themselves in battle, playing a major part is pushing the *Schutztruppe* off the Makonde Plateau, their last refuge in German East Africa, and across the Ruvuma River into Portuguese territory.

London officials proclaimed this a victory since German East Africa had finally been conquered! And as a result many of the imperial troops fighting for that goal—South African, Indian, Nigerian, West Indian, and British—were discharged and sent home. Orders from Nairobi, however, were that the German force still must be "brought to book." So Juma and the other *askari* of the 2nd regiment, King's African Rifles prepared to pursue the elusive *Schutztruppe* until it ceased to exist as a military force. 1/2 KAR and 3/2 KAR again became separate battalions as new recruits were assigned, joining 2/2 KAR in a mostly Nyasaland *askari* regiment, at first encamping at Masasi in the hilly steppes east of the Makonde Plateau. That was the sum total of their victory: five months of continued training and other military preparations. Lieutenant Colonel Giffard took command of the full regiment and, in turn, Juma assumed duties as a true Regimental Sergeant Major.

Although continually busy with preparations for an advance, after months of arduous campaigning the less frenetic pace of camp life was welcome. Juma tried to meet as many of the new recruits as he could, but also took time for conversations with old acquaintances. One who actually sought him out was Captain Rangely, promoted after a year of stalwart service in 1/2 KAR:

"Survival has its rewards, I suppose. I'm a Captain now…" Juma had already noticed the new rank on his uniform. "…but I still command just a single company. And you, while still a Sergeant Major, now have an actual *regiment* as your bailiwick!" He had to explain the latter reference for Juma, somewhat blunting his attempt at humor.

"Ah, yes. I see, sir." Juma replied with somewhat less enthusiasm than perhaps Rangely hoped for, although he was pleased that *Amiri Likwemba* was one of the officers still serving with the battalion after the difficulties they had experienced in the past year.

After an awkward pause, Rangely continued: "Uhh, the *askari* have been so brave. You are the ones who will win this war for us, don't you think?" Juma had indeed been thinking a good deal about victory recently.

"We have a job to do, sir. And most of the men want to do it well. We all look forward to a true victory. For all of us, I hope it comes soon." Neither man knew, or even expected, that another eight months of tough campaigning lay ahead.

∞∞∞∞∞∞

The remainder of their five months "rest period" period passed quickly. Soon on the march south, the entire regiment itself crossed the Ruvuma near Bangalla using an ingenious "flying bridge"—actually a large raft attached to a strong steel cable installed over the river—requiring the *askari* literally to pull themselves across. Once passing into Portuguese East Africa, the regiment marched southeast following the path of the German retreat. Day by day the three battalions took turns leading the column along a route already worn by the advance of the Gold Coast Regiment. Juma usually marched with the small headquarters company just ahead of the last battalion in the line, joining Lieutenant Colonial Giffard, the regimental medical officer and his small staff, plus the adjutant with a few clerks and signalers.

"Sir," Juma spoke to Giffard as they started the second day of their advance. "This Gold Coast Regiment? Are they from the same place as the Asante?" He anticipated the reply:

"Yes, they are, Sergeant Major. Why do you ask?" Obviously focusing on the tasks at hand, the Lieutenant Colonel didn't recall the details of Juma's service record, although he had seen it previously.

"Is it possible some of them are the same Asante warriors I fought against with the Central African Regiment?" His commander was surprised at first by the question, then reflected a bit on the history of the British army in Africa.

"Well, I suppose they could be," he allowed, "although I'm not sure how much recruiting has gone on in the last fifteen years in Asante land. *Mzaha wetu!* Just another irony of this wretched war." He looked downcast as he spoke.

"Yes. Sir." Juma decided to end the conversation. "Indeed it would, sir."

For several days they found little to slow their progress across rolling hills of primarily grass land; no enemy patrols challenged their passage. When they at last neared the *boma* at Medo, the regiment turned southwest in an attempt to encircle the German force.

Hearing the sound of field guns to their north, Giffard ordered 2/2 KAR—then the lead battalion—into action south of Chirimba Hill. He positioned his regimental headquarters on the hillside, overlooking his troops. From there Juma for the first time had a view of how his commanders envisioned their battle plans in action; but from such a vantage point he also realized they couldn't clearly see how their *askari* experienced the fighting. All reports reaching regimental headquarters suggested the battle was extremely fierce and also difficult, with swampy bogs nearly knee-deep in some places hampering movement. After a lull in the firing, he could see Gold Coast regiment attacking from the north; they had fought their way south from near the *boma*, surrounding the *Schutztruppe* detachment. After nightfall, scouts reported Germans retreating to the southwest; come daybreak Juma helped evacuated the wounded and clear the battlefield:

"Every tree and bush I could see bore bullet marks. A clump of bamboo, near the dressing station, was bent over by machine gun fire. Do the Germans not even respect our wounded?" he asked when reporting to Giffard that afternoon. "We evacuated the casualties who remained and buried the dead, including Captain Broom."

"The *Boche* are hardly gentlemen" was the commander's curt reply. Juma wasn't familiar with what the term meant exactly, though he surmised it was a way of disparaging their enemies. He supposed it must be like referring to them as *Washenzi*, which Giffard had done after 1/2 KAR occupied Mingoyo. But this was different: destroying *things* was not a parallel to deliberately trying to kill wounded men and those caring for them.

The next day 2/KAR was again on the track of the *Schutztruppe*, following the Gold Coast Regiment as before. Moving west the track became more difficult—more like a swampy tunnel through the thick bamboo and elephant grass—with little evidence of their prey. Food convoys were further delayed, as the tough going was much more troublesome for the *tengatenga*, carriers with 75 pound or heavier loads on their heads. It was no wonder then that one patrol from 2/2 KAR was welcomed back to the column as heroes: they brought with them chickens and pigs taken from a German food store encountered entirely by accident! For more than two months they continued pursuit of the enemy at the same pace, turning south into a more hospitable terrain of rolling savannah hills. Their progress was blocked only occasionally when the column's van met elements of the German rear guard, who more often than not withdrew after short skirmishes. At a rest stop about half way through this long march—the only pause of more than 48 hours in their pursuit—an exhausted Sergeant Useni came to Juma:

"How long must we continue?" He wanted to know. "Chasing these Germans is like chasing chickens!" Although he couldn't recall seeing Useni Makuta for several years, Juma remembered they had both been assigned to road building duties in Thyolo some eight or nine years before.

"To be honest, I would rather be chasing chickens!" Juma confessed, as he like most of the *askari* continued with empty bellies, weakened by persistent short rations, often half of what they expected.

Useni agreed: "As would I, even if it meant the wrath of *Bwana Chai*!" the plantation master on whose estate they had built several bridges almost a decade earlier. Both of them had a laugh at the thought.

Unlike those duties, which had been temporary and also had a definable end in sight, their current assignment seemed to go on ceaselessly. Soon they were ordered to proceed at an even faster pace, leaving anything unessential behind. The regiment made good time, at least until they reached Korewa where the hills rose precipitously into a narrow gorge. Enemy pickets held up 2/2 KAR's advance briefly then falling back, luring the KAR *askari* further into the narrow pass. Wary of a large scale ambush, Giffard called for an artillery barrage which temporarily cleared a part of the path. That pattern—using mountain guns and Stokes mortars to clear the way for advance—was repeated several times. While he appreciated the caution the Lieutenant Colonel displayed, Juma admired even more his commander's patience, though its application at Korewa didn't lead to anything approaching the victory they sought.

Instead, once the battalion cleared the pass they continued on their hunt for the increasingly elusive German force, stopping briefly for what supplies they could appropriate from the Portuguese *boma* at Vacca. There was little to be had. The *askari* continued with stomachs at best half full. Some of the men in 3/2 KAR started singing a new song, one which soon became a popular diversion in much of the regiment as they marched on:

"When I die, when I die,

"Bury me at Zomba.

"So that my heart should pain.

"Hunger. Hunger is painful.

"When I die. When I die,

"Bury me at Zomba.

"There I'll rest my soul.

"Hunger. Hunger is painful."

It wasn't long before Lieutenant Colonel Giffard also heard the new lyrics and soon thereafter spoke to Juma about it:

"I know we have food supply problems, Sergeant Major, far worse than at any time during this war. It's not surprising the *askari* are hungry. My officers are suffering, too, you know; they're also on half rations and worse. Please speak to the men about this. I am concerned about how the 'hunger'—and especially singing about it—will affect morale, and our ability to continue toward the victory we've talked about before."

"Yes, Sir!" Juma knew the Colonel's concerns were serious. Recalling his recent conversation with Sergeant Useni of C Company in the regiment's 3rd battalion, Juma sought him out. Indeed, Useni identified Corporal Kildon Wajiusa who most likely had first suggested the song's new lyrics. And in further discussions with the men of C Company he realized their sense of desperation and deep desire to return home. So he agreed to take their concerns to Major Edwards, the regimental adjutant, but— without telling them he would so—decided instead to speak directly to Lieutenant Colonel Giffard:

"Sir, the *askari* are indeed hungry. You know they often sing while on the march, and the new song you've heard is a way to let out their feelings without complaining directly to their officers." Giffard put his hand to his head, taking a moment to reflect; Juma paused as he did so, then began again. "Sir, they are very worried some might actually starve to death if they go on with so little food. In fact, *askari* in C Company of the 3rd asked me to tell Major Edwards they wanted to return home rather than continuing to chase the Germans. They are desperate, sir. I know you're concerned…"

Giffard interrupted him: "We are soldiers, Juma! We can't just quit when war becomes hard!" Juma seldom had heard the Colonel quite so upset. "Tell me! What would you have me do?"

"It's not for me to say, sir. I did have an idea that perhaps…"

"Yes, Sergeant Major? Ideas—well, at least your ideas—are welcome."

Juma reluctantly continued: "As our scouts haven't had any success locating the enemy just now, perhaps we might send out foraging parties to find any food the Germans might not yet have taken or destroyed, perhaps some sweet potatoes, a little manioc or millet still in the fields, even cassava which has not yet been dug. If they haven't yet passed this way, there might be something, anything, which might cheer the men, and begin to fill their bellies. Then they'd be more willing to continue."

"And they would be doing something to help themselves. That would surely help morale!" Giffard was smiling. "It is a good suggestion. Thank you, Sergeant Major."

"Sir!" Juma smiled in return. He knew there'd still be additional hard marching ahead, just as soon as the German force was located again.

∞∞∞∞∞∞

The first word 2/KAR received, though, was of a major German success at Nhamacurra, near the port city of Quelimane, capturing a major Portuguese depot. As a result the *Schutztruppe* remnant was effectively resupplied and, thus encouraged, more determined to continue avoiding capture. The British Nairobi headquarters, in turn, ordered all the troops at their disposal to make blocking German return to their east African territory a first priority. As Juma suspected, this meant 2/KAR would continue in pursuit after an only modestly successful foraging effort. The regiment often covered as many as fifteen miles a day when not impeded by rain and the resulting blue/black mud. Conflicting scouting reports also meant occasionally back tracking and changing direction, all intended to accomplish the goal of blocking the *Schutztruppe's* flight.

At one point, as the battalion was preparing to bivouac for the night, Juma was again startled by the "brrraapp, brrraapp" of an approaching motorcycle dispatch rider looking for the battalion headquarters. This time there was news that 1/KAR had managed to engage the main German force at Lioma, a small Portuguese outpost astride the main northbound road. Realizing 2/KAR were only a few miles away, Lieutenant Colonel Giffard organized the regiment to swiftly move out. Juma's orders were to assemble as many torches as possible to illuminate their advance in the approaching darkness of a waning moon. With a small squad, he worked continually as the battalions each formed to begin their march, and as a result he was among the last of the regiment moving to Lioma. Joining the rearguard of 1/2 KAR in pitch darkness, he understood how important the torchlight was in the steep terrain.

When Juma at last caught up with the regimental headquarters detachment, he learned that despite their best efforts the Germans had slipped away … again … this time with significant casualties. The *Schutztruppe*, uncharacteristically, had left their wounded on the battlefield in order to escape being surrounded by the KAR battalions. Juma heard some of them moaning and crying out in *Kiswahili* and, was it *Kijeremani*? Their enemies initially escaped to the south, but as the British East African command was most worried about a German return to the north, that's the direction Giffard sent his regiment while 1/KAR followed the German retreat. In less than a week the regiment had another chance to confront their enemy whom they had actually overtaken and passed in the rugged country north of Lioma.

Marching quickly into the Pare Hills, the regiment maintained its accustomed formation—with the headquarters company just ahead of final battalion—through dry, rocky washes lined with thick breaks of bamboo. Suddenly, Juma and the rest heard gunfire to the rear: the Germans were attacking the trailing elements of 2/2 KAR behind them! Lieutenant Colonel Giffard ran ahead to call back the *askari* of 1/2 KAR, who were only about a half-mile ahead, while his adjutant Major Edwards ran back to assist in defending the column from attack. Ordered to stay with the remaining headquarters detachment, Juma heard ever-increasing machine gun fire accompanied by the bugle calls and shouts characteristic of a *Schutztruppe* attack. Taking the initiative, he organized the *askari* signalers and clerks who were with him and led them toward the firing line. Just then two companies of 1/2 KAR joined them. A Stokes mortar took out one German machine gun. KAR *askari* blunted the German attack. Finally 3/2 KAR came up on the German flank, causing them to retreat.

This unexpected action tested the regiment's resources, with casualties on both sides unexpectedly high. Again, the *Schutztruppe* abandoned their wounded, bringing the total hospital cases to over 200. Juma was put to organizing the building of hospital shelters and additional stretchers necessary to accommodate them all. He was glad that finding food for them all was not among his duties, as once again supplies were scarce. During the week it took to care for and transfer the wounded to a motor ambulance convoy, Lieutenant Colonial Giffard once again sought Juma out:

"Sergeant Major, I'm sending you with the 1st battalion back to Tabora to be in reserve."

"Yes, Sir! If I may, sir: Have I failed you as an *askari*, sir?" he wondered.

"Far from it, Juma! The 1st battalion has served longer than any other in our regiment, and that was your original posting. Our supplies are once again very low, so Nairobi has decided to put your battalion in reserve."

"But who will be your RSM, sir?"

Reluctantly, Giffard told him: "CSM Hemdry will come over from the 1st. He hasn't been with them as long as most of the *askari*." He knew the news would trouble Juma, and the Lieutenant Colonel was right.

"Yes, sir!" Juma replied as he knew a soldier should, though he was clearly downcast as he turned to prepare his kit. A proud man, he thought of himself as a worthy *askari*, and he was—well, not exactly humiliated, but certainly deeply disappointed—being replaced by a *Wasungu* Sergeant Major. So careful was he to disguise his discouragement, Lieutenant Colonel Giffard breathed a sigh of relieve as he acknowledged Juma's acceptance of the change.

Juma remained with the regiment—but now again with 1/2 KAR, which was under the command of Major Wilson for just a few more days until they crossed the new east-west motor track—where once again, even more reluctantly this time—he hauled himself aboard motor transport, this time bound for Port Amelia. From there a steamer to Dar es Salaam, and subsequently the newly repaired train to Tabora, took him away from the war. Though his new battalion would be "in reserve," it felt more like his war was over. His weary body welcomed the rest, but his mind continued to focus on the fact that he had been replaced by an *Angelesi* NCO, and one who was no doubt younger than himself. That, and the military realities he reluctantly accepted, deprived him of the sense of victory which so recently had seemed closer at hand than ever.

∞∞∞∞∞

"Is this what a victory celebration looks like?" Juma queried Captain Rangely in the midst of shouting *askari*, many firing their rifles aimlessly in the air, while the entire battalion danced—if that's what their otherwise seemingly random gyrations could be called—around a huge bonfire. After several months in Tabora as a reserve force, 1/KAR received word the war was over: first, news of the armistice reached in Europe, and finally, a few days later, a report the scrappy *Schutztruppe* leftovers they had been chasing in Portuguese East Africa also surrendered.

"Well, the men are celebrating the end to their war. So it must be our victory celebration!" Captain Rangely understood his cautious reply wasn't fully satisfactory. Certainly the nature of this celebration differed markedly from those he remembered as a boy following the end of the Boer War. He recalled seeing fireworks on the main green in Northampton, people marching through the streets of the city carrying lanterns, singing patriotic songs, waving flags, and ultimately standing with his parents during far too many speeches. But this celebration was clearly different, as was this war. Their more confined military encampment in Tabora—within what, after all, was a captured enemy town—would almost naturally beget distinctly different expressions of joy marking the end of their arduous campaign.

The battalion did get its victory speeches within a week or so. General van Deventer came from Nairobi to mark the allied victory officially with his reserve troops. He told the battalion they, and indeed their entire regiment, had "marched further and fought longer" than any others involved in the effort. He led the battalion in cheers:

"Huzza!" At first the *askari* repeated his words:

"Huzza! Huzza!" Then, spontaneously they improvised, picking up the spirit of their commanding General and broke into song, dancing, rather than marching, in place:

> "He has failed, the German has failed.
>
> "He has failed, the German has failed.
>
> "The German has failed!
>
> "Take the machine gun and leave it at the door.
>
> "The German has failed! Oye! Oye!"

Singing was almost in the Nyasa *askari* DNA, a way to put their collective emotions on display. Their South African commanding general was impressed.

On his orders, the next day the battalion had double rations of meat! That gesture did feel much more like a real victory celebration, not just to Juma, but to almost all his fellow *askari*. And within a week the paymaster also had the various accrued payment accounts available for everyone, especially for the senior men whose long service awards were considerable. Juma's account showed he was due a little more than £60, a larger sum than he ever received before! Wisely, he elected not to receive a cash settlement, opting instead to collect his accumulated largesse only after returning home to Zomba. Some, perhaps those who were owed much less, were happy to spend their new wealth in Tabora, frequently in stereotypical ways as have many soldiers before and since. Juma, however, had plans for his sudden windfall! But those would await his retirement from active service, which he once again postponed by re-enlisting to continue as an *askari* even though this most recent war—at least the actual fighting—was over. His expectation was for a final two years in Zomba, allowing him time to fashion a new life for himself.

Preparations for full demobilization of the battalion were well underway when a sudden arrival put an abrupt halt to much of the activity: the "Spanish" influenza hit the KAR encampment with unexpected ferocity. Many of the men were sick, coughing with high fevers, overcome with nausea and frequently uncontrollable diarrhea. Within three weeks well over half the battalion was ill, and the medical officer didn't have any solutions to their complaints. Juma's case wasn't among the most severe, but he was only able to watch as far too many in the KAR camp visibly turned blue and could not breathe, their coughs often producing a frothy discharge tinged with blood. It was heartbreaking to see brave *askari* who had survived a long campaign succumb to this scourge.

"It must be the war air which has lingered, bringing on this new suffering," Juma told several of the *askari* who shared the tent in which he was recuperating. Private Amos Isaac offered a variation on that theme:

"Maybe it's the smoke and blood of the dead which has caused this plague." But there was another connection with their recent experiences which appeared to garner the most support:

"It's must assuredly be *chipindupindu!*" Lance Corporal Brakson Chimwala spoke confidently. "We have made a profit [*pindu* in *Chiyao*] from this war, have we not? No sooner were we paid, then we were struck by this awful sickness. *Malweso kwa mulungu!!!*" Curses from god? Juma was unsure about that idea, and was similarly doubtful if the affliction was a result of any greed on the part of the *askari*. More than anything else, he hoped to be well enough very soon for a return to Zomba, and then home to Majowa! Only when he was at last able to clamour aboard the converted railway freight cars for Dar es Salaam did Juma feel his war was truly over. And as he listened to the "tchjkity, tchjkity, tchjkity" sound of their wheels on the rails he was mesmerized, and he thought—or did he dream?—perhaps this is the sound of victory.

∞∞∞∞∞∞

The long journey by sea, rail, and river back to Nyasaland did not seem quite as long as it had in the past. Once they marched into Zomba, the battalion gratefully went on leave. Juma immediately started toward Majowa. He fairly flew along the path around the mountain only to encounter Mtindiso running toward him. Word had already reached the village that the long war was at last finished, and the battalion was home, so Ambikanile quickly rushed her son off to meet his father. Mtindiso was now—in almost every way—no longer really a boy. Juma greeted him warmly, walking cheerfully with him nearly stride for stride along the path toward his mother's home, trying to answer his son's many questions. Juma's reunion with his wife was equally warm and, he thought, marked a reaffirmation of the part Ambikanile played in his life. In sum, he was overjoyed to be home!

Ambikanile soon took him to another small home on the edge of the village for a bittersweet reunion with Apesile and to meet her new husband, Chisulo Bakali, a nephew of his old friend Issa. Experiencing the joy of this marriage was, it suddenly struck him, another casualty of this war. Once again, an important event in his children's lives passed while he was away! It was perhaps his greatest regret about his long service in the KAR, but also was reason to value this, likely his last home leave. For a time he was almost able to forget going back to Zomba even though he was due to report in only a fortnight. There was much to be done to make his return an official reality, not least to claim the cash settlement of his gratuities left unpaid in Tabora.

Lieutenant Colonel Soames, now in command of the Zomba garrison, was the first to greet him when he did make his way back to the KAR cantonment in Zomba:

"Juma, we both know the fighting may be over, but the work we started in this war is not yet finished!" Yes, he agreed with his commandant, the war was over, even if it had been hard for him to celebrate a victory. But what was unfinished, he wondered?

"We… " Soames continued, somehow including Juma in his understanding of the totality of the British Empire, "… must now make good on our occupation of what was a German colony. We must transform it into a much better, a *British* territory! And to do that, we will need a stalwart occupation force. Your old second battalion will become the backbone of that effort. We would like you to be a part of the process. Therefore we are posting you back to Tabora." Juma's heart sank. This wasn't what he expected when agreeing to re-enlist, extending his service well beyond the usual twenty-one year limit expected of an *askari*. As a soldier, though, he knew orders were precisely that and he was expected to follow them. Moreover, he did not want to jeopardize the gratuity payments he was expecting!

"Yes sir," Juma replied with less than his usual enthusiasm, hoping his reticence wasn't too noticeable. "When will I be leaving, sir?"

"The details are not final yet, but I should think you might have another fortnight or thereabouts. Of course, the paymaster is holding some of your funds. You'll want to collect those first, won't you?"

"Yes, sir. Thank you, sir." Juma hesitated. "Though I don't know if I can use that money as I've planned in so short a time."

"I am sorry, Sergeant Major." Soames wanted to commiserate. He thought a moment, then offered: "Well, there is always the Post Office Savings Bank!" Juma thought he'd heard of it, but wasn't at all sure how it worked. He appreciated the Lieutenant Colonel explaining a bit more, especially the part about deposits earning interest: "like acquiring cows or goats and having more of them to sell once calves or kids are born" was how Soames put it. The idea that he might even have a bit more money when he returned from Tabora was an attractive option. Since he was not going back into combat—and the obvious dangers that might have entailed—Juma agreed to put the monies he was due into the Bank. Saving for the future seemed it might be a good idea. He hoped it was a wise choice.

There was another concern which troubled Juma about returning to Tabora, so with the Lieutenant Colonel seemingly in a cooperative mode, Juma simply put it to him:

"Sir, if I am returning to Tabora, might I also be allowed an officer's tunic? Other Regimental Sergeant Majors I have seen there and elsewhere in East Africa—including the police at Nairobi—wear such uniforms. Even in the old German forces I have seen the same. Would our *askari* not think I am less important than the others if I did not do so? What about the people who formerly lived under German protection? And how would that affect our ability to create, as you say, 'a British territory'? Having such a coat would, I am certain, better help me be a part of that effort. So may I have your permission to receive one before I leave?"

So unexpected, even uncharacteristic, was such a request from the Sergeant Major, Soames was at first taken aback. Quickly gathering himself, though, he thought about it. Indeed, he trusted that Juma was almost certainly correct in his observation of practices in other units, and the argument for its effect on his performance had merit. Without any doubt he was the only real Sergeant Major—African or European—in the entire Second Regiment!

"I understand, Juma, and give you my permission to draw such a tunic from the supply sergeant and henceforth to wear it on duty. However, when you arrive in Tabora the commanding officer may ask you not to do so, and I cannot be responsible for any consequences. Do you understand?"

"Yes, sir!" Juma paused ever so briefly, then added another request: "Perhaps you might write a letter explaining that you have given your permission, sir, and I could carry it with me to Tabora, sir?" The forthright request again reinforced Soames opinion of the Sergeant Major, and he quickly jotted a note on regimental letterhead. As he accepted the sealed envelope, Juma smiled broadly:

"Sir! *Asante sana*, sir!" He was, indeed, thankful, and on his arrival in Tabora three weeks later, Juma encountered no opposition at all to his new khaki tunic. It was, as he had told Lieutenant Colonel Soames, just like those worn by his peers in the police and other regiments. Some also wore boots, though Juma continued to eschew them preferring his still serviceable bare feet.

∞∞∞∞∞∞

Juma found his service with the occupation headquarters detachment in Tabora at best merely underwhelming. Battalion offices in an old German administrative building proved adequate, but the same could not be said for *askari* accommodations. The war-worn tents passing for barracks did little more than shield their occupants from view but were no protection at all from insects—scorpions, flies, and of course mosquitos—nor from rain. Almost everyone one of them leaked, subjecting occupants to frequent drips or dripples depending on the severity of the rains and the precise condition of individual tents. And in keeping more with *Schutztruppe* practice rather than that of the KAR, there were many local women—far too many and especially too many of dubious virtue, Juma believed—living within the camp or very close by. As he inquired about these women, he learned that the ravages of war, followed by influenza, had created a pall over the local Nyamwezi community. "There came a darkness," was a phrase repeated many times by local residents with whom he spoke. Somehow many of them hoped, or perhaps even expected, the British *askari* to deliver them from their troubles.

A few of his fellow *askari* brought their wives with them to Tabora, but Juma was relieved he had not asked Ambikanile to join him. Although he missed his wife terribly, her sorrow at being away from their grown (or nearly grown) children would have left her deeply downcast; in fact, Juma feared she would have been disconsolate. The entire atmosphere in the town—not just the newly created occupation military encampment—was nothing short of toxic. Once a transportation hub of sorts even before the German railway cemented its place at the colony's center, the town itself declined precipitously following its transfer to British control. Shopkeepers were wary of the new *askari* who were also less than welcome in the local markets.

As Sergeant Major of the occupying force, Juma also saw the situation as a trap, or at least a series of temptations, for his men. Too often, some of them stayed away from their tents when they were supposed to be on duty; at other times, many wandered back to their base in terrible states of drunkenness. Quite a few also were drawn into altercations with Nyamwezi men, frequently over the affections of one local woman or another. As a result, Juma far too frequently found himself presiding over punishments for the most egregious offenders, acting the role of the headquarters detachment's Provost Sergeant. Whenever the battalion's Adjutant, Major Collins, ordered a man caned for a serious disciplinary infraction, Juma was required to organize the disciplinary ritual. The offender's platoon formed a square on the parade ground while he lay face down in the middle, with a moist towel over his otherwise bare buttocks. Juma was then required to strike with the cane, first on one side and then the other, until the prescribed number of blows was reached. The offending *askari* was then expected to don his uniform, stand at attention and salute. It was all Juma could do to keep from being physically ill on every such occasion. Finally, it became too much for him, and he sought out Major Collins:

"Sir!" He saluted the Major. "I am the Sergeant Major, not an ordinary Provost Sergeant. When I am required to dispense such harsh justice with the cane, I believe it diminishes my effectiveness in leading the men. I am asking your leave not to be assigned such duty in the future, Sir." Juma could see that Major Collins was taken aback by his request. The Adjutant was an old school officer who saw little wrong with corporal punishment. Juma understood their present situation—as representatives of a victorious army operating in conquered territory—required considerable discretion from the *askari* which, perhaps too frequently, they failed to adequately display. Nonetheless he was concerned the strict discipline meted out by Major Collins could be counterproductive.

"Sergeant Major, you are an old soldier and have seen much discipline in the ranks during your service. It is true we are not at war, but we must ensure the proper behaviour of our *askari*. We *are* an occupying army. The local people must not see us being as callous in our occupation as were the *Wajeremani*. What would you have me do, Sergeant Major?" Juma saw the question as an opportunity:

"Sir, I agree we must be certain *our askari* do not treat the local Nyamwezi as did our former enemies. Yet, as I understand it, the *Wajeremani* themselves engaged in such beatings for the slightest of crimes. Should they see us do the same to our own, what might they think we could do to them? Sir, can we not, at least, enforce discipline for our *askari* outside of public view?" The Major brought his right hand to his chin as if in thought.

"I see," he began slowly. "You make a fair point, Sergeant Major. You may erect a punishment tent for use in future. And you may appoint another to serve in your stead as Provost Sergeant. Dismissed!" Juma saluted, turned sharply, and strode away in thought. He was thankful for the first order, which he quickly put it place. As for the second, he considered it unseemly to order one of his lesser sergeants to assume a duty which he found so distasteful. He did not appoint another Provost Sergeant, opting instead to deal with all of the headquarters detachment *askari* individually, urging each of them to show greater respect for the local population—as well as for themselves! He hoped his standing among the men was such that he might avoid using the cane on any of them.

During his final two-year enlistment—spent in Tanganyika, as the British referred to the former German East Africa during their post-war occupation—Juma was most pleased when his duties took him away from Tabora to either of the other 2/KAR outposts in the Territory. He especially enjoyed going to Mwanza, near the shore of Lake Victoria. There he was reminded somewhat of the land between his home near Zomba Mountain and Lake Nyasa. The terrain near Mwanza appeared much more hospitable to him than the steppe grasslands surrounding Tabora. When Major Collins at last showed him the formal discharge order—reading, in part, "time-expired, character exemplary"—the prospect of at last returning home for good cheered him even more! He had confidence in his own character, but perhaps did not realize how significant that official endorsement of his unquestioned integrity would prove to be in his life as a retired *askari*.

∞∞∞∞∞∞

Book Three

Departing Nairobi only after the influenza epidemic had subsided, Captain Rangely's return to England was hastened by the reopening of sea lanes through Suez. He longed to see the familiar woods at Althorpe and rejoin his family, though he knew many of his school chums wouldn't be there—or perhaps worse—would hardly be recognizable after their wartime experiences. Rather than reducing him to a charity case, his own wounds at Aubers Ridge had inexplicably opened up a new opportunity. He was uncertain if he'd now be welcomed to remain in the Northamptonshire Regiment, sure to be reduced in strength once the armistice was ratified. Thus he was surprised when, at the regiment's ceremonial inspection prior to participation in a Northampton victory parade, the Regimental colonial—Major General Browne—quietly said to him "We've heard good things about your service with the KAR."

Shortly thereafter, he was heartened by orders to join the 2nd battalion in India, with the promise of at least a five-year tour. A second followed, and it was a dashing Major Rangely who made the rounds in Northampton after a full ten years in India. That was the man who swept Sarah Carnham—the second daughter of a Northampton solicitor—off her feet. They were soon married and then off for Wellington's third tour in India with his regiment. On his return for an administrative assignment in regimental headquarters, he and his wife began to think of a life after his retirement. Though Sarah remained enamoured of her role as a military officer's spouse, Wellington did not expect he would be offered another tour of duty.

All that changed with the collapse of Prime Minister Chamberlin's Munich agreement. Another war looming on the horizon, Wellington assumed command of the 2nd regiment's D company, part of a new British Expeditionary Force bound for France. A near disaster followed, and his evacuation from Dunkirk was not only a reprieve but also a chance to reprise his earliest success: another secondment to the King's African Rifles. Army authorities believed he might best, and more quickly, contribute to the war effort in East Africa. Sarah's eyes were tearful as she bade him goodbye at Castle Station.

"You will simply love Africa, my dear!" Wellington tried to cheer his wife with promises that they might visit East Africa once this new war was over. She found it all but impossible to look that far ahead, knowing only too well that she was sending her husband off to his second war.

"I just want you back, safe. I love *you* too much to think about fanciful promises just now." They kissed, then—as a soft refrain from Vera Lynn could be heard in the station waiting room—embraced as long as they could before he had to board his train for Southampton.

Rather than Mombasa again, this time he was bound for Zomba to begin his new assignment in command of a Nyasaland training unit. What Rangely didn't expect was the reunion which awaited him shortly after his arrival at Zomba's Cobbe Barracks. Among the old soldiers called back to the colours, waiting to help train the many expected new recruits was Sergeant Major Juma!

"Sajini Nanyula!" Recognizing his companion from the previous war, Rangely broke military protocol to embrace the veteran,

using the nickname his fellow *askari* had given their brave and steadfast companion. Juma was embarrassed by the attention, and as soon as he could, came to attention and saluted!

"Sir!" He followed the expected greeting with a smile. "*Amiri Likwemba ...*" Juma blurted out the *askari* name for his former commanding officer, then stopped himself. "... ah, Major!"—he recognized Rangely's promotion—"I did not expect to see you again!"

They didn't have time for reminiscences; instead they now shared a determination to prepare new *askari* for another war. For Juma, it was a temporary assignment; he soon returned to Majowa. But for Rangely the new war would involve further service in East Africa, Egypt, Celyon, and finally in Burma, where he was promoted to command a battalion of Nyasa soldiers. His 22 KAR was, however, much like the old 1/KAR with whom he had campaigned in the Great War, with veteran *askari* NCOs shaping the fighting character of the entire unit. But this was a decidedly different war than the one which first brought Wellington and Juma together: the savannah grasslands of east Africa replaced by the rain-glistened hotbox jungle of East Asia, and the determined *Wajeremani* colonial army swapped for the *Jampans* and their attempted "Co-prosperity Sphere." If there was anything which might have made it appear similar perhaps it was the mud, more often than not ankle-deep and—at least in the thickest pockets of the jungle—not receding even as the incessant rains subsided. Just as in East Africa, the result elevated issues of feeding and supplying his troops to the most consistently critical matter facing the new battalion commander. In Burma the solution to overcoming the muck and mire which threatened to stall or even stop his troops struck Rangely as an exquisite irony. On the one hand was the workhorse of air transport, the C47 Dakota, and on the other was the down to earth and indefatigable army mule. By turns—the first flying through blinding rain, the second slipping on muddy ooze beneath hooves—these two provided all that was needed to keep his men in the field.

Wellington understood his *askari*'s enthusiasm for the new *ndege,* much larger than those some of them had seen in East Africa, so he tried to capture one of their praise songs for Sarah including, perhaps incautiously, this verse in one of his letters home:

> Our great brown bird
>
> Flying high
>
> Drops white flowers
>
> From blue sky.

After the war he was amazed to discover it had not been deleted by the regimental censor! That made him wonder what sort of comments some of the *askari* might have written in their many letters to family, especially about the other side of their supply dichotomy. When he realized the *Chichewa* word for pack mule, *bulu,* borrowed from the Portuguese, had another near cognate, *mbulu,* referring to an unpalatable uncooked lump of flour in their *nsima* porridge—which comprised a good share of their usual rations—Wellington could imagine all manner of *askari* jokes lost on those reading them in Nyasaland despite passing a censor's scrutiny!

It was precisely their generally indefatigable cheerfulness which had endeared his Nyasa soldiers to Lieutenant Colonel Rangely. More than any other East Africans, they were the joyful singers, often in camp but especially on the march. And whenever queried about how things were going, *"Mzuri sana"* seemed their bywords. If they worried about anything not being "very good," it seldom was their present circumstances. Rather, things at home were their greatest concerns. As one of his young subalterns once told him when asked how his men coped with the unremittent rain:

"In their tents the *askari* whisper, 'the crops are coming up now in Nyasaland.'"

Wellington had always found it such with his Nyasa soldiers, accounting for his great anxiety whenever required to order them into battle. Despite the joy with which they sang, whenever he heard them reach a particular verse in one of their favourite songs, he cringed:

"Let's move off;

"By whose order?

"By whose order?

"By the orders of the Colonel,

"The orders of the Colonel,

"The orders of the KAR."

He could scarcely bear the thought of any one of them becoming a casualty.

In Service

Returning to Majowa from garrison duty following the war, Juma received a hero's welcome. The village headman—perhaps spurred on by the elderly Chief Chikowi—organized a lavish welcome. Beer was brewed; not one, but *two* goats roasted. There were ululating women, including his own wife and daughter, making such noise he heard them long before coming upon scores of children lining the road into the village. The boys, especially, were delighted to fall in step, as if marching with him home. Gratified, yet not embarrassed, Juma was greatly pleased with the welcome. As he was escorted to a place of honour, dancing began. Tired after his long journey from Tabora, followed almost immediately by the familiar walk from the barracks, he was glad to rest a bit, and happy to accept the beer offered to him. Along with the libations, the sumptuous feast put everyone gathered in the small village into a festive mood. The highlight of the event was yet to come. Slowly rising from his place of honour, Chief Chikowi motioned for quiet from the crowd. His people, as usual, obliged. Standing as tall as he could manage, the elderly chief spoke:

"Juma, we welcome you home. Your journeys have been long, your trials many. Yet you have come back to us! We are grateful." Juma smiled in acknowledgement, but remained silent as he assumed the Chief had more to say. Indeed, he did:

"You have seen many things, met many challenges. Many men have followed you, believing you would lead them through troubles. Now, it is time for you do the same for me and my people." A frown, ever so slight, came to Juma's face. He was looking forward to being released from such expectations.

"I have for you this *mlangali*," the chief continued, handing him a ceremonial scarlet headband. "Henceforward it will mark you as one of the most honoured men among us!" Juma, as well as the gathered assemblage, were stunned, none more so than the forty or so headmen of the Chikowi chieftaincy who had also gathered for this celebration. Usually such an honour was bestowed only on the most favoured of the chief's *ndunas*. Juma did not have such rank or position, nor did he expect it. *Ndunas* only held their office among the Yao by inheritance.

"Nanyula!" The shout from the edges of the crowd took everyone by surprise, but not Juma who recognized the voice. It was Issa, reaffirming the strength and steadfastness of his old friend and, at the same time, attempting to lend his support for the retired Sergeant Major's elevation to such standing in the community. Not aware of the nickname Juma had earned from his fellow *askari*, many in the crowd were only further dumbfounded by the interjection, giving rise to whispers and murmurs all around.

Without being prompted to do so, the Chief quickly countered the disbelief he sensed from the crowd. "Juma!" He waited for quiet again. "Juma, in the times of our ancestors, this honour was given only to the bravest warrior leaders among us. You have proven yourself a great warrior. You are a leader of men—*nanyula,* as Issa has now told us—but not just among the *asilikali*. Now it is time for you to be a leader among my people as well. I am nominating you to become *lipunga* and serve in court as one of my advisors. And *Bwana Disi* has already agreed for you to do so!" Juma knew only too well, after his time in Tanganyika, that a chief was no longer a chief by the people but also needed British acquiescence, so it made sense to him that he could only be one of the Chief's assessors if the British District Commissioner approved.

∞∞∞∞∞∞

Proud of her husband, and also aware of the expectations of a Yao wife, Ambikanile didn't press Juma for more than a perfunctory greeting after his return. Ever since word reached the village that he was coming home for good, the plans for a public welcoming feast had been underway. As word of those plans was left for him at the barracks, he had rushed his return home to Majowa as soon as he could. Ambikanile understood the importance of the Chief's welcome—not just to Juma but also to their future—so apart from joining in the initial chorus of praise, she held back as he assumed his elevated status. His new position almost certainly guaranteed their basic needs would be provided for, but she did not know what, if anything, remained of his KAR gratuities. Many *asilikali* returned from the war no longer had anything left of theirs. And she was aware of much that needed doing, not least involving Mtindiso's future. So when the feast was well and truly over, she insisted they retreat to their home.

"I am glad you are home, with me and with Mtindiso," she began, only to observe that he was quickly falling asleep, his traveller's drowsiness fueled by the celebratory beer! A quiet snore was the only response she received that evening, resolving to try again the next morning.

A habitual early riser after years as an *msilikali*, Juma was awake well before his family. His first thought was to make his way around the mountain to the Post Office, but he knew his wife would be upset to find him gone when she awoke. And it was not long before Mtindiso—now a strapping young man almost the same age as was Juma when he began his military career—also awakened. He was alert and almost immediately began:

"Father, I have much to discuss with you, and mother has assured me you will listen." Why would he not, Juma wondered. Did he, too, want to become an *msilikali*?

"Of course, my son! I am pleased to have time again to speak with you."

"There are many changes in my life and decisions I must make, and I want to tell you about them and seek your advice."

"But what about your uncles?" Juma was quick to ask.

"That's just it, father. I am now *Mkhristu* and Bwana Anderson said I must speak with you rather than my uncles." Juma was dumbfounded. The surprise in his eyes and speechless response conveyed far better than words his reaction to this news.

"Please do not be hard on our son, Juma!" Ambikanile was now also awake and joined in the conversation. "Mtindiso is a gentle and obedient young man. He knows you may be inclined to disapprove, but he seeks—more than anything—your approval."

"This is my fault. I have not been here to guide him." Juma was trying to remain calm, as he had learned to do when facing even graver dangers in battle. "It is yet another price my life as an *msilikali* has cost me ... has cost *us*, actually." He realized his voice was raised, and was glad that Mtindiso interrupted him, though actually trying to diffuse any anger.

"Please, mother. These are matters for me and my father to discuss. Even Bwana Anderson says we must approach this as men, and that is what I shall do."

"Who is this Bwana Anderson?" Juma blurted out. However, once he spoke the name he remembered: This was the man who demanded the KAR provide a Christian school for the *askari*. Juma knew him as an *amishoni* who, in his zeal, had over-represented the concerns of Christian *askari*, causing the men to be harshly disciplined. Had he now done the same with his son? Juma was able to supress his sense of rage, though the tone of the subsequent question scarcely hid his contempt:

"What has this *amishoni* told you I must do?"

"Nothing, father. He has only told me to discuss this with you as it is how we should do so now. It is the *Mkhristu* way!" Juma knew the customs as well as the laws of the *Angelesi* were increasingly dominating their lives, and that he had surely been a part of bringing that about. "Like you," Mtindiso continued, "I have wanted to embrace what the *Wakhristu* have brought to us." There it was! Confirmation that perhaps his entire service in the KAR had been in vain. Had he actually failed in carrying out the assignment Chief Chikowi had given him years before?

"So you have been caught in their net? Are you no longer Yao?" Juma's voice rose again as he continued questioning his son.

"I am Yao," Mtindiso did not hesitate in making reply, matching his father's insistence with the intention of forestalling any continued questioning. "But I know our world has changed. At least mine has! I remain proud to be Yao. But I am also *Mkhristu* and want to be married in the church as well. I wish to bring Njimile to our home to meet you—tonight—before we are married!"

"Just when will that be? Does her family know? Have you built a house for her?" Juma would have asked more questions had not Ambikanile intervened:

"Mtindiso and Njimle have made all the arrangements! They have been waiting for you to return home, as I've asked that they do. I knew how disappointed you were to miss the wedding feast for Apesile and Chitsulo." Juma wanted to be pleased his wife had thought of *his* feelings, but was almost overcome with the thought that he had lost Ambikanile as well. Was he to be alone in his own family?

"Do not worry, Juma," his wife went on, having anticipated her husband's reaction. "I also remain Yao like you, but respect that our son has made another choice." She softened her voice and addressed just her husband:

"I'm just pleased he won't also be an *msilikali* so his wife need not worry if he will return to her." Her parting shot hit home. Juma's displeasure quickly turned to despondence. Not only would his son not follow in his footsteps. His wife revealed the distress she had felt but carefully had not conveyed to him. What might he do now that would redeem him in her eyes and, at the same time, convince his son he understood the new parameters of their lives?

Indicating he wished to complete his morning ablutions, Juma left his wife and son for a few moments, then quietly returned. The few moments away were sufficient for him to recognize these new challenges couldn't be won by a frontal assault, but instead would best be met with a slow and steady advance, a tactic he'd learned well as an *msilikali*.

"You have made your decisions, Mtindiso, and I shall respect them," Juma announced as he returned. He paused, raising his hand, and before either his son or wife could respond, he continued. "Will you live in the village, or in the town? If you will not join the KAR, will you work for the *boma* or the *Wamishoni*? Or have they taught you a skill?"

"The arrangements we have made, father, are for the wedding. But I wish your advice about the other matters you mention." How could this be? Juma thought it little more than the arrogance of youth. Nonetheless, he remained resolute that he should weather this storm with calm. Then the embryo of an idea came to mind: the money he had saved might be put to use to help his son! He had planned to use his gratuities to purchase land for himself. But why not for his son as well? And perhaps even the wherewithal for him to begin a life for himself and his bride? He was suddenly aware Mtindiso had been continuing to speak:

"…and I have purchased a *njinga*—a used one—but it will be sufficient for me to ride bringing fish from Lake Chirwa to sell in town." This sounded more promising to Juma.

"As I had saved just a little money, mostly from your wounded gratuity, it seemed appropriate to help Mtindiso with just a little of it. Surely you will think I was wise to do so?" Ambikanile addressed her husband. His mind speeding ahead, but with a steady voice—one he had practiced often when in command of his *askari*—Juma acknowledged he had no objection and then added:

"A fishmonger? Our forefathers were traders, so that would be a noble occupation. But if you truly wish to embrace the new world of the *Angelesi*, why not a repairer—and perhaps later a seller—of bicycles?" Mtindiso eyes opened wide in a pleasing compliment to his widening smile. "I am willing to purchase some tools for you as a start…" His son interjected with something Juma hadn't yet thought through:

"And Bwana Jackson at the mission can help me learn how to make the repairs! I should like that. Father, you are too kind!" Juma was pleased, both by his son's thanks, and to have resolved—at least for now—this family dispute.

"We can tell…" Juma had to pause for a moment to recall her name, "…Njimile…tonight at dinner!"

∞∞∞∞∞∞

The first few months after Mtindiso's marriage were joyous ones for Juma. He withdrew his gratuities, plus the earned interest, from the Post Office Savings Bank, quickly putting them to use. He expanded and remodeled his home at Majowa. At the same time Chief Chikowi helped him acquire land for Mtindiso, and working with his son, they built a small home and a bicycle repair shop. As a confirmed *Asikotilandi*, Mtindiso began his training at the Scottish mission. The plans they had made were coming to fruition. Yet a lengthening shadow soon fell over their lives: two seasons of failed rains led to a general famine all around their mountain. Having invested much of his savings, Juma and his family—along with many others in the surrounding district—were troubled by the increasing cost of basic food.

During his wartime marches in Portuguese territory, Juma became familiar with soldiering on while at the same time eating very little. But asking Ambikanile now to do likewise deeply troubled him. He could live off the pounded cassava leaves that were generally available, but didn't relish her doing so as well.

"Perhaps I too should go to Mulanje for work," he finally suggested to her, relating that's what his old *msilikali* friend Funsani had finally decided to do in a desperate attempt to buy food for his family. "Or maybe it would be better to go with *Wenela*," he mused despite his aversion to the idea of joining the many men—including Stambuli—who had left for South Africa or Southern Rhodesia to work in the mines. He really didn't want to work for men like the many South Africans he encountered during the war, especially the abusive officers in the Cape Coloured regiment he met in southern Tanganyika. Perhaps he needn't have worried:

"NO! Absolutely no! I will not have you leaving again!" Ambikanile was adamant in her response. "If you want to work, can you not find something near here?" Her challenge set Juma thinking: Might not there be a role for him with the KAR, despite his retirement? He had heard Colonial Soames himself had retired and returned to Britain, though perhaps the new Commandant could help him. The only way to know for sure would involve going to the barracks and asking Colonel Hawkins, whom he learned was the newly arrived KAR Commandant in Zomba. And that is precisely what he did!

"Is there a job for me here, Colonel?" Juma asked after introducing himself. He always thought it best to be direct when dealing with officers. The response made him feel a little foolish for not having thought of it himself:

"You certainly could join the KAR Reserve, Sergeant Major. The pay would be minimal, but it might help. Are you, too, concerned about the increasing prices of food? We've been seeing many recruits the last few months—many more than usual—most saying the cost of food is their reason for volunteering." Hawkins was silent for a moment, before leaning toward Juma: "But between you and me, few of them even come close to having the makings of such a good *askari* as you've been!" Juma was flattered that Hawkins had already learned about his record with the KAR, and he openly acknowledged buying food for his family was his concern. He readily agreed to join the reserves, receiving a new cap and shield for his old uniform. Carrying them back to Majowa he was sure Ambikanile would approve, which she did, as he assured her it wouldn't mean time away from home. He also thought it wise to report this new development to Chief Chikowi, proudly showing him the new additions for his uniform!

"I have tried to serve you well and honour our people by serving in the KAR," he reminded the Chief. He also cautiously broached the subject of Mtindiso's conversion to Christianity which—though Juma had come to grips with it himself—still gnawed at his conscience. He then shared his latest news: "I have now joined the KAR Reserve forces."

"I am delighted ... you have done so," the Chief replied somewhat haltingly, adding: "Do not ... be concerned about ... Mtindiso. There are many ... *Wakhristu* among our people now ... as well as *Wasilamu*." Juma acknowledged Chief Chikowi's reply, while trying not to show his concerns for the elderly Chief who surely showed signs of having aged even since Juma's return from Tabora. But when he spoke again, there was no mistaking his continued commitment to promoting his people's welfare:

"Juma, you are one of my advisors now ... a court assessor ... but we all know you are respected ... loyal and steadfast ... *nanyula* to your *asilikali* comrades ... but also to me! You have helped form a connection ... if not exactly a bridge ... between the Yao, my people ... and the *Angelesi* ... Yet you, if anyone ... also knows there remain ... the troubles and tensions between us ... indeed between all *Waafrika* ... and the *Wasungu*." The Chief paused a moment, then began again:

"I have been asked ... to endorse a new organization—called the Southern Province ... Native Association—joining other chiefs and educated men ... in making our voices heard. What do you think? Would this be a good idea?" To Juma it was a surprising request, especially for his opinion, but he didn't hesitate in replying:

"Indeed, it seems another valuable opportunity. We must do whatever we can to ensure our voices are heard!" He recalled the many times that he had fought to suppress African voices both directly—at Lake Chilwa, Mpezeni's, Asante, Somaliland and elsewhere—or indirectly by merely supporting British rule. His most recent service with occupying forces at Tabora especially came to mind. What had his service brought? His answers were demands, more demands: for taxes, for labour, and even for the minds of his people, even his own son! Were there any benefits? Even after the long war was over, what had the British government done to end the famine and suffering of the people? He was tense and troubled, too! What might he do to calm this situation, just as Chief Chikowi was proposing to do? He could only hope there would be answers and, in some measure, he might be a part of them.

∞∞∞∞∞∞

The first time he made his way to the KAR Barracks to meet Mrs. Metcalfe, Juma wondered why Colonel Hawkins had summoned him. He was accustomed to travelling from his home at Majowa to regimental headquarters. But to meet an *mzungu* woman? Nothing like that had ever, *ever* happened before! The regiment was a man's world and had been so for as long as he had been an *askari*. Of course, there had been a few female nurses he encountered during the Great War. He recalled the young *Mjeremani* woman tending to his wounded KAR officers on Mafia Island, and Sister Whitworth, wasn't it? He tried to remember the name of the woman who had briefly cared for him in Nairobi during his last few weeks in hospital. But he wasn't at all sick just now. At least he didn't think so, but perhaps the Commandant knew something of the complaints he constantly heard from Ambikanile that he was slowing down and couldn't do nearly as much he used to! He didn't want to admit it, but there might have been at least a sliver of truth to her concerns.

But that didn't explain the order to bring his old dress uniform. Luckily he still was, just barely, able to fit into the khaki shorts and tunic which Ambikanile carefully kept cleaned and pressed, set aside in a special cupboard with his leather belt, dress sash, braided shoulder cord, felt hat, and, of course, his coveted *nishani*, those hard won medals to pin on his uniform. Though he now seldom had reason to don his "*Msilikali* clothes," as his wife called, them, she knew he wouldn't ever put on that uniform without his coveted *nishani*! When he entered the Commandant's office, Juma quickly discovered he would, indeed, have need of his uniform again. Mrs. Metcalfe was to *paint* his portrait!

"*Andika picha?*" Juma was quizzical. What could this be all about? He was familiar with photographs. He had many times stood as still as possible for photographers and the almost magical boxes they used. More than just a few times he had, as well, seen the resulting photos. As the Colonel soon explained, this would be different.

"Mrs. Metcalf will use her paints and brushes to create a likeness of you so that all of us in the KAR can remember exactly what our very best *sajini* looks like! Once you have that uniform on—My, it looks as nice as it did at your last parade!—Mrs. Metcalfe will want you to stand at attention for a while so she can observe you and make sure she has your likeness exactly right. Can you do that, *Sajini* Juma?"

"*Ndiyo, bwana!*" Juma knew that saying "Yes" was the only possible response. He had been a loyal *askari* far too long to have done otherwise. The standing at attention part, however, turned into multiple sittings—or "standings," as it seemed to Juma—asked for by Colonel Hawkins, who was still, in a manner of speaking, his commanding officer. What he did not know, however, was that Mrs. C.C. Metcalf was well known, at least among the British colonial settlers in central Africa, for her portraits, especially of children and families. Juma was to be another of her subjects, but for a series of "native types" she had recently begun. And while he might have been—what was it? "The very best *sajini*" in the KAR—he ultimately was just one of three such Africans of that rank she painted for her series.

Gradually, he came to be more comfortable—if not with the standing for such long periods—at least in making conversation with Mrs. Metcalf. His English was limited, even after lengthy service in the KAR, and her knowledge of *Chichewa*—or any other African language, for that matter—decidedly paltry despite dealing with local servants for years. They did manage to communicate a few ideas. Juma came away with the sense she was genuinely impressed by the *askari* she was painting. She understood Juma and the others were proud of their service, and she attempted to convey that in her portraits. What he did not realize, though, was the impact these paintings would have once they were on view in London at the 1924 British Empire Exhibition and later in the 1/KAR officers mess in Zomba.

Ambikanile had a hard time understanding why he was making the trip around the mountain, time after time, always in his dress uniform. Juma tried to explain, but his wife's familiarity with either the changing world their son had embraced or her husband's *asilikali* domain was decidedly limited. Nonetheless she did her best to be sure he looked his best each time! He did look smart each time he set out, and always smiled for the young boys who greeted him and frequently lined up behind him, pretending to march in step. He welcomed their attention. Yet the frequent "standings" for the demanding artist did grow tiresome! And when he saw the finished painting he was somewhat uncertain if all the effort and those many trips had really been worthwhile. It seemed to him a photograph, made with one of those magical boxes, might have been just as good!

∞∞∞∞∞∞

The journeys around the mountain continued even after the painting was completed, so Mtindiso offered him a restored bicycle from his growing stock. Out of respect for his son, Juma tried riding it around the mountain, but his balance soon betrayed him and he quickly set it aside preferring his time-tested feet. As a member of the KAR Reserves, Juma was always welcome at the KAR Barracks though he much less frequently wore his dress uniform, and only when invited to attend formal parades. As a result he drew considerably less attention on his treks, but perhaps that was all to the good. More and more his journeys extended well beyond the army cantonment, as he began seeking out others among Zomba's growing African community whom Chief Chikowi encouraged him to meet. His walks from Majowa gave him time to plan where he would go and whom to visit, while the return stroll allowed time for reflection. Consequently, he gradually came to understand better the issues facing the Yao and other peoples of Nyasaland from a perspective broader than just that of an old *askari*.

Among his first new acquaintances was Levi Mumba, whom Chief Chikowi mentioned when asking Juma about joining the new group for expressing African voices. After a few pleasantries even in their first meeting, Juma came right to the point:

"What is this new organization Chief Chikowi tells me about?" he wanted to know. "Is it only for chiefs and those who have been to school?"

"The group I mentioned to Chikowi is called the Southern Province Native Association," the senior government clerk told Juma, then explained further: "Its goal, as that of similar groups in other regions of Nyasaland, is to get the government's attention about what concerns all of us. To the *Azungu* mind"—Mumba lowered his voice a little, as if communicating a secret—"traditional chiefs are best able to know this, although those of us who have succeeded in English schools also hope to have the ear of the *boma* as well." Then, more boldly, he added: "Of course in some cases—in the KAR, public works, and perhaps the police—the *Wazungu* sometimes listen to others with experience, particularly people such as yourself." Juma wasn't sure if he'd always been that influential. But as he thought about some of his most recent interactions with officers—Lieutenant Colonel Soames, Major Collins, and Colonel Hawkins—he recalled feeling they had indeed respected his concerns and acted to help him in resolving particular problems.

Impressed by the clarity and confidence with which he spoke, Juma gradually grasped there was some truth to what Mr. Mumba said. Yet, as he was born and educated in the northern part of Nyasaland, Juma wondered how well Mumba actually understood the situation of the Yao people. Juma knew there were many *askari* who were Yao and some in the police as well, but working for the *boma* Public Works Department? He queried Mumba about that and learned that a Yao, Che Msoma, was a long-serving senior roads *capitao*. Thankful for that information, Juma made a special effort to meet Msoma on his next visit to Zomba town. As it transpired he was somewhat younger, and had begun working on the roads about the time of Juma's service in Somaliland with the KAR. Moreover, he was also from Chief Chikowi's area! That happy coincidence brought them together as friends, and the two talked whenever they could. When Juma told Issa about his new acquaintance, he was surprised to learn that Msoma was a nephew of the Chief—the son of his younger sister—who, after years of government service, was actually relatively wealthy.

Unlike Msoma, Juma's new standing among Chikowi's people wasn't based on his wealth, but his newly awarded scarlet headband and appointment as one of the Chief's "assessors." Making judgements concerning the disputes between people who lived in the Chief's area was among the hardest of tasks he undertook after retirement. Though some of his fellow *askari*, especially the younger ones, had occasionally referred to him as *mwalimu*—he didn't consider himself a teacher, continuing to prefer *nanyula*—Juma felt more wily than wise. After all, he was a soldier. That had been his life. But Chief Chikowi told him it was precisely those experiences that led to his nomination as *lipunga*. Now the chief, and indeed most of those among whom he lived, looked to him for quick and fair resolutions to even their most contentious disagreements. For a man of action, the transformation into an elder, from whom contemplation was expected, became a special trial. "I can do this, too!" he reminded himself more than once in the first days of his appearance as what was, in effect, a magistrate. Though not recognized precisely as such by the District Commissioner, his decisions would nonetheless have—with the chief's concurrence—the binding power of law, not only for his own Yao people but also in the eyes of the British government of Nyasaland. It was a responsibility he took with earnest humility.

On occasion he passed the time on his journeys to and from town to reflect on the most troublesome cases which came to him in his new role as *lipunga* for Chief Chikowi. The cases causing him the greatest consternation were not those from among Chief Chikowi's Yao people, but the few stemming from the very heart of the colonial reality in which they lived. Within Nyasaland, boundaries between various Africa societies were now fixed by British fiat, even if the people were not. On one occasion, a Yao woman came to him wishing to divorce her Ngoni husband, seeking custody of their child. Mesi met her husband when he was working in Zomba, where they married. She then set up housekeeping with him in his father's village far away in Mzimba. Finding her situation there intolerable, she relocated to her own home village in Chief Chikowi's area, along with her infant son Chabwera. Her Ngoni husband, Onani, pursued them wanting to return with the boy to Mzimba. Appealing to Chief Chikowi, the mother claimed her Yao matrilineal rights superseded the patrilineal claims of the boy's Ngoni father.

Juma was assigned the task of assessing the claims for the Chief. First Mesi and then Onani argued for custody, followed by heart wrenching stories supporting their claims. Juma listened to everything each had to say, then listened some more as their arguments became increasingly bewildering and bitter. Juma finally put a stop to the bickering:

"No more of these long stories!" he firmly insisted. "We are actually conducting this case according to the customs of the *Wazungu*." He went on to explain the ties which bound mother and child that he observed as the norm among English families. Though he didn't mention it, Juma was especially thinking about the conversations he had long ago with Lieutenant Brogdan—his own son, Mtindiso's namesake—about family life. Such thoughts promoted him further to note that Mesi had apparently suffered greatly in her husband's village, causing her to flee Mzimba if only to protect her relationship with Chabwera. Then Juma announced his recommendation to the Chief: "Mesi should receive 10/- shillings compensation from Onani and custody of the child." Onani's reaction was one of almost immediate hostility toward the assessor.

"How can you, a Yao, deprive me of my son? Who are you to take my son from me? What do you know of Ngoni ways? Nothing! Absolutely nothing!" Onani became so agitated; several of the men present at Chief Chikowi's court that day had to restrain him as he otherwise would have likely struck the Chief's assessor, a truly troubling offense. Juma, though, remained calm.

He had faced far greater dangers in battle. And he also knew the outburst would do little to win the Chief's sympathy!

Indeed, when the time came for Juma to present the case and deliver his opinion, the elderly Chief Chikowi not only affirmed his decision, but went out of his way to praise Juma's balance of judgement and personal restraint in handling the matter. And as the principals left the court, the Chief motioned for Juma to stay behind:

"You are wise ... to see the need ... for us to balance ... our ways with those ... of the *Angelesi* .... All our neighbours ... Chewa ... Lomwe ... Ngoni ... Tonga ... and all the rest ... we live together ... but under the law ... of the *Angelesi*." He paused for an even longer breath. "I believe ... you've learned well ... as an *msilikali*. I .... Thank you." The Chief began to cough and wheeze, motioning Juma away, preferring the ministrations of his young grandson who led him out of public view to his home. It was the last time Juma saw the Chief alive.

∞∞∞∞∞

When news of the Chief's passing reached him, Juma was worried—not about his position—but for the entire community. His first instinct was to turn to the quarter he knew best, so hurried to KAR *boma*, explaining his concerns to Colonel Hawkins:

"We Yao worry about what will happen when our chief dies," Juma began, sharing the news of Chief Chikowi's death with the Colonel. Juma continued about the heightened anxiety he felt: "Too often there is a brief time of troubles. My father called it *chipinimbe*, when there can be some social disorganization, even lawlessness, in our community. I want to do what I can to see the worst doesn't happen." The Colonel welcomed his concern, assuring him the District Commissioner would manage the succession expeditiously and not permit any disruptions to local life. Despite offering these reassurances, he could see the matter still weighed on the Sergeant Major's mind. Leaning back in his chair, the Colonel thought a little more and then had a further idea:

"Perhaps we could ensure *you* would be able to intervene, if nothing else to protect the regiment's cattle which graze just south of Majowa." He then sat up to the desk, penning a note to the Zomba District Commissioner authorizing Juma "to carry a carbine rifle with a view to protecting the King's African Rifles' cattle at Nkanda from '*zirombo*'." Handing it to Juma he added, "We needn't tell *Bwana Disi* exactly which wild beasts might be about! I trust your judgement and discretion. Once the DC agrees, you may see the armoury sergeant to claim a carbine and a little ammunition."

"Yes sir! Thank you, sir!" After leaving Majowa for his walk around the mountain to the *boma*, he'd almost thought better of going directly to Colonel Hawkins, but Juma was now glad he'd done so. Following orders he went to the DC's office—where Juma's permission was recorded—but before heading back to the armoury he stopped to see Mr. Mumba, sharing all of this recent news. Unlike the Colonel, Mumba had already heard of Chief Chikowi's death and shared some further gossip from his government contacts:

"Indeed, the word around town is that Che Msoma is likely to be agreed by the *boma* as the new Chikowi. Not only is he a relative of the former Chief—God rest his soul—he also is known to and trusted by the government. Once he is confirmed and installed, I'm sure he will want your counsel."

Juma's first reaction was discomfort that the *Angelesi* would decide who would be the new Chief. Then, recalling Chief Chikowi referred to getting permission from *Bwana Disi* before appointing Juma himself as *lipunga*, he thought better of his reservations. This was the new reality of their lives. He told Mr. Mumba how he felt and added:

"For now, at least, we must continue to find ways to accommodate our masters." It was as harsh an assessment as Juma had ever confessed to anyone, even Ambikanile. But Levi Mumba agreed with him, cautioning they might best discuss any future disagreements with the *boma* only through official channels! Juma took his leave, returned to the Barracks, and stopped at the armoury before making his way around the mountain and back to Majowa.

His arrival in the village with a rifle did not go unnoticed. Long before—even before the great *Chiwaya* War in which Juma fought was finally over—the *boma* had confiscated all the remaining rifles in the village, indeed throughout the district. So Juma's appearance with the carbine he'd been issued was of particular note among his peers. As it turned out, he didn't have any occasion to use it; word the new Chief Chikowi would soon be installed calmed any jitters in Majowa and the surrounding villages. There was no unrest, and Juma reported to Colonel Hawkins that the KAR cattle were all safe! All the same, he kept the rifle and regularly exchanged the few rounds of ammunition he'd been given for a fresh supply. The newly installed Chikowi took note of Juma's elevated stature as an arms-bearer, and—but not precisely because of it, Juma liked to think—asked him to continue in his position as *lipunga*. Juma readily accepted, as he had gradually become more confident in hearing cases, and regularly offered advice and counsel to his new Chief.

∞∞∞∞∞∞∞

For several years, Juma's life continued much as it had since his return from Tabora. The rains were good and the previous food crisis wasn't replicated. Mtindiso's bicycle business grew, perhaps a little more slowly than he and his father had hoped, yet not so slowly as to prevent the widespread joy when he and Njimile welcomed Juma's second grandchild, Mary, a girl to join Chitsulo and Apesile's son, Thenga, in competing for Juma's affections. In truth, their grandfather doted on them both! Ambikanile, increasingly in ill health, was of little help with the grandchildren, and—although he was loathe to admit it—neither was she to Juma. One day when Ambikanile was away visiting Apesile and Thenga, a woman whom he previously encountered on the path to Zomba, appeared at his home with a pot of porridge.

"Why have you brought me this *ugali*?" Juma asked her.

"You told me your wife sometimes was unable to prepare it for you," she replied. Lowering her face slightly, she smiled and added: "Besides, I want you very much!" Juma was surprised and slightly embarrassed, though he knew she spoke truthfully.

"Don't your already have a husband?" He inquired of her, dismissively.

"I do not. My husband left me a long time ago. You might not know since you have been away so long yourself! You may ask my brother and he will tell you." Juma did, discovering she had again spoken the truth. Then, reluctantly, he discussed the situation with his own brother and, with his approval, went to the woman himself.

"Chotsani," he asked her, "Would you truly wish to be with me even though I am growing older and you may someday be the only one to care for me?" She was surprised, while insisting he would never be a burden. Juma then suggested they might spend some time together, a common trial arrangement among the Yao. When she agreed, Juma began making arrangements, though he knew his decision would not sit well with Ambikanile. Still, he wanted to be sure someone other than his children would take care of him should his first wife's health continue to decline. He was careful not to mention the situation to Mtindiso, fearing his new-found faith would lead him to disapprove. However, when Juma did mention his plans to Apesile, she offered to deal with Mtindiso, eventually succeeding in softening whatever opposition her brother might have had.

In due course they were married, with Chotsani becoming Juma's third wife. The matter of a home for the newlyweds was a little contentious, however. Juma's home—well established and now extended well beyond its original limits—was in Ambikanile's village. He wanted to stay in his well-established home and didn't want to move to Chiradzulu, Chotsani's home. And what of Ambikanile? In an act of great kindness, the new Chief Chikowi himself intervened, encouraging Juma's in-laws to accept his continued residence at Majowa while allowing Ambikanile to live at their daughter's home on the edge of the village. It was not entirely a selfless act on the part of the new chief, as he wanted Juma to be nearby and happy in his now more expansive role as a favoured elder. And Chikowi also wanted to be sure Juma would remain well-connected with the authorities in the KAR *boma*.

His own position—both within his family and the chiefdom—somewhat stabilized, Juma turned his attentions his own fortunes. With an additional area of land allotted by Chief Chikowi, Juma soon began a new endeavor as a tobacco farmer, not so much because he was adept at farming but out of a desire to seize an economic opportunity. Perhaps because of his military background and respect for authority, he turned to agricultural agents from the *boma* for advice, enlisting Mtindiso and Chitsulo for help with the initial preparation of his fields. By his third season, he was already one of the larger small holder producers in Zomba District, earning a sizeable income by selling his crop to the Native Tobacco Board. Proud of his success, he was maybe a little full of himself in bragging to Levi Mumba:

"I'm *sona kwa sona* now even more than just an old *askari*," he announced proudly, forgetting Mumba wasn't a *Chiyao* speaker who completely missed Juma's attempt at a pun. So he explained that in *Chiyao* the word for tobacco—*sona*—had a cognate—also *sona*—indicating the act of becoming famous. Despite the embarrassing moment, Mumba quickly congratulated Juma on his new initiative and especially his willingness to adopt many of the newer planting methods which had been opposed by some other tobacco farmers who also began growing tobacco at about the same time. Juma took the compliment well, as he knew Mumba was becoming one of the leading advocates for a variety of government efforts promoting the education of Africans in the Protectorate.

Despite his respect for Mr. Mumba—who again urged him to maintain ties with the Barracks—and even in contravention of similar advice from his new Chief, Juma felt so busy with his new ventures he decided to forego his next re-enlistment in the KAR reserve. The small extra KAR income was no longer so important. And nothing was said about relinquishing the carbine he'd been issued a few years before.

∞∞∞∞∞∞

Holding on to the rifle soon proved to be strikingly significant when to Juma's surprise—but not, he learned later, to KAR officers and other government officials—a call went out mobilizing the reserve and seeking new recruits for the KAR: The British Empire was again at war with their old enemies, the *Wajeremani*. Even though he was no longer formally a member of the reserve, Juma reported to the Barracks where he was welcomed with thanks and put to work indoctrinating the first new recruits. He actually volunteered to assist with their formal military training, at least until a full instructional company could be formed. What he didn't expect was the surprise when the new commander of the company arrived at Cobbe Barracks.

Hearing the shouted greeting *"Sajini Nanyula!"* out of the blue so startled Juma it was a moment before the many memories associated with that voice flooded into his mind! His old commander, back again, and in Zomba! Juma could scarcely believe it, but was gratified *Amiri Likwemba* recognized him and recalled their service together. Both of them nearly allowed their personal emotions to overcome military protocol, though soon enough they were focusing on the serious mission that yet again drew them together. As he went through some initial drills with the recruits, Juma thought of his first days as an *askari*. How different those experiences had been! Along with Issa and Stambuli, he'd had no idea what it was to be a British soldier. But now the entire country had memories of a long war and, as a result, the preparation of recruits was much different.

No longer were *askari* taught *Kiswahili* as they learned *military* drill. Gone were the marching songs about a farmer and his dog, replaced by familiar lyrics—even to civilian ears:

"Sole, sole, sole, sole

"There's war again in Kenya..."

and continuing in a sorrowful lament, usually embracing the *asilikali's* most recent concern or complaint, like many of the refrains Juma remembered from his last war. Gone too were the regimental *Kiswahili* commands, replaced by *Chichewa* forms more familiar to the new recruits, starting with even the basic march step:

Imodzi,

Awiri,

Atatu,

Anayi.

Yet it was clear to Juma that—especially under Major Rangely's leadership—the fundamental purpose of their rigourous training remained unchanged: instilling the new *asilikali* with the discipline needed to face a determined enemy. As a few old soldiers, including many who had eschewed joining the reserves, answered the appeal for troops and rejoined the ranks, the training went more smoothly. And once the recruiting company was properly squared away, Major Rangely thanked Juma for his veteran presence and invaluable assistance:

"We couldn't have managed without your help, *sajini*! Once again, you've distinguished yourself as an *asilikali* asset to the regiment." Juma knew he'd done his best at short notice and was grateful the Major had taken notice.

"*Asante sana*, Sir!" Juma replied as he would have previously, then quickly added, "*Zikomo*," adapting his thanks to the shifting patois of his regiment, which brought a smile to Rangely's face. But Juma also hoped this would be the extent of his service in the present emergency; he'd already been back far longer than expected.

"Might I return to Majowa now, sir?"

"Yes, Sergeant Major! Return to your family and fields. We will call on you should we need any further assistance. *Pitani bwino, Nanyula!*" After biding Juma goodbye, Rangely paused for a moment, then added: "I have been ordered to Kenya, to join the regiment for the advance to Addis Ababa." Then, almost absent-mindedly, continued reassuringly, "We'll meet again," even though he had no idea if they ever would. Rangely felt a little foolish as he knew the *asilikali* often were far more literal in their understanding of what Europeans said. Perhaps it was his affection for Juma, particularly, or maybe a fleeting memory of the song playing in the waiting room of Northampton's Castle Station when he said goodbye to Sarah as he left for Africa. He needn't have worried:

"*Pitani bwino*, Major!" Juma replied quickly. "*Zikomo!*" His was a cheerful farewell as he briefly returned to his temporary quarters before hurrying back to Majowa. Yes, he wanted to get back to his fields; it was time he saw to the fire-curing of his tobacco crop. Yet getting back to his family loomed even larger in his mind. His wives needed him. Ambikanile was still ill, and

Chotsani, too!…how he missed his new wife! Of course, the youngsters, Mary and Thenga, in whom he delighted as well. As grandparents often do, he felt certain they needed their grandfather to play with them more than any others. So he was indeed happy this latest regimental assignment—though not as short as he had hoped it would be—was at last over!

∞∞∞∞∞∞

His respite was short-lived, however, as a need for further assistance, hinted at by Major Rangely, came much more quickly than Juma would have liked. First, messengers from the *boma* brought a directive to Chief Chikowi—signed not just by the District Commissioner but also by the Governor!—demanding he recruit men for the KAR. At first the Chief appealed to some of the younger war veterans to re-enlist, but many of them made it abundantly clear they had no intention of agreeing to fight again. In fact, one of his *ndunas* was extraordinarily blunt:

"I survived the *chiwaya* war. But I'm no fool. You don't attempt such things again!"

Faced with such marked recalcitrance, Chief Chikowi almost in desperation turned to Juma for assistance, not expecting him to re-enlist, but hoping he might convince others to do so.

No sooner had he offered to assist his Chief, Juma faced an even more urgent call to duty, one which even Chikowi agreed took precedence. Their friend, Levi Mumba called Juma to a similar mission. He'd been directed to organize recruiting tours—*ulendos* as they were commonly known—throughout the nearby districts drawing upon former *asilikali* as agents to attract young men into the KAR ranks. Would Juma join the effort? Governor

Mackenzie-Kennedy, responding to pressure from the Colonial and War Offices, insisted these efforts should employ "every kind of theatricality" short of outright compulsion to muster even more *asilikali* than in the last war. Leading the effort, the KAR band marched through many villages—as they had during the previous conflict—followed by a cinema team stopping to show what at least passed for "patriotic" films. Their appeals to a greater Nyasa identity as part of a British imperial bond seemed a bit strained to Juma, perhaps because of his experiences in actually expanding colonial power. Following the films was when the old soldiers were supposed to come in, supplementing the entertainment with rousing speeches and patriotic appeals for recruits. For Juma, it meant wearing his full dress uniform once again—complete with his medals and even his new cap and badge from the reserves—which now Chotsani dutifully made ready for him.

Juma looked as immaculate and imposing as he had in Mrs. Metcalfe's painting and easily might have stolen the show when the old soldiers were invited forward before the potential recruits. But the featured speeches could be an unexpected and sometimes unpleasant wildcard, as Juma discovered all too soon. For example, during one meeting at Ncheu *boma*, former CSM Neza, whom he barely knew, became so wound-up his appeal devolved into a crass and—at least to Juma, a needlessly bloodthirsty—inducement to service:

"You'll love going into battle!" Neza almost yelled. "It's more exciting than anything I've ever known. I worked a machine-gun in the last war," mimicking the action of firing the weapon. "Men fell in swathes before the spray of bullets." Neza shook his fists in the air in a parody of a victory cheer. "Such a surge of power came over me! I can think of nothing more intoxicating in my entire life!" A few cheers erupted from some of the younger men in the crowd, much to Juma's disgust.

Trying to escape any attention on himself, Juma slipped away from the main group of former *askari* and sought out Levi Mumba, who'd also drifted to the edge of the crowd:

"What is Neza trying to do?" he complained. "Arousing young men to think of killing as glorious will NOT produce good *asilikali*. Nor will it make our lives any better once this latest war is over. I have no desire to continue in such company," he fumed.

"I wouldn't ask you to endorse those sentiments, Juma. But please, please help us!" Mumba pleaded with him. "We must press on, trying to find tenacious and thoughtful recruits for our cause which, I think you'll agree, is a just one." So when it came time for him to speak, Juma walked slowly to the front of the crowd and made a very different appeal:

"Yes, there is excitement at times if you go to war, but that comes with fear as well. Make no mistake. War is hard and not for the faint of heart. And when the fighting is over—if only for a few moments—it is your comrades, your fellow *asilikali*, to whom you'll turn. Who else is there? They alone can help you feel braver than you really are, instill you with the courage to continue. And why do you keep going? It is for those whom you will leave behind. Because choosing to join the KAR now will mean making sure your loved ones will be here so you can return to them when your war is over. That's why I'm asking you to join now, to prevent any enemy from coming here! Oh yes, you'll soon enough have a uniform to impress the girls! And there will be money, too. But those are fleeting, flighty and tattered, or squandered on trifles. Preserving our place and people is why I joined so many years ago. And it's why I call on you to join today. Please help to save our land!"

His speech was met with silence from the crowed. Gradually one or two men made their way to the recruiting sergeants as the KAR band began again, this time playing "God Save the King." As he turned to Levi Mumba with a resigned look on his face, believing his efforts had accomplished little, the distinguished government clerk bade him look again toward the crowd. More and more men were joining the queues in front of the recruiters' tables.

"Yours is the appeal that is genuine. You speak for the needs of the people," Levi Mumba assured him. "Your heartfelt honesty will not be forgotten, I assure you! Please carry on."

One of the final stops on the recruiting tour came at the Thyolo *boma* where, to Juma's surprise, another old soldier joined the entourage: none other than Sergeant Useni Makuta.

"You're a long way from Zomba, my friend!" were Useni's first words, prompting not an explanation from Juma, but instead a query of his own:

"It is good to see you're alive, well, and at home. But why are you here?"

"*Bwana Disi* here in Thyolo knows me as I'm now working as a *capitao* on the very Bandanga Estate where we first met. Since our plantation is so close to the *boma*, the DC asked my estate manager allow me time to help recruit *askari* for this new war." Juma was pleased to see his old compatriot again. Their encounter brought Juma back to what the former Chief Chiowi said, when learning he'd met Useni, something like: "Being his friend may be a part of our future." The thought set Juma to musing about the old Chief's sagacity.

∞∞∞∞∞∞∞

Not long after the recruiting *ulendo* was completed, Mr. Mumba sent word to Juma their efforts were a resounding success! Even more men had agreed to become *asilikali* than in the previous war! So Juma made certain to make his way once again around the mountain to see the first group leave on their way to East Africa. As did so many Nyasaland *asilikali* in this latest war, they left singing:

"We don't know where we're going

"But now we must go away.

"We're sorry we are leaving home."

"You will stay.

"This is war!

"Time of trouble."

"We young men are going away

"To defend Nyasaland and Africa

"Because the enemy is near"

"This is war!

"You will stay.

"Time of trouble."

"We are leaving Nyasaland.

"And if God allows it,

"We will meet in heaven."

Juma found the lyrics both uplifting in spirit, yet also somehow disheartening since he knew too well the realities of war. Mr. Mumba sensed his ambivalence, reminding him there was little he now could do:

"The effort will be theirs, not ours," he assured Juma. "Most are off to East Africa to drive the Italians out of Ethiopia and return Haile Selassie to his throne. Though they are a British army, they will actually be Africans helping Africans!" He was quiet for a moment, then added: "That's a little different than your service in Asante and Somaliland, don't you think?" On reflection, Juma had to agree.

Once his recruiting efforts concluded, Juma's life returned to the new normal he enjoyed after marrying Chotsani. As a tobacco smallholder he was successful. The small plot he carefully cultivated following Native Tobacco Board advice was a model of efficiency, his leaf fetching ever increasing prices. His flourishing enterprise improved his financial standing, while the birth of Njimile and Mtindiso's second child—his second grandson, Titus—buoyed both his spirits and that of his still ailing wife, Ambikanile. Those positives, however, were somewhat negated by news of the war which he followed with anxious intensity. Yes, he was especially proud of the heroism shown by *askari* of his old battalion, 1 KAR, in defending their base at Moyale on Kenya's northern frontier against an immensely larger force of Italians. But the frequent lists of casualties as the war dragged on—even the deaths of some of the very men he had recruited—was a conspicuous counterweight on his mind.

However, nothing—absolutely *nothing*—affected him more profoundly than receiving word Ambikanile had succumbed to the considerable maladies plaguing her for several years. Yes, Chotsani had been taking good care of him and meeting his everyday needs. For that he was grateful. But Ambikanile! Her devotion was different. She had remained faithful during his long deployments. She had born his children, cared for them, and ensured they did not despair of their father's love despite his extended absences. She truly had been a rock and a joy. Now she was gone. His sorrow was honest, open, and heartfelt. Understanding this, Chotsani wisely left him time and space to grieve.

But Mtindiso rushed to his father's side, offering to arrange a "proper" church funeral for his mother, though Juma swiftly rebuffed that idea. Appreciating his son's concern, Juma still preferred the more traditional Yao ways. So he asked Apesile to help prepare her mother's body while he notified Chief Chikowi, and then he arranged for the necessary *awilo*, or burial officials, who would actually carry her body to the place of interment, dig her grave, and attend to other details. While Mtindiso and Njemile weren't entirely comfortable doing so, they acceded to Juma's wishes, participating in the funerary procession and actually assisted Chotsani in preparing food for the many mourners. But they drew a line at participating in the *chindimba* funeral rituals of singing and dancing which continued in the village well into the night. Instead, at Mtindiso's insistence, they left the village early, taking the path 'round the mountain and past the Barracks to their church where they privately offered prayers for his mother's soul. The whole experience—Juma was coming to realize—offered a symbolic blending of the old and new orders of their lives.

Chief Chikowi's absence from the funeral, though, was for Juma a respectful recognition that not everything was changing. He well knew it was unseemly for a Chief to attend a commoner's funeral so he was actually pleased not to meet with Chief Chikowi until several days after the event:

"Is it well with your family?" the Chief inquired, with Juma replying as expected with news that all of them were well, with the children and gardens thriving. Juma was particularly thankful his tobacco operation was by now for the most part in the capable hands of others—some relatives and other carefully selected and trusted employees—easing any immediate burdens. He was continuing, as best he could, to ensure the success of his primary enterprise. Receiving reports several times a week and regularly inspecting the well terraced gardens, he also insisted on supervising the fire curing of the hand-selected leaves.

"My fields are prospering, as am I," he assured the Chief, "though it is disheartening to learn of casualties among the many young men I helped persuade to join in this war. That, too, leaves me with a heavy heart." The Chief took his hands and they commiserated together over the anxieties the second war had brought to their land.

With Nyasaland KAR units increasingly deployed at greater distances from eastern Africa—first to Egypt, then Madagascar and Ceylon, finally even a far-off place now known to them as Burma—many of their apprehensions and anxieties seemed to diminish in corresponding fashion. When at last they could join in celebratory parades with marching bands, fireworks, and even massive bonfires on the hills to mark first VE day and finally VJ day, Juma, all of Majowa, and nearly everyone among Chikowi's people cheered the prospects for a better tomorrow!

Their euphoria lasted almost a year, maybe a little more, as the rains were good and produce was readily available in the markets. Juma's crops brought greater yields and businessmen like Mtindiso continued to do well, especially with returning *asilikali* ready to spend their discharge bonuses on consumer goods such as bicycles. Yet there were glimpses of trouble. On one of his visits to Mtindiso's shop, Juma met a returned solder—Sergeant John Mandwiso—complaining about trying to buy goods from one of the long established stores in Zomba, a major outlet of the African Lakes Company which had been doing business almost from the start of *Angelesi* and especially *Asikotlande* settlement in Nyasaland.

"I went to the Mandala Shop and they didn't want my business!" Mandwiso told Juma. He used the name by which the ALC store was popularly known. "Guards were at the door and wouldn't let me inside to see what I might purchase. 'Go to the back,' they said, 'Ask for your bread there! They will give it to you through the little window.' Only the *Wazungu* are allowed to look for what they want!" Juma was in disbelief:

"You were *msilikali* and they treat you like that!?" Visibly upset, Juma was only able to contain his anger with the assistance of his son. He continued to fume as he left his son's business to seek out his friend Levi Mumba, only to discover on reaching Mumba's Secretariat Office that his friend had only recently taken ill and gone home to Mzimba where, sadly he had recently died. Instead he found Charles Matinga, a clerk from Blantyre who recently arrived from the Southern Province on a temporary secondment. Juma hardly needed to have introduced himself, as clearly Matinga knew of him from conversations with Mumba. But Matinga motioned that they might walk in the nearby gardens for a more private discussion.

After brief personal introductions, Juma launched directly into his immediate concerns: "How can this be true? A Sergeant in the KAR dismissed as if he were a common thief!" Juma remained livid. "Surely our Nyasaland is a better place than that!" He almost seemed to demand a solution from the senior government clerk. Matinga's was a friendly ear, and he didn't hesitate to react as if he had known the retired Sergeant Major for many years:

"Please try to remain calm, my friend. We are—or at least have been—a better place, you are correct. But this new war has changed our lives, much more than your war ever did. These new *asilikali* have seen so much more, both bad and good, and they're now expecting their lives to change, to be better. But the *Wazungu*—especially those who have been here for a long time—simply expect these *asilikali* to come back just the same, as if they know nothing else, simply returning to their homes and fields just as before. Yours was a great adjustment, my friend, as I well know. After this latest war, how much harder will it be for all of us to find our way in a new Nyasaland?"

This was a far more pessimistic prognosis then Juma expected. His own return from the last war and his post-war duties in Tabora were troublesome enough, but he also felt his possibilities had been decidedly more promising. Then it hit him. What they were facing now must just be the "time of trouble" the young *asilikali* sang about as they left for war! Even if they didn't have precisely the prescience to know exactly what they would be facing, this was their new reality—and it was his as well! What difficulties might it present for him and his family? Just how, he wondered, might he manage to navigate through it?

∞∞∞∞∞∞

Juma was only beginning to entrust his concerns such as these to Chotsani when one evening, after they'd been talking about their new Nyasaland for what must have been several hours, extraordinarily loud thunderclaps quite nearby startled them both. Then the rain began and didn't stop at all during the night. Even the next day the deluge not only continued, but became more intense and insistent. It was more rain than Juma could remember since he was at war in East Africa—well, he couldn't actually remember when—but it was filling up all the streams and every other possible, even if unlikely, watercourse near Majowa. At one point in the afternoon he heard what at first he thought must have been thunder in the distance. But the "Bwoosh" he heard sounded almost like explosions of heavy artillery preparing for an offensive, just as he remembered from his great war. But how could that be:

"What is that?" Chotsani asked, but he had to admit he had no idea. Clearly frightened, she meekly offered an explanation likely reflecting more alarm than erudition:

"*Napolo?*" It sounded to Juma as more a question than an assertion. He had not thought much about the story for many years, of the great snake living in a fissure underneath the mountain. *Napolo* was the same creature invoked in explaining the earthquake just before Juma agreed to become an *msilikali*. But if the specter of that serpent were a factor in this latest downpour, the distant rumblings he heard must be a sign of some greater danger than merely the torrential rain. Though he knew it would be an unpleasant journey, he was determined to make his way around the mountain at least to the KAR Barracks where he knew someone could tell him what might be happening.

The path from Majowa was nothing less than treacherous, even more difficult than he'd imagined. Slick from the rain, it was actually washed away in a few places, with large boulders and massive tree trunks blocking his way at other points. As he came upon one newly formed gully near Nitya village, he could hear wailings from below the road.

"*Pokola!*" First a hearty male voice, calling for help. But that was not all; again:

"*Pokola!*" This time a woman, or perhaps a child. The multiple pleas for assistance were distressing. At first it was hard for him to imagine what might have happened. No longer as nimble as he once was, Juma made his way down the washed out hillside trying to find the people whose voices he was hearing. It was clear many of the small houses had been swept away, although one or two were smashed by disloged rocks and a couple of others twisted against large trees. In the first one he came upon he found a young girl, hurt but alive and not unexpectedly sobbing. As he carried her out, several *asilikali* approached who had come from the opposite direction. The Barracks were spared the worst of the devastation, they quickly explained, and their officers sent them out to help anyone they might. After Juma joined a group of the soldiers, each carrying or supporting one of the surviving villagers, he suggested they move them to the relative safety of the Barracks before returning to what was left of the village.

A young Lieutenant recognized the now well retired Sergeant Major and welcomed them, praising the *asilikali* for their actions—including Juma for his continuing devotion to duty—and reassuring survivors they would be cared for. Then he took Juma aside for just a moment:

"*Sajini*, I fear many from Nitya village have lost their lives. I know you have seen such horrors in war. Would you kindly lead a few of these young *asilikali* back below the village seeing if you might find bodies of some who did not survive?" It wasn't at all what Juma was thinking about when he left Majowa, yet he knew this was what he now must do. With so many men just having returned from Burma and on leave, the KAR battalion was bound to be short-handed. It didn't at all feel like an order, in any case. It was just what he might do to help. So he did. In all, the *asilikali* accompanying him found fifteen bodies of villagers who died in the disaster. Later he learned there were seven other fatalities, all but one from the same village. And most of the bridges and culverts in Zomba town were destroyed, though many of the old buildings were almost miraculously still standing, even though many were damaged.

He decided to find out what had happened to cause this, even though he knew Chotsani and many others would be hard pressed to accept any other explanation beyond the vicissitudes of *Napolo,* whose existence was fixed in their minds. A week after the disaster, he went back to the KAR *boma* and, using the pretext of checking on some of the survivors he had helped rescue, made some further inquiries.

"A tropical cyclone from the Indian Ocean," the Battalion Adjutant told him. Juma wasn't certain, but it sounded much like the storm he'd sailed through on the British-India steamer *Dwarka* coming back from his first tour in East Africa, before his war. "Damnedest thing," the Adjutant went on. "Blew right past Madagascar and for some crazy reason didn't turn into the Mozambique Channel." That's where Juma remembered his encounter with a tropical cyclone took place. "Went straight across Portuguese East and made a beeline for Zomba. Never heard of anything like it before," he concluded. "All that's left is to clean everything up, I guess!" Juma was correct; Chotsani didn't give much credence to that explanation. If it hadn't been for his previous experience Juma, too, might have thought it was just a silly *Angelesi* story!

∞∞∞∞∞∞

Juma later confirmed with Chief Chikowi that the flood was not nearly such a calamity in the rest of his lands. Relieved, Juma turned their discussion to the concerns troubling him just before being diverted by the disaster. Juma relayed his discussions with Sergeant Mandwiso and with his new acquaintance, Mr. Matinga, whom he discovered was also well known to the Chief.

"If this truly is a new reality, what can we do to find our place in this world?" Juma wondered aloud to Chief Chikowi. "The charge given me by your predecessor so long ago—and which you've recently affirmed—was to remain true as a Yao while also serving the *Angelesi*, seeking a means of preserving ourselves amidst the ever-increasing powers which encompass us. I have tried to do so, but if Mr. Mumba was correct, perhaps that way is now lost. We may instead have found ourselves in a time of troubles." Chief Chikowi could read the concern in Juma's eyes and also detected it in the timber of his voice. He didn't exactly want to disagree, but did wish to convey a strong element of doubt. Therefore he chose his response very carefully:

"*Kwaliko*," was the word he used in *Chiyao*, knowing Juma would understand that, while saying perhaps he was right, the Chief held some significant reservations. He then began to explain:

"You will know, of course, that even before this second war had ended, the *boma* created several Provincial Councils—even an African Protectorate Council—to better understand ideas held by the African peoples of Nyasaland, primarily voiced through their Chiefs. Of course, all of us called to these meetings have been circumspect in expressing our concerns officially." As he paused briefly, he could see Juma rolling his eyes just a bit as if in disbelief. "But," the Chief hesitated, wanting Juma to recognize his shift in emphasis, "our meetings have given us a chance to talk privately among ourselves as well…Yao, Chewa, Ngoni, Tonga and other leaders of our peoples. That is when we have discovered how much we agree about—what was it you called it, this new 'time of troubles'?—in which we find ourselves." Juma could scarcely believe that perhaps he had found a friendly ear for his concerns. Chief Chikowi continued:

"We know—virtually all of us—that there is much we have learned and gained from our associations with the *Wasungu* who have come to our lands. But we also know it would be folly to follow blindly every European idea or adopt everything the Europeans taught us. I'm sure you'd agree, we must also have respect for what our peoples have practiced and our own many achievements. As Chiefs of our peoples, we think it's also a time for a revival of our quality of African life!" The two men exchange smiles indicating a sense of mutual agreement. "But of course we must do so carefully," the Chief concluded, prompting Juma to add:

"We can't follow the example of Che Tungawe, right!" Almost immediately both of them broke into uproarious laughter as they recalled a well-known Yao folktale:

Once upon a time, there was a farmer who was bedeviled by a troop of baboons stealing his crops. So he promised to pay a well-respected wizard to rid his fields of the troublesome creatures. One night shortly thereafter, all the baboons suddenly disappeared, and the farmer prepared to pay the wizard. But his nosey and overbearing neighbour, Che Tungawe, insisted the farmer make a sizeable over-payment to the wizard as a symbol of gratitude. But the wizard—angry at the farmer for not following his instructions precisely—instead of being grateful, punished the farmer by sending even more baboons to ravage his fields.

Their mirthful demeanor wasn't founded in any disbelief. Far from it! In fact, they shared a widely held Yao sentiment in the power of wizardry—*usaŵi*, as they would have called it—but their amusement arose from their simultaneous appreciation of the import they both recognized in the tale: "A man can't serve two masters!" It was one of the basic stories of virtue they heard as children and which was imbued in their consciousness following the initiation instruction both had received as very young men.

"And so," Juma added after reflecting on their conversation, "We must advance our cause slowly and deliberately." It was much the same approach he had found valuable as an *msilikali*.

∞∞∞∞∞∞∞

Any notions either of them might have had about springing into action, however, were soon sidetracked as a new food crisis gripped not only the Zomba district but much of the Shire Highlands. Two years after the Zomba flood came the year of the locusts, followed by complete failure of the rains the next. The resulting environmental emergency was by far the greatest since Juma had returned from his postwar assignment in Tabora. With prices paid for tobacco, especially, steadily increasing during the latest war, Juma and many others had turned away from maize, sorghum, and even cassava to fill their grain stores. Instead they counted on buying food in the markets as did clerks, artisans, and tradesmen, such as Mtindiso. But with little to buy, prices skyrocketed. Even the attempts made by the *boma* to import maize seemed to have little effect; those prices too quickly went beyond the reach of many, including Juma and his family.

"What am I to do?" Juma complained to Chief Chikowi. "Not only are prices for food too great for me to pay, when there are more than two of us queuing at a stall to purchase what little we can, the sellers raise the price even as we are standing there! Something must be done!" he pleaded.

"There is little in my power," Chief Chikowi opined, knowing not only the District Commissioner but also the Governor had been trying to import food for sale at fixed prices in the markets. "I certainly object to greedy profiteering among my people! But I shall try again. Perhaps *Bwana Disi* will send *capitaos* to each of our local marketplaces to make sure those selling grain only ask fair prices for what they have to offer. But as you know, there are far too few such officers available to police every transaction. If I could send you to do so, I would. But…" His voice tapered off. Juma knew the Chief despaired about his capacity—even though recognized as a Native Authority by the *boma*—to right every injustice he saw afflicting his people.

As the famine intensified, there was a good deal of desperation in Majowa. Many plants seldom used as food—at least not since the great famine following the *chiwaya* war—became staples in otherwise inadequate diets. One day Juma saw Chitsulo hard at work on the edge of a banana patch, wondering what he could be doing.

"Digging up the roots of these bananas, of course," was his son-in-law's matter-of-fact explanation. "I will dry them in a spot of full sun, give them to Apesile, and she'll pound them into flour. Then we will at least have something to eat!" Juma grieved at the obvious level of desperation which had reached his own family. At least, he thought, Chitsulo hadn't traveled to Mulanje as had so many other men, working for a few measly cassava roots to feed their families. But there was another alternative which occurred to him:

"Why not go around to the Barracks and enlist?" Juma asked his son-in-law. "The KAR is seeking more men to go to Malaya in an effort to put down a local rebellion there against the *Angelesi*. Now they'll pay even more than they did soldiers in the last war!" It seemed a natural alternative to him, as had his own decision to join the KAR Reserves during the last famine.

"Malaya?" Chitsulo seemed incredulous.

"Somewhere near Burma, I think, where the KAR fought in the most recent war."

"Why would I want to go there?" Juma wasn't surprised with Chitsulo's reluctance, causing him to think about Ambikanile's relief when Mtindiso had chosen not to follow his father as an *msilikali*. So Juma continued, without thinking carefully about his words:

"I'll promise to take care of Apesile and Thenga while you're gone!" Oh no, he thought. I've made matters worse. So he tried again: "Don't fret about any fighting! This won't be a real war. It'll be much more like my first campaign against Chief Serumba at Lake Chilwa—so Apesile needn't worry!" Juma could tell from the look of disbelief on Chitsulo's face his effort might well have been a mistake!

So he was surprised just a few days later when his daughter, son-in-law, and grandson came for a visit, announcing that indeed, Chitsulo would be going to enlist as an *msilikali*! But as Juma congratulated him and renewed his pledge to take care of his wife and child, he also detected a note of consternation on Chotsani's face. He knew she, too, had been struggling to find enough food for even the two of them. In recent weeks often all his wife was able to prepare for their meals were some wild yams, grasses barely fit to eat, and a few fruits she'd been able to forage. And he simply couldn't salvage any more tobacco from his withering fields to sell in an effort to buy food, even if there were any affordable supplies of grain and other commodities available for sale in the markets. He knew that when the few district *capitaos* were on duty enforcing price controls, all too often there was nothing to purchase. Moreover, even if there were enough rain in the future, the Native Tobacco Board was now enforcing a ban on smallholders growing leaf for sale, insisting instead that they produce maize and other food crops.

Juma didn't want to disappoint another wife by even suggesting he go to Mulanje for work. Nor did he want to let his daughter down after promising to care for her and his grandson. Recalling what he had done before, he hatched another plan! This time he knew there would be nothing for him at the Barracks, although perhaps he might look elsewhere for an opportunity to put his skills to use. So he asked Chotsani to prepare his dress uniform—complete with all his medals—including the new socks and boots he'd been issued and seldom worn. He wanted to look his very best as an *asilikali*! Donning the full kit, he set out early on a journey—this time not around the mountain but to the west, toward the big river—though his destination was only to the sub-district *boma* at Chingale. Word had reached Juma a new *Bwana Disi* was on his way there and would no doubt be looking for district messengers. He certainly would be just the man for such a job!

Arriving soon after dawn at the very small sub-district office itself, Juma stood as erect as he could facing Bwana Calder Robinson, who himself had only just finished his first cup of morning tea:

"Sir, I have come for a position in your esteemed office! As a veteran of the KAR I know that I can be of help to you." Juma saluted smartly even though he knew the gesture wasn't truly necessary. Robinson, taken aback by the visage of such an impressive figure obviously from the Protectorate's past, inquired further about this imposing man. Juma described not only his service—though Robinson himself quickly noted the Distinguished Conduct Medal proudly pinned to his chest—but also his unfortunate present circumstances. The initial response was far less than Juma hoped for:

"I very much regret that I have no authorized vacancies in my staff," were the first words Robinson spoke as Juma finished the disquisition he had practiced on his journey to the small outpost. Expecting the old veteran to be downcast, ADC Calder Robinson was instead greatly impressed with Juma's respectful and almost reverential reply:

"I understand, sir! Thank you for considering my request. I would not wish to displace any of your trusted staff. It is my sincere hope we may have cause to meet again! *Zikomo kwambiri!*"

It was that the final warm thanks which especially touched Robinson, whose young wife, Myra, had come across from their cottage to see who had called so early. Overhearing the final bit of conversation, she whispered in Calder's ear, "Is there nothing you can do, my dear?" Though not a remonstrance, his wife's concern prompted Robinson to think of the small discretionary budget available to him, specifically for district agricultural duties, so he quickly called out as Juma turned sharply to take his leave:

"Sergeant Major!" Juma turned back to Robinson. "Perhaps I could add you as a sort of Head Messenger to assist me with a variety of special tasks! The salary would not be much." At that, a broad smile overtook Juma's face. Then Robinson asked simply, "You did mention you have a wife?" Juma replied in the affirmative. "There is one more junior staff house available—I'm sorry, but it's an old one—though the two of you might have use of it." Robinson assumed a man of Juma's age wouldn't have children at home. "Would you be willing to join us on such a basis?" Now a palpable sense of relief was easily visible in Juma's already proudly filled-out uniform:

"Indeed sir!" He almost needn't have added, "*Lero ndi tsiku losangalala,*" which Calder slightly mistranslated for his wife. "He says it's the happiest day of his life," causing her to smile in return, feeling as though she had done something positive in support of her husband's charge to care for the people of his district. As he later confessed to her, he primarily hoped the old *msilikali's* self-assurance would lend a significant measure of prestige to the sub-district's establishment. He had explained the situation a little differently to Juma, however:

"Strictly speaking, yours will be a supernumerary position," prompting a quizzical look from the Sergeant Major. How to explain an English bureaucratic term for someone in excess of the usual number of staff yet employed for other significant tasks? Simply being an extra messenger wasn't exactly right; the ADC wanted Juma to understand there was something special he was hoping Juma's presence would bring to the office. Finally Robinson hit on a word in *Chichewa*: *"Zozizwitsa."* That brought an expression of true joy to Juma's face:

"Kwenikweni!" Juma responded, though saying he now knew exactly what the Robinson meant was most likely based more on each's rudimentary knowledge of the other's language, Juma almost certainly understood his new superior describing the position offered as nothing less than a "miracle," which it surely seemed to Juma! They happily bade each other farewell, with Juma hurrying back to Majwoa with the good news, asking Chotsani to make preparations for their move to Chingale as soon as possible. Her pleased reaction, however, was a marked counterpoint to those of Mtindiso and Apesile, even though both his children understood the importance their father put on this new venture.

∞∞∞∞∞∞

Chotsani understood her husband's desire to move as quickly as possible, hurrying to make sure all their essential belongings would be ready within a few days. In doing so, she came across the carbine rifle and ammunition which Juma had been keeping in a safe place, wondering what she should do with them:

"Are we to take this to your new position as well?" Juma didn't hesitate in his response:

"*Ngawa*! I must not keep this, but return it to the armoury sergeant before we go. I'll no longer have need of it, and Bwana Lobisani would not wish his Head Messenger to be carrying a gun!" So before the day was out, Juma once more made the trek around the mountain to the Barracks where he returned the carbine and ammunition. He also made time to drop by the Secretariat Office where he had met Mr. Matinga, finding his new friend also preparing for a move, back to the Southern Province Commissioner's Office in Blantyre.

"We shall once again be far from each other!" Juma's tone was clearly sorrowful as he responded to his new friend's news. "You will once again be in Blantyre, while I will be in Chingale." Describing his new duties, though, left Matinga very impressed with the full import of Juma's news:

"Perhaps, but I feel certain our paths will cross again." After a short pause he added, "And it likely will not be long indeed!" Completing their goodbyes, Juma returned to Majowa expecting to be off to Chingale with Chotsani in only a day or too. And when they finally did arrive at Chingale—a day later than Juma had hoped—ADC Robinson and his wife welcomed them to the small square in front of the *boma* proper:

"We have been expecting you," Myra Robinson said as she moved to help Chotsani toward the old staff house which she had attempted to tidy-up slightly in expectation of its new occupants. Much more businesslike, Calder Robinson, asked Juma to come into the small office:

"Juma, *Bwana Disi* in Zomba tells me that by special permission of the KAR Commandant you have a rifle. I am sorry, but must..." he couldn't finish his sentence before Juma, slightly embarrassed for doing so, interrupted him:

"*Ayi, Bwana*!" choosing the *Chichewa* interjection, he immediately wanted his new superior to know, and in no uncertain terms, he no longer possessed the firearm, telling him it was safely back in possession of the KAR armoury. "I know that none of your messengers carry guns. So I would not want to set a bad example for any of them! And I wanted to be ready to begin work as soon as I arrived!"

"That is fine, Juma," Robinson told him with a relieved smile; "We needn't start work today. Please go prepare your quarters! There will be time enough tomorrow for you to join me on our first *ulendo* together. Of course, I would hope you might wear your uniform on our rounds!"

Indeed, for more than a fortnight Juma set out with ADC Robinson and at least two other messengers almost every other day, generally following one side or the other of the Shire River tributary flowing by Chingale. Not that they seemed to carry any messages! Nor did they collect taxes or apprehend any miscreants. Their treks seemed more like pleasure junkets, greeting minor local officials, greeting farmers in their fields, or smiling and waving to women collecting wood or berries. Juma began to wonder what could be so important or difficult to this work. He was becoming increasingly curious: Why was it a job at all? Finally he asked Dauda Linyama, one of his more friendly colleagues:

"What is it we are actually doing by going out on these *ulendos*?" At first he didn't understand the answer:

"Getting to know the land and letting the people get to know us," was all Dauda said. But as Juma asked him further questions, the answers started to become clearer. "The *bwana* looks carefully at all the fields. Every evening or the next day he draws pictures of them. And he also wants to make sure all the people get to see that you—a retired *msilikali* who's had much experience—are one of us." Juma looked puzzled. "Once all the pictures are down he will take you with us to mark the fields and have all the farmers hoe them again, exactly as we mark them. That's the new *malimidwe* for all the fields." Juma had heard the word but was uncertain exactly what it was. "The Bwana's hoping if you are with us no one will object very much!" Juma could hardly believe this, so he at last asked Robinson to explain it to him.

"Yes, Juma, the Governor has told us—me, you, all of us who work for the *boma*—to do exactly that." Robinson continued, making it clear, "We must enforce these new conservation rules: *malimidwe*. It is a plan to keep more water on the fields and prevent too much soil from flowing down to the big river. But it is a great deal of extra work for the farmers, and they don't appreciate being told to do it. At the same time, the Governor has also told us we should not compel people to do this, even though he expects us to be sure that it is done!"

"So as an old *asilikali* you expect me to make them do this?" Juma wanted to know.

"Well, not exactly, Juma. I'll not ask you to force anyone to do so. But you are such a respected man, one whom people know was a brave *msilikali*! I am hoping when people see you are with us they will be—how shall I say this?—perhaps they will be more willing to comply with the new rules." Then Robinson changed the subject abruptly.

∞∞∞∞∞∞

"You recall, Juma, I told you there would be a variety of tasks I might ask of you. There is another—not *malimidwe*, at least for the moment—which I think would be equal to your vast experience! The new KAR Commander, with the Governor's blessing, has decided to sponsor a new Boy Scout Troop at the KAR Barracks. He has called for suggestions and volunteers to lead these activities for boys of this district, and I would like to suggest your name, hoping you would be willing to volunteer! Well, I would make that part of your official duties, of course." Was it shock, amazement, fear or trepidation that overcame the Sergeant Major? Robinson couldn't decide, but then Juma spoke:

"Sir. I have heard of these Boy Scouts before. But they are for *Wazungu* lads. Surely I am not the one to lead them."

"Ah, Juma, I understand. This is the first Boy Scout troop in all of Nyasaland which will be open to every boy—European, African, even Asian—and we hope many will join. I was a Boy Scout in my youth; it was a very positive experience in my life. I particularly recall one of the ten basic principles of scouting as set out by General Baden-Powell who founded the movement:

"A Scout is a friend to all and a brother to every other Scout, no matter to what social class the other belongs."

"We believe—all of us, the Commandant, the Governor, Captain Braxley who will be the Scoutmaster of the KAR troop, and myself—that this means we shouldn't merely *invite* boys to join, but to seek out *all* boys and set an example by having an African as Assistant Scoutmaster! Who better to do this than *you*!" Juma shook his head in disbelief, pointing to his chest in wonderment.

Then Robinson asked simply, "Haven't you commanded Europeans, even in battle, Sergeant Major?" Juma had to concede that was true. "And you know this land, especially all around this magnificent mountain, better than all of us. Who better to share this knowledge with boys of all sorts than you?"

"Sir! This is an order, sir?" Juma asked just as he would have had ADC Robinson been a KAR officer.

"No, Juma. It is not an order. But I hope you will agree to do this as a gesture showing how much we all hope to change Nyasaland for the better." Juma thought first of the *malimidwe* he had just been discussing with ADC Robinson. Quickly, though, the charge he had been given by former Chief Chikowi years before overcame him. He hoped agreeing to this assignment now would be a way to help fulfill the promise he had made then.

On first being introduced to Captain Braxley, Juma realized he was the now-promoted young Lieutenant he encountered at the time of the great flood. This second meeting went so well that the entire Boy Scouts idea seemed to gel in Juma's mind, particularly as the young officer reminded him so much of Wellington Rangely, whom he had not seen since the second war was finally concluded. Juma's excitement about these Scouts even led him to ask Mtindiso's permission for Titus to join, though he would be one of the younger members. Several boys from the Barracks—two or three sons of officers as well as several whose fathers were *asilikali*—were soon enrolled. A son of one of the prominent Indian shopkeepers also agreed, though Juma wondered if it only was because his father was insistent. Among the most enthusiastic recruits may have been three sons of local missionaries. The entire group met just once a week, although Juma and the Captain conferred one other day in between meetings to plan activities. At first language was a bit of a problem, but gradually between *Chichewa* and English the generally eager youngsters gradually came together as a group. Juma's commitment largely focused on leading hikes in the vicinity of the mountain and telling them about vegetation, animal life, and a little history. At one point Captain Braxley even shared with the boys that their Assistant Scoutmaster was once known as *Sajini Nanyula*, cementing that nickname in the minds of those Scouts forever!

With all the troop activities, plus travel to and from Chingale, Juma was away from his official duty station almost half of the time. Chotsani was very understanding, seeing how pleased her husband was when engaged in this latest pursuit. But she did ask him:

"Won't *Bwana Lobosoni* be angry with you for missing so much of his work?" Juma wondered too, but always seemed to receive support from the ADC for his engagement with the scouts. Even when he asked for permission to be gone nearly an entire week for a hike to the top of Zomba Mountain on a camping expedition with the troop, Robinson readily gave his blessing to his Head Messenger, only asking:

"Will you lead them up the Potato Path?"

"Of course!" was the confident reply, as Juma knew well the commercial track which farmers and their agents used to bring produce from fields on top of the mountain to markets in town.

Indeed, the Scout Troop began their mountaintop adventure climbing that very track to the top of the mountain. Despite his aging legs, Juma felt exhilarated as he showed the boys up the crude pathway: how to select carefully each spot to place their feet so they could avoid slipping on rocks occasionally wet from a tiny stream; which branches were safe and strong enough to grasp for added leverage; and when to jump from one ledge to another while also knowing when to avoid such risks. Though he didn't climb as fast as some of them probably could have, none seemed to mind the pace he set as it allowed him to offer lessons about the mountain while they made their way to the top of the plateau. When they at last came to a meadow near Mulunguzi Dam, Captain Braxley—who had been following at the rear of the column just in case any of the boys needed assistance—chose a flat, dry area to pitch their tents and an adjacent spot for a campfire. The boys went out in search of firewood, returning to make first a cooking fire and then a large, controlled bonfire around which they gathered to talk about their experience.

In the next days, the entire troop explored the extent of the plateau, starting just to the northeast of their initial campsite, where they could look across the plain to Lake Chilwa, smaller than it once was. Juma explained the important role the lake played in feeding the town. First he mentioned the lakeside fisherman and then the bicycling fishmongers who, from the plateau, were just barely visible on the path between lake and town. Titus chipped in with the story of how his father supplied and also repaired the bicycles vital in that enterprise. Then, the group followed a well-worn trail further to the northeast, where they could look down on Zomba town itself with an even better view to the southeast of the even larger Mulanje Massif. Captain Braxley explained to the scouts about the ecological importance of Mulanje as an ideal environment for tea production, while Najeer proudly told his fellow scouts about the varieties of local teas found in his father's shop. Their path continued near the edge of the escarpment, bypassing Mulunguzi Swamp and heading to a forestry clearing where they made their second camp, again revisiting the day's discoveries by a campfire. The next day's hike was probably their longest, taking the troop first north and then west to another forestry encampment where they again pitched their tents, this time just a bit before sunset. Their view north, across the Domasi Valley, was spectacularly lit by rays of the setting sun peeking through wispy clouds, inspiring oohs and ahs from everyone as they waited for what they hoped would be a beautiful African sunset. The clouds cleared just enough so they were not disappointed. During their campfire that evening, their Scoutmaster pronounced it the most awe-inspiring sunset he had ever seen and Juma—whose experience included more sunsets than any of the rest—didn't disagree.

Another long trek the next day took them west, where they had a panoramic view of the Shire River—looking like the highway which had originally brought Scottish missionaries in the wake of Dr. Livingstone's explorations—a story Donald, whose grandfather had been one of them, happily retold everyone. As darkness fell on that fourth day of their journey atop Zomba Mountain, they were approaching Chingwe's Hole when the two leaders called a halt, promising the scouts a visit to the famous site the next day. Though both Juma and Captain Braxley had prepared them to understand the many legends surrounding this seemingly bottomless pit, the stories made for fascinating campfire chatter. That evening reminded Juma of the visit he had made there with Mtindiso, when he had been about the age of these scouts. Their Assistant Scoutmaster was determined to help these boys learn the same lesson he had imparted to his own son. The entire troop anxiously awoke at dawn, eagerly ate breakfast—and not-so-eagerly tidied-up the camp—then hiked toward what was to be a highlight of the trip, Chingwe's Hole itself. The troop hiked to within about thirty yards of the entrance, stopping as a group, awaiting a chance to explore the mystery. Their leaders invited each boy in turn to advance to the very edge, throw a stone into the hole, every time listening for the inevitable "thud" as it found the bottom. None of the mysterious legends confirmed, both the European Scoutmaster and his African Assistant echoed what Juma told his own son years before: "Listen to the stories, but test the reality for yourself!"

The weary troop moved on to a forest clearing near Williams Falls where the Mulunguzi River begins its cascade down the mountain to Zomba town, and all of them were content to make camp for the last time rather than rushing their descent from the idyllic and nearly perfect plateau. All the lads, and their leaders, were quietly contemplative and considerably less chatty during their final campfire. Every one of them—perhaps none more so than *Sajini Nanyula!*—rested well having completed an extraordinary adventure they all hoped, in their own ways, foreshadowed a better understanding of how common experience might build a more vibrant new Nyasaland.

∞∞∞∞∞

With all the boys safely returned to their parents, the tents and other supplies secured in their storage hut, Juma said goodbye to Captain Braxley with the understanding the Cobbe Barracks Boy Scout troop would take a few weeks respite before convening again. Juma took a few moments to stop by the Secretariat Building before beginning his journey to Chingale. Though his friends—Levi Mumba, now deceased, and Charles Matinga—no longer worked there, he had several other acquaintances among the slightly more junior clerks his friends had introduced to him.

Juma was glad he made the stop as one of them, McKinley Chibambo, was especially anxious to alert him that—while he was away with the Boy Scouts—the British Parliament had voted to force Nyasaland into a federation with Northern and Southern Rhodesia. Juma knew Mumba, Matinga, and their protégé Chibambo had long feared such a plan and even Chief Chikowi worried any federation with the Rhodesias would prove detrimental to the position of Africans in the Protectorate. Juma understood their arguments and did not disagree, but hoped still there might be a way to satisfy everyone who lived in their beautiful land.

This conundrum troubled him during his entire journey back to Chingale. He first greeted Chotsani, but immediately went to *Bwana Lobosoni*'s small office. All the ADC wanted to talk about was the Boy Scout trip. Juma answered all his questions:

Yes, the boys got along well. They visited the entire plateau. Their nightly campfires gave everyone a chance to talk, gradually getting to know one another. They managed to cook food for themselves which everyone ate. And they helped the boys learn about the myths of Chingwe's Hole. There were other questions, too, which seemed to fade in his memory as that was not the conversation Juma wanted to have with his employer:

"Sir," he asked frankly, "Is it true there will be no more Nyasaland? Are we instead to be a Federation together with Rhodesia?" It didn't seem as though Calder Robinson was at all pleased to be facing such a blunt question from a member of his African staff.

"First, there still will be a Nyasaland and, I hope, it will still be like the one you and the boys experienced this past week. But no doubt there will be some differences." Juma wanted to know what those might be:

"I certainly hope an end to *malimidwe* will be one of the differences!" Juma confessed.

"Sorry to disappoint you, Sergeant Major. In fact, I was glad to see you back with us fulltime as I truly am hopeful you can help us in implementing these new agricultural rules. I've been reduced to chivvying owners of local gardens to begin work on those projects. I certainly hope you understand doing so can only improve agricultural production in this country, of both food and export crops. You were a tobacco farmer, didn't you tell me?"

"Yes sir!" Juma replied. "I did get help from the agricultural department before I began planting, but that was before *malimidwe*. By using their suggestions along with the farming wisdom I learned from my father and uncles, I made a success of my small plot. I even managed to keep the earth from washing away in the rains! Until, that is, the *boma* told me I could not produce leaf for sale anymore." It was the same story he had told Robinson on their first meeting.

"Indeed, a hard decision for the Tobacco Board, but it is true we must encourage people to produce more of their own food. But I do hope with your own agricultural success you might help persuade some of the reluctant farmers in this district to assist with the new plans for their fields. And," Robinson was quick to reassure Juma, "as I told you before beginning work with the Boy Scouts for a while, I do not expect you to force anyone to comply. My hope is that you will help us win the farmers over to this sensible new approach." Juma didn't speak in reply, but his downcast eyes must have indicated his doubts. His only promise was to make an effort.

Indeed, the next day Juma joined the ADC and the entire team on *ulendo,* beginning work on terracing of a new section of the sub-district. The local Manganja farmers were dismayed as agricultural *capitaos* marked appropriate ridgelines about three feet apart following the natural contours of the land, then about every six feet indicated where transverse closure ridges should also to be constructed. The farmers were instructed to begin making the changes. None of the agricultural staff stepped in to help, presumably moving on to another field. It was left to Robinson and his messengers to encourage the local farmers to put their *makasu* to work hoeing the dirt into place, sometimes chiding them to work more quickly and also chastising those who didn't follow the instruction marks. Almost alone among those from the *boma,* Juma began walking among the farmers, talking with them in friendly tones, recounting his own experiences:

"You must keep the soil from going away down to the river," he tried to tell them. "You won't be able to grow anything if the good earth is gone away!" But when they asked if he made the same ridges they were being told to make, he had to admit he did not. "But I did connect the mounds of my tobacco with small trenches so the rain wouldn't take so much soil with it." Many of the local men complained, though, that what they were expected to do disrupted the *chiswe,* as they called the ubiquitous termites found throughout their fields, causing further problems. One farmer made the case:

"If we destroy their *chulu,* the termites will move to another part of the garden and starting building a new mound. Then they will disrupt the new crops we plant. *Chiswe chimaononga chimanga.*" That the termites would destroy their maize, Juma understood, and was not surprised when another farmer chimed in:

"We will actually be able to grow less. It is better we live with the termites where they are rather than encouraging them to move around and make bigger troubles for us!" Their concerns captured his sympathies:

"*Inde!*" Juma emphatically agreed! In his own fields Juma left the termite mounds alone, connecting his own tobacco mounds around them. As he thought about it further, it struck him the termite mounds actually absorbed the rain. That would prevent erosion, wouldn't it? And wouldn't that send the rainwater to the crops all around the mounds? The more he thought about it, the less inclined he was to continue any efforts to persuade the farmers that all the extra effort in the name of *malimidwe* was worth it.

Bwana Lobosoni took notice of the change in his approach as well. Any persuasive powers he anticipated Juma's presence might bring were instead delivering diminishing results among the Manganga farmers. And as an officer of the British administration, he knew that would redound to his detriment. When they were back from *ulendo* he summoned Juma into his office:

"As you know, the farmers do not seem to accept your exhortations and encouragement of the new agricultural rules. Perhaps I was wrong to expect more of your presence on our *ulendos*. How am I going to be able to continue your employment as a supernumerary Head Messenger?" It was clear *Bwana Lobonsoni* was unhappy, but Juma thought he could explain:

"Sir. The farmers don't see *malimidwe* as an improvement." He tried to explain about the termites. Robinson was having none of it:

"Whatever do you mean? Termites are nothing more than pests! That is the silliest and sorriest excuse for refusing to comply with sensible modern farming methods I've ever heard of! And to think I thought you, of all people, a decorated war hero, might actually help? What am I to do with you?" Juma hadn't heard such a dressing down addressed directly to him since he first began *askari* training! But he did want to keep his job, so he made a counter-offer:

"I could continue with the Boy Scouts, Sir! I believe that has worked out very well!" Robinson conceded that was likely true, but no matter:

"I am paying you to work with us implementing these new agricultural rules. If the KAR want you to continue with the Boy Scouts, they will need to arrange it with you. I simply do not believe I can continue with you here at Chingale on your present terms of service. Of course you and Chotsani may take a week to vacate your house, and I will pay you until then. I do wish you well, and I'm sorry it has come to this."

∞∞∞∞∞∞

After their return to Majowa, Juma soon was able to meet with Chief Chikowi who expressed no surprise at all about Juma's situation. He, too, had been hearing complaints concerning *malimidwe* from almost all of his people. He told Juma that almost all the chiefs of "*dziko la Nyasaland*"—clearly implying a new political unity of all the peoples who spoke the great variety of languages heard in the Protectorate—had already met in Lilongwe and sent a delegation to meet the new Queen hoping to convince her to stop plans for the recently announced Federation even though, they'd been told, the new political arrangement was already fully approved.

"They will remind her that many men, just like you, fought to protect her country. Then they will ask her to protect ours!" Chikowi also told Juma the Nyasaland African Congress—the political movement started by their friend Levi Mumba—was quickly gaining support, but its leaders nonetheless were pessimistic about the success of the Chiefs' mission. Even more than food and family, such matters dominated the thoughts of both men for several months. When they learned the delegation on which they had placed their hopes had been refused an audience with the Queen, both were despondent. Their disappointment was widely shared throughout Nyasaland, and soon the well-known Chewa Chief Mwasi was chosen to lead a new Supreme Council uniting all the Nyasa Chiefs with leaders of the more overtly political Congress.

"I myself nominated Mwasi to be leader of our Chiefs Council, and he was elected unanimously," Chief Chikowi proudly told Juma. "Perhaps he may help the new Council bring some hopeful resolution of our problems." Only a month later, though, Chief Mwasi and the new Council made a determined call for all Africans in Nyasaland to cease cooperating with the government: no *malimidwe,* no taxes, no court cases, nothing that might indicate they supported the power of the *boma* over their lives. Both men knew—as did many of their Yao compatriots—that the dilemma of Che Tungawe they had discussed after the last war had become a reality for their lives. Chief Chikowi was blunt:

"If I live with what the *boma* expects of me, I'm a *Mzungu* with a black face to my people. If instead I encourage my people to live as they will, I am no good to the *boma* and *Bwana Disi* may be forced to remove me as Chief." Indeed it was not long before two or three of his fellow chiefs—though none from Zomba district—were removed for encouraging their people neither to pay taxes nor do any *malimidwe* work. Wishing to avoid such a fate, the Chief turned to his old friend and counsellor for help, thinking Juma would help organize a meeting of some of his fellow Yao chiefs along with a few others whom he trusted. His intent was to encourage opposing the idea of a Federation but, at the same time, to agree to help the *boma* in continuing to serve the people. Little did Juma realize when he agreed to help it would open perhaps the most tumultuous year of his life since the one he spent chasing the stubborn scraps of *Schutztruppe askari* through Portuguese East Africa.

Juma went to Zomba seeking assistance for arranging such a meeting. As he explained the plan to McKinley Chibambo he was shocked by the reply:

"You may be an *msilikali sajini* but if you do anything like this you'll be playing with fire!" Juma realized he had made a mistake in speaking with this man whom did not know well, but whom he believed supported the political ideas of his old friends Levi Mumba and Charles Matinga. Before long, Chibambo was hurrying about Chief Chikowi's area urging anyone who would listen to demand their Chief be removed, telling people Chikowi was one of those who actually had proposed this new federation.

"Lies! It's all lies!" Juma told as many people as he could. "Neither I nor the Chief like this Federation idea, but neither do we wish you to be hurt by stubbornly resisting the *boma*. We wish to work for better ways to improve our lives." When finally the chief's forum met at Chief Chikowi's court, McKinley Chibambo arrived to disrupt the proceedings with further demands that the Chief be deposed. But the District police also came to the meeting, arresting Chibambo on charges of obstructing government business. And it was with some relief Juma learned the trouble-maker was soon thereafter convicted of the more serious charge of sedition and exiled to Port Herald at the very southern tip of the Protectorate.

"Good riddance!" Juma proclaimed to Chotsani. "He got what he deserved." However, the Chibambo incident was not the last of the disruptions during his turbulent year!

∞∞∞∞∞∞

Just a month later, a KAR messenger arrived at Juma's door in Majowa with a message from Captain Maculay Braxley. Expecting to be called back to duty as Assistant Scoutmaster, Juma was surprised instead to be summoned—in uniform—for special duty with the KAR in, of all places, Thyolo! No, Braxley explained as Juma rode beside him in a KAR Landrover, it was unlikely the Boy Scout Troop would be meeting again any time soon, not at least until the present unpleasantness was over. While Juma didn't particularly agree with the characterization of Nyasaland Africans as unpleasant for insisting they be treated as respected citizens of their own land, he made nothing of the Captain's comment. Rather, he merely expressed his hopes the Scouts might meet again soon. Then Braxley got to the point of their present trip:

"There's been some sort of disturbance at one of the estates in Thyolo as well as continuing opposition to the agricultural rules, so the DC has asked for our assistance. I really doubt all this"— he nodded toward the half platoon of *asilikali* in a Bedford truck followed by two yellow-coloured iron armoured cars in the line behind the Landrover—"are really necessary. But I've been ordered to take them with me to defuse whatever sort of disturbances we might find once we get there." To Juma it looked almost like an invading army!

"But why me, sir!" Juma wanted to know.

"To tell the truth, I'm hoping maybe you can help make all the rest of this useless!" He again gestured back at the truckload of *asilikali* and the armoured cars. "The Commandant didn't think you'd be of much help, but he had no objection. You understand how the army works, and I also knew you'd been working with ADC Robinson on some agricultural projects." Juma wondered if he knew Bwana Lobosoni had dismissed him. He must, since the messenger found him in Majowa.

"But sir! I've left that work now, sir." He didn't want to sound as if he were protesting; rather just being sure his situation was clear to the Captain.

"I know, Juma. I saw your work firsthand during the Zomba flood. But most of all, I saw how you worked with those boys—young men, really, some of them not much younger than the *asilikali* we've got with us today—and I trust how you deal with people, how well you understand Nyasaland and its peoples." He smiled at Juma, pausing for a moment. "Frankly I'm hoping you can help in talking down some of these protesters."

With the din of the Landrover and the clattering of the vehicles behind them, their conversation had taken them all the way into Blantyre. It wouldn't be much longer before they reached Thyolo. Juma was grateful for the opportunity to think a few minutes about the situation he'd unwittingly been drawn into. As an *msilikali* he'd always—at least to some extent—been seen as with the *boma*, though he also felt as *lipunga* he was respected by Chikowi's people for his judgement. Of course, the people in Thyolo would know nothing of that, yet having served as a court assessor boosted his confidence for the situation in which he would soon find himself. Driving though the Thyolo hills, Juma was again amazed at the lush green hillsides of tea bushes with only the occasional tall tree breaking the spectacular view. But as they moved closer to the Thyolo *boma*, large boulders and felled trees blocked the road. *Asilikali* muscle moved the boulders sufficiently out of the way, and the Landover winch handled the trees. It was clear something was afoot!

A multitude of African demonstrators had gathered in front of the *boma* itself, just barely kept at bay by the district police. Juma overheard enough of the conversation between Braxley and the local police commander to understand the crowd believed—incorrectly the police commander stoutly claimed—that the sons of a local European plantation owner had killed two African men the day before, carrying away their bodies in sacks. The protestors demanded the bodies and the arrest of the supposed murderers. Many in the large crowd were also shouting something about the agricultural rules. Juma understood that well enough: "*nkhonda ya mitumbira*." The war of the ridges sounded very similar to the denunciations he had heard in Chingale objecting to *malimidwe* enforcement.

Captain Braxley ordered his *asilikali* out of the truck and lined up at rest; he also sent the two armoured cars driving about the town in some sort of demonstration of the army's presence. But before Braxley set him a specific task, Juma spotted his old friend Useni Makuta at the front of the crowd. Greeting him, Juma asked about the situation, more or less confirming what he had heard thus far.

"Did they really carry dead men away in sacks?" Juma first wanted to know.

"Not really," Useni admitted. "They were caught taking oranges and ran away. The sacks most likely had the oranges the men picked, dropped as the *Wazungu* chased them away" Though that explanation made sense to Juma, he still wanted to know more.

"*Nkhonda ya mitumbira*? Is it really a war, my friend?"

"Not like our war," Useni admitted. "But it is like the war of *thangata*,"—the demands of landowners for the labour of Africans living on their land—"the way in which the *boma* took *tengatenga* to carry the loads for us. Now the agricultural *capitaos* come to the villages at night, forcing people to work on *malimidwe* on into the day. No one is at peace nor can they rest. Some people even run away and hide in caves or graveyards." Juma remembered hearing people did the same when the *boma* was grabbing carriers during his war. These new rules amounted to forced labour again, *thangata*, in Zomba, Dedza, Chiradzulu, Mulanje, and—as Useni said—in Thyolo too. No wonder people were angry!

"But you have a job on the tea plantation, right? So they didn't come for you?" Useni shook his head in response.

"I have not paid tax, as part of the non-cooperation campaign," he admitted. "So I've lost my job, too!"

"*Pepani*" Juma was sorry and wanted to be sympathetic. It was difficult for him, seeing the dilemma he and Chief Chikowi discussed, from another's perspective. The conversation with Useni, however, was interrupted as a loosed spear head struck Juma, cutting the side of his scalp. Clearly it wasn't thrown at him, but merely became unattached from a demonstrator's "spear" which—almost without question, given how poorly it had been made!—was not really intended as a weapon but a photogenic prop for the demonstration. Instead it had felled an honoured Nyasaland veteran who was not even meant to be there!

Captain Braxley had the *asilikali* company's medic tend to Juma's "wound" which seemed to be minor enough, yet he also remained restrained in his response, not even trying to search out the "spear" chucker. The mere presence of the KAR itself, and the *asilikali's* non-provocative behaviour, quieted the crowd, preventing them from degenerating into a full-scale mob. As the demonstrators began to melt away, Useni apologized to Juma for his injury, but also urged him to reconsider his apparent support for federation policies. How else might he interpret Juma's presence in Thyolo? And after listening to Useni, Juma also began to wonder about his position himself! Without such a sense of urgency, the return trip to Zomba was decidedly longer than the initial rush to Thyolo, giving him time to nurse his injuries to both his scalp and scruples.

∞∞∞∞∞∞

Once he arrived back in Majowa, Chotsani ably tended the cut on his head, determining he would soon enough recover. But when he was able to relate his Thyolo experiences to Chief Chikowi, he was less certain about recovering his convictions.

"In Thyolo, *malimidwe* is seen as *thangata*, almost the same as slavery," Juma told the Chief who, in turn, reported learning it was being viewed similarly in Domasi where there had also been demonstrations. Then Chief Chikowi spoke more directly:

"But the Federation is now a reality and, as you have seen, Juma, the *boma* will use even the army to crush us if we fail to obey. If we are to survive we must urge people to obey the law. That is why I have decided to join a new organization of Chiefs and others, the Nyasaland African Progressive Association. Our friend, Charles Matinga, will lead this new group; I hope they will help us look to the future with hope, not hatred. Won't you join with us?" Juma respectfully declined. When he did, Chief Chikowi pointedly asked him:

"Has that wound on your head softened your brain?" Juma felt hurt more by his own Chief's implied criticism than he was by the misdirected "spear" in Thyolo. Matters might not seem as bad in Zomba as elsewhere, but he wondered what had happened to that "*dziko la Nyasaland*" the Chief had been so proud of scarcely a year before? Was he now only concerned about the Yao Chiefdom of Chikowi? Juma knew he had started his journey for the former chief with just the latter in mind. But he also knew there was something much larger now to fight for, an idea reinforced when his son-in-law Chitsulo returned from Malaya.

The joy of family celebrations with Apesile and Chitsulo dominated his concerns for a few days. But Juma was pleased when Chitsulo sought him out—as well as his own uncle Issa—to discuss his experiences, *asilikali* to *asilikali*. Chitsulo, promoted to corporal, had been a radio operator with 22 KAR operating mostly in jungle clearings on the Malay Peninsula. His stories of unreliable communications were echoed by both Issa and Juma who remembered similar problems in the East African Campaign.

"I remember giraffe would tear down the radio lines while walking to their waterholes," Issa recalled.

"And then we had to restring the wire still higher between the trees," Juma laughed with them.

"It's new times now," Chitsulo assured them. "Our radios have batteries—when they work!—and only the long-range antennas we had to string up, mostly at night, so the CTs won't see them." Both Juma and Issa looked at each other quizzically:

"CTs?" they asked in unison.

"Communist Terrorists!" Chitsulo explained further: "The *Min Yuen*, fighting for freedom from British rule." The idea struck home with Juma immediately. He had heard some *Wazungu* talking about communists in Nyasaland. In fact, several of the KAR, police, and other officers in Thyolo had said something about the demonstrators at the *boma* being communists. He wasn't sure what exactly communists were, though he was certain the epithet wasn't a compliment, so he asked for some clarification.

"Well, Sergeant Matthew talked with us a lot about that," Chitsulo began, though Juma quickly interrupted him:

"Sergeant Matthew is a *Mzungu*, right?"

"Oh no! That's just what we all called him because our KAR officers did. He's actually a Chewa, Graciano Matewere. He told us Matthew was his mission name! We talked about the CTs, how violent they were, actually working against the Malay peoples, denying them food unless they also fought against the British. Then we talked about *dziko la Nyasaland,* how we wanted freedom here as did the *Min Yuen*, but how lucky we are to have the Nyasaland National Congress instead! Congress will work with the people and our chiefs to get freedom for us."

"*Kwacha!*" Issa immediately shouted, raising his fist in the air, as did Chitsulo. It was exactly what Juma had seen and heard in Thyolo. But hearing it from his friend and own son-in-law offered him a very different perspective, as did an unexpected visitor to his Majowa home about a week later. On that afternoon, following a knock on his door, Chotsani came back to inform Juma a Mr. James Sangala was looking to meet him. As he hurried toward the door, Juma spoke warmly:

"*Takulandirani!*" He wanted to offer a warm welcome into his humble house for this man about whom he had heard so much. "Did Chief Chikowi send you to me?" he asked, assuming that must be the reason for this visit. But Sangala slightly bowed and shook his head:

"No, Sergeant Major, he did not," and after a short pause, adding "The Chief and I are a bit estranged just now. In fact, some of my friends in Thyolo asked me to see after you when I was next in Zomba. And here I am! They wanted to be sure you were not seriously injured during an unfortunate accident at Thyolo *boma*. I also wanted to take this opportunity to meet someone my dear departed friend, Levi Mumba, used to speak of so highly." Juma was flabbergasted that he, a simple old *msilikali*, might draw such attention! But he had enough presence of mind to ask Chotsani to prepare a pot of tea for their guest.

"Please sit down." Juma directed Mr. Sangala to a chair. "I am well, but hope we might talk for a few moments."

"*Zikomo,*" Sangala thanked Juma as he sat. "Perhaps just one cup of tea, as I must meet some others before evening. In fact, I believe you know Issa Bakali, who is expecting me." He didn't elaborate—leaving Juma wondering about Issa's business with Sangala—instead explaining that, as the newly elected President of the Nyasaland African Congress he wanted to ensure any political activities of the group would be non-violent and, in furtherance of that end, the organization was lifting its previous call for non-cooperation with the government.

"But we will stop short of endorsing this stupid Federation, and we will do all in our power to make certain it fails. Therefore—and this is where the difficulties between Chief Chikowi and myself come in—we are condemning the sort of accommodation the so-called Nyasaland Progressive Association has reached with the Federation." His blunt manner of coming directly to the point reminded Juma of Levi Mumba, the first overtly political figure he had met. It was, as well, the sort of plain speaking he valued in his own dealings with others.

"Are you asking me to choose between my Chief and your Congress?" Juma decided he could be equally blunt.

"I am asking that you join the Nyasaland African Congress. My friends in Thyolo tell me you understand how the *boma*, now the Federation as well, is denying the land is ours by insisting they can tell us how we may use it!" What friends did Sangala have in Thyolo, Juma wondered? It took just a few moments of reflection to realize it must be Useni! Sangala spoke again:

"I am not asking you to renounce Chief Chikowi. He is a good man who truly wishes to support his people. Frankly, I believe that his present dalliance with Matinga and his so-called Progressive Association will soon fade and your Chief will—sooner, I hope, rather than later—join us in Congress. Our numbers are growing, with Nyasas in Rhodesia, South Africa, and even Britain itself. Perhaps our strongest supporter is Kamuzu Banda, a doctor in London. I do hope you, too, will join us now. And if you will, I have but one additional request of you." Juma knew from experience that on any battlefield a soldier needed to seize the initiative, so Juma agreed to join with the Nyasaland African Congress and listened intently to Sangala's final request.

∞∞∞∞∞∞

After they made their fond goodbyes with Mr. Sangala, Chotsani turned to her husband. She was skeptical:

"I am afraid you will be hurt … again!" She made her unhappiness with his agreement to distribute Congress literature abundantly clear. Juma tried to calm her, confident in his choice but even more certain he would come to no harm as a result.

"It is only a little newsletter! People between here and the Barracks know me and it's nothing for me to travel back and forth, often carrying parcels. And I expect Chitsulo will help me, and maybe even Thenga and Mtindiso." He was uncertain about the latter two, but was confident, after their previous conversation, that he could count on his son-in-law in such an endeavor.

Kwacha may have fancied itself a newspaper for their true believers, but it was no more than a cyclostyled newsletter put out by the Nyasaland African Congress. James Sangala explained—though he probably didn't need to—that they couldn't send copies in the mail as the Post Office likely wouldn't deliver them. But since he was planning to expand Congress' communication efforts, he was searching for other means to get copies of *Kwacha* into the hands of more people. Once Juma agreed to join Congress, Sangala's additional request was one requiring a significant commitment. Would Juma take on the task of making sure new issues were handed out in Zomba, and especially in the *askilikali* lines at Cobbe Barracks?

The task proved considerably more complex than Juma initially envisioned. First, he was sent a list of names, Congress people for the most part, to whom he should deliver the papers. Some he knew, but others he would need to find. Second, he needed to meet a Congress courier with bundles of papers every week, changing their rendezvous destinations regularly to circumvent any attempts by the police to confiscate all the copies. Third, he was expected to take issues by hand to every person on his list, doing this for each of them every week. In fact, it was a large and tiring job for a man not nearly as young and spry as he once had been! Juma hated to admit it, but every task was now more difficult than he anticipated. He tried not to complain, but Chotsani noticed nonetheless.

He did manage to enlist Chitsulo to carry some issues of *Kwacha* to the KAR lines, which lessened his burden somewhat. For several months he hesitated to ask Mtindiso for help. He knew the bicycle shop kept him busy, but as a result his son also knew people who used their cycles for work—fish from Lake Chilwa and firewood from the top of the plateau—who might be willing to help with the distribution efforts. But he had to know if they were trustworthy, and to do that Juma had to speak to Mtindiso about his own political views:

"Have you heard of this Nyasaland African Congress?" he tried to ask innocently, shocked that Mtindiso wasn't at all puzzled by the question.

"Of course! They have been trying to stop this Federation which may bring even more troubles for us!" Mtindiso sounded as though he might actually have joined as well, but on further questioning it was clear he had not. So Juma asked further:

"What about this Nyasaland African Progressive Association of Chief Chikowi's? Do you know what they are about? This time Juma wasn't as shocked by Mtindiso's response:

"Yes, father. They also disapprove of this Federation, but don't think blindly opposing it will help us. Instead, they—and Chief Chikowi as well—don't want to upset the government any further. They think cooperating with them may be a better way to help our people, but I just don't know what to think is best! Do you believe all your service has made things better for us?" Juma was dumbfounded. He had misjudged his son and, in doing so, realized he was not as well informed himself as he ought to be. He missed the regular rounds he used to make in Zomba! And especially his conversations with Levi Mumba. Despite finding it harder and harder to do so, he resolved to visit town more often and try to meet more people, even those who weren't on his regular *Kwacha* delivery route!

For the moment, he didn't ask Mtindiso for his help. He even took on some of the tasks he had previously been giving over to Chitsulo. When his son-in-law asked why, Juma had a ready explanation:

"I am getting older, I know. But I don't want my mind to slow down like my body. I need to know more about what is happening! So I need to ask people about their views, talk with them, even if that means much more walking about. My only worry is that Chotsani will try to put a stop to my doing so since I'm always so tired when I return home." Chitsulo, though, knew there might be another way to solve Juma's information problem!

A few weeks later, Apesile and Chitsulo came to visit Juma along with Mtindiso and Njemile. The grandchildren, of course, came along as well. Though pleased to see them all—of course especially Thenga, Mary, and Titus!—Juma was perplexed by this unusual visitation. It wasn't a usual feasting time; nor did he know of any wedding or other celebration. Soon after their arrival he discovered there was a special purpose for the visit. His children had brought Juma a present! It was his very own radio: a "Saucepan Special" which Chitsulo and Mtindiso had repaired after it was discarded by one of the missionaries leaving Nyasaland. Juma's son, by now a skilled bicycle mechanic, was also renowned as a *fundi*, a "fixer of things"—as Chitsulo described some of his particularly clever comrades from his KAR days—while Chitsulo himself was more specifically a KAR radio operator. Together they'd come up with a new way for Juma to stay in touch with his world; at least that's what they hoped would happen!

Juma was enthralled with the new device—the *wayaleshi*, Mtindiso and Chitsulo called it—despite only being able to clearly hear one station. As he tried turning the little dial to point in other directions, all he usually heard was the fizzzz fizzzz fizzzz of radio static, rarely combined with sounds which might have been intended as something else. So Radio Lusaka it was! He enjoyed listening, appreciating the music as well as the stories, some told with many voices. One of the first such stories he heard was about "Mumba and his new Bicycle" which reminded him how thankful he was to Mtindiso, and of course Chitsulo. However, news stories were his favourites! He anxiously awaited those reports whether in English, which he could sometimes understand, or in *Chichewa*, which was easier for him. The absence of any news in *Chiyao*, though, was a great disappointment.

As word spread around Majowa that Juma, too, had *wayaleshi*—just as did Chief Chikowi—many visitors came to see and listen to the new device. Not one of the first curious visitors, his old friend Issa turned out to be one of the least impressed:

"You do know that is the Central African Broadcasting Station you are listening to?" he asked sarcastically. Juma nodded to acknowledge he did. "It may be from Lusaka, but it really is just the voice of the Federation!" Issa sounded triumphant, but Juma was unfazed:

"Still, it is good to listen, and I enjoy much of it. When they sometimes talk of London, I try to remember if what they say describes what I saw myself. At least once or twice it was. Zanzibar, too!" He also told Issa about the story of "Mumba and his new Bicycle," particularly the moral about foolish pride, especially in things. "So I listen, then try to find out for myself what is true. If the Federation helps *me* learn things, perhaps it really *is* stupid! I do not like it, or our own Nyasaland *boma* either, and Radio Lusaka has further convinced me of that view. I simply feel proud that now I have the whole world—well, at least more of it—to learn from in my own house!"

∞∞∞∞∞∞∞

Chotsani, too, was happy the *wayaleshi* had come to their house, as it meant Juma was happier staying at home. He gradually had been growing weaker and unable to walk so far, carrying copies of *Kwacha* as far as he could. She was relieved, too, when word came that Congress would no longer send the newsletter out to members. Juma, though, was disappointed, but for a different reason. He was becoming more convinced in the arguments Chitsulo, Sangala, and even Issa had been making. But the most forceful voice for those arguments—the Nyasaland African Congress—now seemed to be in disarray. The news from Nyasaland on Radio Lusaka made that evident as did reports he received from Chitsulo. Paradoxically, when he came to check on Juma's health, Chief Chikowi brought word too, along with predictions the voice of Congress would only become more strident as Sangala was eased out of a leadership role. Much as he still respected his Chief, Juma continued to believe that Congress—even without Sangala—held the best hope for the aspirations of his people. When word reached him—and not long after confirmed on Radio Lusaka!—of Dr. Banda's return to Nyasaland after more than four decades, Juma expected greater progress, though the results, at least as reported on the radio, seemed to him merely more fiery protest rhetoric.

So when a scant few months later news came—prominently announced on Radio Lusaka—of Dr. Banda's arrest and detention along with the banning of the Nyasaland African Congress, Juma's hopes dimmed. The defiant launch of a new Malawi Congress Party and especially its new organ, the *Malawi News*, lit a fire in Juma. He was ready to begin distribution again, despite both new prohibitions for doing so and his own continuing ill health. He was determined that people know what the new Party was thinking and what they would do in the uphill struggle against colonialism. To him, it was almost a crusade to undo the results of some of his own previous battles as an *msilikali*. Chotsani was not having any of it, however:

"You are no longer an *msilikali*, not beholden to any cause," she insisted, hoping he would instead continue to rest at home. But even Chotsani could see he was energized and quickly stopped begging him to desist. Juma sent word that Chitsulo should bring him copies of the *Malawi News* every fortnight. And he gave them to like-minded friends and family.

"Take this! If you can't read it, have someone who can, read it to you. This is news you won't receive on the *wayaleshi*." It was the same message he had for everyone he saw, discovering that many were pleased and happy, as they agreed with him. Gradually he came to see it as a duty to extend his distribution efforts to nearby villages. Once he even went with Chitsulo to Cobbe Barracks hoping to engage other old *asilikali* to embrace the cause. When he returned coughing and weak from that journey, Chotsani renewed her protests:

"You should not have made that trip. This consumption you have—isn't that what the health care nurse called it?—won't allow you to be so busy on this cause." Juma wanted to answer, to tell her he saw no other way, but could only cough. Finally able to speak, he signaled his resignation:

"Could a man die better than trying to preserve his own people?" He asked his wife. But he also resolved to rest, for her sake if not his own. His resolution lasted almost a year which coincided with what the *boma* called an Emergency in Nyasaland. In addition to Chotsani and visits from family and a few friends, Juma contented himself with the music and stories from Radio Lusaka as there was no *real* news broadcast due to the Emergency. What news he could piece together from friends and from Radio Lusaka was gloomy, at best: Congress organizing protests. The *boma* responding harshly. Hundreds of people put in jail. Rhodesian military units firing on Congress demonstrators. Almost fifty of them killed!

One fateful day, though, he heard a mournful song on the radio, described by the announcer as an Ndebele chant from Rhodesia. Uncharacteristically, the announcer then offered an English version of the words:

"Where are you our fathers?"

"Where are our cattle?"

"You, oh great lover of cattle,

"Where are they now?

"Where are our fathers?

"Where are our cattle?"

"That world has been overthrown!"

The melancholy melody, in addition to what Juma could make out of the English words, struck a chord in his heart. He knew the importance of cattle to the Ndebele way of life, having met several Ndebele soldiers during his war. Just as the song bemoaned the loss of their "world," the preservation of his own fathers' land and way of life—the entire Yao world which he had been charged to help preserve by becoming an *msilikali*—had instead been overthrown. He knew, after hearing that song, he must not stop his efforts despite any, even well-placed concerns his wife might have.

When the announcement came—one that Radio Lusaka did broadcast!—that the Nyasaland Emergency would be lifted, Juma rejoiced. As Congress leaders, released from detention, negotiated for change, he waited for an ideal moment when an old *msilikali* might make a difference! When at last direct African elections for government representatives became a reality, Juma saw this as a call to action. Even with his physical limitations, he wanted what limited efforts he could make to have the greatest possible impact. So when asked to distribute *Malawi News* special election editions, not merely to friendly neighbours, but to carry them to Zomba market as well, he was ready! His wife attempted to prevent him, to no avail. Because the *boma* had agreed to this election, it was not against the law. So he didn't anticipate any difficulties in carrying out his assigned mission. But after his long, slow, and more painful than expected walk to the market, he was harassed—not by police, but by others who opposed the Malawi Congress Party slate of candidates—and was actually knocked to the ground and kicked several times before the police intervened.

"Don't come around here with your papers, old man!" a young policeman warned him. "Next time we won't protect you." Juma didn't feel as though he'd been protected at all! Indeed he barely was able to stagger more than a few feet, wondering how he would manage to return home. As the afternoon sky turned to dusk a worried Chotsani sent word alerting Mtindiso his father wasn't yet back from Zomba Market. Only as the sun was finally setting did anyone find Juma, walking a few steps at a time, then resting, before taking a few further steps along the familiar path from Zomba to Majowa. Mtindiso and young Titus found him, and while Mtindiso steadied his father as they walked together Titus ran ahead to tell Chotsani his grandfather was alive and, if not truly well, would soon be home so she might tend to his needs.

Seeing Juma in such a state frightened Chotsani! She did manage to get him into his bed and attempted to make him comfortable. He was not. He continued to cough, awakening himself as he occasionally drifted off to sleep throughout the night. The next day he continued to sleep and, to Chotsani at least, seemed more comfortable. That evening she insisted he try to eat a little, and he made an attempt, complaining about how sore he was. Apesile came to be with her father for a time, allowing Chotsani herself to rest. That pattern continued about a fortnight as Juma—even though he remained weak and still prone to coughing fits—regained a little of his strength. He began again listening to his radio, as always enjoying the music, but especially relished the reports of the election: the MCP slate of candidates for whom he campaigned were elected to the Nyasaland Legislative Council! He did feel he had made a difference, not merely at Zomba market, but in all that he had done since Mr. Sangala called him to action.

Perhaps the greatest joy was when Chief Chikowi, himself not entirely well, came to see Juma with news that he was now supporting the efforts of the party he had previously shunned:

"Congratulations, Juma. You have been victorious! I only regret your efforts have come at a great cost to you and your family. I have for long valued your advice and counsel. Now I also have a real regret that I was not attentive to your opinions about the best way forward regarding the Federation. Our people have made clear their choices; I shall conform to their wishes. I am also asking that you agree again to serve as *lipenga* for my court." Juma was pleased the Chief had humbly come to him in this way and agreed to once more assess cases for the Chief, as long as he might be able to do so.

∞∞∞∞∞∞

Juma remained in fragile health for some time, on occasion rallying, seeming better for a short while, but much more often confined to his bed. Managing occasionally to attend the Chief's court, he continued to assess a few cases. Those visits also offered opportunities to confirm the dizzying developments in Nyasaland's changing political landscape. It had once seemed impossible, then only unlikely, but finally a reality: Britain agreed to self-government for Nyasaland! As the day of independence—when the Nyasaland he had actually been a part of creating would become the independent nation of Malawi—grew nearer Juma, unfortunately grew even weaker. Chotsani almost never left his bedside, not merely because that was expected of a Yao wife. She truly cared for this man who had warned her that, as his wife, she might be left with little more than such an obligation. And her reward was in knowing he, indeed, was one of the savers of his people. Finally, she sensed it was time to inform his old regiment, only to discover Chitsulo had taken it upon himself to carry word of the Sergeant Major's deteriorating health to Cobbe Barracks.

"Vroom.... vroom... vro... ssssk" The sound of a motorcar arriving and then stopping at their home alarmed Chotsani, although Juma barely reacted. He was scarcely awake, just as he had been for most of the day. Since the incident at Zomba market—even though it was many months ago—she remained fearful the Police Special Branch would one day come for Juma. In the twilight, as men in uniforms stepped out of the automobile, she first thought her fears had been realized. Surely, they wouldn't take her husband away in his present condition!

Chotsani need not have feared for her husband. Juma, though, recognized at once the men Chotsani let into their home weren't police, but KAR officers. The shock on his face transformed to a smile when he recognized *Amiri Likwemba*, now a colonel! His instinct was to stand and salute, but he couldn't come close to moving his body even as it was apparent he was trying to do so. Chotsani motioned him to stay down in his bed and Colonel Rangely did the same. Though they struggled to find the words both could readily understand, Chotsani communicated her husband's grave condition to the man she could only see was a sympatric *asilikali* officer. The two old soldier's greeted each other warmly, if briefly.

Lieutenant Lipenga, who followed the colonel into the house, then spoke briefly with Chotsani, and with greater ease than his commanding officer as he was fluent in *Chiyao*:

"The Colonel is concerned for the Sergeant Major's health and wants to do what he can to make him comfortable." She expressed her thanks as profusely as was formally appropriate to a *Chiyao* speaker:

"Nanga!" And as Juma began coughing, the Lieutenant moved to more delicate matters:

"Is the Sergeant Major resting comfortably..." Before he could continue, Chotsani interrupted:

"E-e-e," adding, "As comfortably as can be expected. I stay close by him, and he has the radio he enjoys so," pointing to the "Saucepan Special" in the corner of the room. "His face lights up when there is music, but he's been suspicious why there seems so little information about what is happening in Nyasaland."

"And how long..." Lipenga paused, knowing it was especially delicate to speak about an impending death. However, Chotsani understood.

"Who can know such things?" she shrugged, almost in an effort to forestall the inevitable question. "Tonight? Tomorrow? It is unknowable...but soon. I've sent for his family."

Rangely put on his cap, saluted toward Juma, then motioned for Lieutenant Lipenga to follow him out of the house. Without speaking, the two officers knew Sergeant Major Juma Chimwere would soon join his ancestors as protectors of the Yao people.

∞∞∞∞∞∞

Epilogue

Though he'd only met the Lieutenant three weeks before, Colonel Rangely implicitly trusted that Resten Lipenga would follow through in meeting the needs of RSM Juma. His confidence came from many years of military experience, including this, his third assignment with the King's African Rifles. So there was no need for further discussion of the matter. The two officers, and their driver, returned from Majowa to Zomba in near silence as an evening fog started to descend on the mountain. Rangely spent the time reflecting on his career, especially the fondness he had developed for the Nyasa—soon to be Malawian—soldiers it had been his good fortunate to command. In his mind those *asilikali* were among the elite of the British army, none more so than RSM Juma whose sickbed he had just left.

He recalled a letter from his mother—it must have been almost forty years ago—about the "lovely portraits of distinguished native soldiers" his parents had seen at the British Empire Exhibition. They had traveled to Wembley primarily to get some idea of the far reaches of the British dominions in which their son was making his new military career. Mrs. C. C. Metcalfe's painting of RSM Juma was one of those "native types" on display in the small Nyasaland pavilion. That same work was now hung proudly in the Officer's Mess at Cobbe Barracks, though perhaps somewhat faded from the tropical environment. From his perch on that wall, a much younger and fit Juma would soon look down at his now aging former company commander returning to the welcome dinner he had left to visit the old soldier. The Colonel fondly hoped Juma's memory, and service, wouldn't fade and, instead, be forever commemorated there for future officers to see. Was there a more distinguished *askari* veteran in all Nyasaland? Rangely knew of no other. Were his chest full of medals still in his possession? Might he allow the battalion to put them on display as well? Rangely briefly put it to the Lieutenant:

"Lipenga. Please inquire if RSM Juma and his family will permit us to showcase his medals next to his portrait in the officer's mess."

"Yes, sir! Very good sir." In the silence which once again filled the staff car as it was enveloped in a not unexpected *chiperoni*, Wellington Rangely returned to musing about the RSM, and especially one of the most cherished memories of his commands with the KAR. During the first war when the battalion's trenches near the Rufiji River were inadvertently bombed by a British aeroplane, RSM Juma calmly—or so it appeared to Rangely—reassured frightened *askari*. Juma's words still resonated in his recollections:

"I too have been fired on by enemies and friends. It is our enemy's and not our fellow soldier's fire which should most concern us. We must depend on each other to survive the confusions of combat. I will always support you, and I am counting on all of you to protect me. Can you remain calm and join me in helping each other?"

At least that was how he remembered what RSM Juma said to the men in those trenches. Years later, when his own battalion in Burma was also troubled by a friendly fire incident, Rangely recalled borrowing almost those exact words in his attempt to reassure another generation of Nyasaland *asilikali*. Had he been as effective as the Sergeant Major in doing so? He was uncertain then, and he remained uncertain now. He had always thought his men respected him—and he didn't mind they called him *Bwana Likwemba* when they thought he was out of earshot—but he also understood how his best African NCOs were better able to connect with their soldiers. And he had no doubt RSM Juma had been among the very best at doing so!

Sarah Rangely greeted her husband as he walked up the steps to the Officer's Mess.

"How is he?" she asked, in an almost pro forma way, following her question with a more cheery note: "You're back in time for the Baked Alaska!"

"What on earth?" He seemed incredulous. "Have I missed the entire dinner?"

"No, no!" she attempted to reassure him. "You've returned just in time for the pudding. For this special occasion the chef most wanted to offer something quiet spectacular!" Then she whispered to him as they made their way back to the dining room: "Some of the officers told me the chef has been practicing this new recipe on them for the past week!"

With a sigh, followed by a smile, he acknowledged the waiter who placed the warm meringue in front of him at the table. Sarah leaned over once again to explain there was actually ice cream inside the warm concoction. Gently assuring her he was aware of that gastronomic detail, Rangely began to sample his desert, a formal signal to the assemblage that they might do likewise. And when he had consumed most of the delicious concoction—a surprising treat on this warm tropical evening—he positioned his wine glass immediately in front of him, and stood to address his officers.

∞∞∞∞∞∞

"Thank you for honouring Sarah and me this evening. I also appreciate our chief mess chef for this cool delight!" He paused as the officers and their wives applauded politely.

"As you no doubt are aware, Lieutenant Lipenga and I have just returned from Majowa where we visited with Regimental Sergeant Major Juma Chimwere." He noticed heads nodding in agreement before continuing. "Despite his frail condition, he would want me to greet all of you with a smart salute. That was his way." All of the officers stood to return the salute Rangely offered on Juma's behalf.

"Many of you knew RSM Juma, as for decades he was a regular visitor here. However, I gather he hasn't been to the barracks quite as frequently in recent years." Hesitating, he looked down reflectively for a moment. "Juma was my Company Sergeant Major during my first command. But his distinguished service long predated that of the King's African Rifles itself." As he spoke without notes, *Bwana Likwemba* realized he knew the old *askari* better than he had ever assumed. Recounting Juma's experiences during and after the Asante Campaign, his exploits at Mafia Island (which earned him the nickname *Nanyula*) and Mbuyuni (where he won his African DCM) in the Great War—as well as all he continued to do for the battalion and his homeland since. He especially commented on Juma's service with the KAR Boy Scout Troop, an episode he had only recently learned about himself. The Colonel concluded simply:

"We should have given him the Victoria Cross all those years ago. It was our mistake to assume Africans could never serve with such bravery and distinction as did General Sir Alexander

Cobbe—for whom our own barracks are named—or Corporal James Upton, who saved my life at Aubers Ridge during the Great War." Again, a hesitation as he turned to face Juma's portrait, looking down at him from its place of honour. "Without a doubt, RSM Juma has been as great an institution as his regiment itself." He picked up his wine glass from the table.

"Ladies. Gentlemen. A toast." Raising his glass toward Juma's likeness, he glanced around the room to be sure everyone else had found theirs, then continued: "To Regimental Sergeant Major Juma, whose entire life was one of distinguished conduct."